Hong Kong's Chinese History
Curriculum from 1945

Hong Kong University Press thanks Xu Bing for writing the Press's name in his Square Word
Calligraphy for the covers of its books. For further information, see p. iv.

To my parents

Hong Kong's Chinese History Curriculum from 1945
Politics and Identity

Flora L. F. Kan

香港大學出版社

HONG KONG UNIVERSITY PRESS

Hong Kong University Press
14/F Hing Wai Centre
7 Tin Wan Praya Road
Aberdeen
Hong Kong

© Hong Kong University Press 2007

Hardback ISBN 978-962-209-836-7
Paperback ISBN 978-962-209-837-4

Secure On-line Ordering
http://www.hkupress.org

British Library Cataloguing-in-Publication Data
A catalogue record for this book is available from the British Library.

Printed and bound by Liang Yu Printing Factory Ltd., in Hong Kong, China

Hong Kong University Press is honoured that Xu Bing, whose art explores the complex themes of language across cultures, has written the Press's name in his Square Word Calligraphy. This signals our commitment to cross-cultural thinking and the distinctive nature of our English-language books published in China.

"At first glance, Square Word Calligraphy appears to be nothing more unusual than Chinese characters, but in fact it is a new way of rendering English words in the format of a square so they resemble Chinese characters. Chinese viewers expect to be able to read Square Word Calligraphy but cannot. Western viewers, however are surprised to find they can read it. Delight erupts when meaning is unexpectedly revealed."

— Britta Erickson, *The Art of Xu Bing*

Contents

Acknowledgements

This book would not have been possible without assistance and support from many people. They cannot all be named here, but the following require specific recognition. I am extremely grateful to Professor Paul Morris and Dr Pong Wing Yan for their inspiration, advice and encouragement throughout the course of this work. They have provided me with an invaluable learning experience. I would like to thank also Professor Anthony Sweeting who offered very constructive comments to improve the manuscript. A special vote of thanks is extended to Mr Ivor Johnson and Dr Edward Vickers who read and commented in detail on drafts of all the chapters. My heartfelt thanks also goes to Ian for his unfailing support, both emotionally and mentally, throughout the entire process.

Abbreviations

AI	Advisory Inspectorate
A-L	Advanced Level
AS-L	Advanced Supplementary Level
CCP	Chinese Communist Party
CDC	Curriculum Development Committee
CDI	Curriculum Development Institute
CUHK	The Chinese University of Hong Kong
ED	Education Department
EC	Education Commission
EMB	Education and Manpower Bureau
CEE	Certificate of Education Examination
HKEA	Hong Kong Examinations Authority
HKEAA	Hong Kong Examinations and Assessment Authority
HKSAR	Hong Kong Special Administrative Region
HKU	The University of Hong Kong
H-L	Higher Level
KMT	Kuomintang (Nationalist Party)
PRC	The People's Republic of China
STC	Syllabus and Textbook Committee

1

Introduction

> One purpose of teaching Chinese History to Chinese children would
> be to get rid of this [inferiority] complex by reviving what is good in
> Chinese culture, thereby instilling fresh confidence into, and restoring
> the self-respect of her people. This, however, must not be identified
> with the promotion of vanity and anti-foreignism which is to be strongly
> deprecated. (Report of the Chinese Studies Committee, Government
> Education Department, 1953: 18)

> We will incorporate the teaching of Chinese values in the school
> curriculum and provide more opportunities for students to learn about
> Chinese history and culture. This will foster a stronger sense of Chinese
> identity in our students ... . As we face the historic change of being
> reunited with China, for every individual there is a gradual process of
> getting to know Chinese history and culture, so as to achieve a sense
> of belonging. (Tung Chee Hwa, Chief Executive, HKSAR, Policy
> Address, 8 October 1997)

These excerpts illustrate the views of the Hong Kong government on the role
of Chinese History in the school curriculum during two distinct periods. The first
quotation comes from the colonial era and shows the government-sponsored
committee's ambivalent attitude: on the one hand, it agreed that Chinese History
was a source of cultural revival and self-respect but, on the other, it cautioned
against possible xenophobia and unrest. The second quotation is from shortly
after the handover of sovereignty to China and reveals the government's aim of
using history to foster students' national identity and sense of belonging to China.
In addition to their interest as statements of colonial and post-colonial
governments' attitudes to the aims of teaching Chinese History, these extracts are
an indication of the important political role that history plays in a society's school
curriculum. Of all the school subjects, history may be the most politically sensitive,
and the one which most reflects the culture and politics of a society; it is a

legitimating phenomenon serving to define national identity and ideology, and to contribute to nation-building (Slater, 1989; Jenkins, 1991; Goodson, 1994).

This has been particularly true in colonial and decolonised countries. There are several conflicting theories about the impact that colonialism has on a country's history curriculum, the most extreme and perhaps simplistic being the classic view of scholars such as Altbach and Kelly (1978, 1984) and Said (1994), who tend to assume that colonial curricula invariably devalue and alienate 'native' history. Several commentators have adopted this view in the case of Chinese History in Hong Kong. For example, Pennycook (1998) sees Chinese History as having been distorted and devalued by the colonial authorities, while Luk (1991: 650) refers to the Chinese cultural curriculum, including Chinese History, as fostering '... a sense of being at the periphery of both the Chinese and World worlds — which no doubt assists the consolidation of colonial rule'. However, those holding such negative views on the influence of colonialism on Chinese History in Hong Kong seem to overlook two important points: first, most people came to Hong Kong only after it had become a colony, which is an unusual feature of colonialism; and second, even if there were restrictions on the content and scope of Chinese History, this might not have been due solely to the actions of the colonial government. Moreover, such claims have not been supported by in-depth studies. Therefore, although it may be tempting to draw such stereotypical conclusions, it is important to look at the possible effect of factors other than colonialism on the nature of the local curriculum. There are several indications that the situation may not be as clear-cut an example of cultural imperialism as the above writers suggest. For example, successive colonial governments were willing to allow Chinese History to be used as a source of cultural renewal (as can be seen from the first quotation). Also, Chinese History enjoyed an independent status as a subject during most of the colonial era.

With regard to decolonisation, the tendency is for the political authorities to remove all signs of colonialism and use education to build up a sense of patriotism and belonging in the newly independent state. However, in the case of Hong Kong, the situation is rather different: after 156 years of colonial rule, Hong Kong did not follow the typical pattern of decolonisation by becoming independent, but was 'handed over' to another sovereign state, becoming a Special Administrative Region (SAR) of the Peoples' Republic of China (PRC). These unusual aspects of Hong Kong's colonial past and decolonisation make the study of the development of the Chinese History curriculum in Hong Kong of special interest as they allow us to compare it with the practice in more typical colonial and post-colonial countries, in this way perhaps broadening our understanding of colonial and post-colonial education.

There have been very few studies of the history of school subjects in Hong Kong, and this is the first attempt to analyse the development of Chinese History through the colonial and post-colonial eras. Also, whereas previous work on curriculum development has confined itself to the effect on the curriculum of educational interest groups, or socio-economic-political forces, or colonialism/ decolonisation, the present study attempts to analyse all three types of influence, and the way in which they interacted in determining the nature of Chinese History in Hong Kong. In addition to providing contemporary curriculum planners with an understanding of how the subject has evolved over time — including the major issues, problems and influences in its development — this investigation offers an opportunity to look at the social, cultural and political changes that Hong Kong has undergone through the years of colonial rule, and during and after the transition from British to Chinese rule.

The purpose of this book is to examine how the aims, content, teaching, learning and assessment of the Chinese History curriculum have evolved over the past 60 years, and what the major influences involved have been. Some of the questions the study attempts to answer are:

- To what extent, if at all, has its development conformed to the various theories of colonial and post-colonial curricula, especially the 'classic' theories of colonial history curricula mentioned above?
- How much has curriculum planning been determined by the government, and how much has it been in the hands of educational interest groups?
- How has the curriculum changed since the return of sovereignty to China?
- What part has the government of the People's Republic of China (PRC) played?
- What were the motives and actions of the parties who were most closely involved in curriculum development?

This study reveals a rather different situation regarding the development of Chinese History than might be supposed. It does not support theories of colonial cultural imperialism, in which colonial governments dictate the nature of school curricula in order to diminish the culture of the local population, or theories which see curriculum development as a power struggle among local interest groups. Rather, it is argued, the development of Chinese History was largely the result of a collaborative effort on the part of the three key parties involved — the colonial government/SAR government, the local subject community and the government of the PRC — and of attempts to strike a balance between their interests. Also, the development of the curriculum did not follow the traditional pattern of decolonisation; instead of the Chinese History curriculum being strengthened, after the handover its status was actually threatened by the reforms of the SAR government. However, recent developments have forced the local subject community to make drastic changes to the Chinese History curriculum and re-secure its independent status in the school curricula.

This book also reveals three dominant themes which have typified the curriculum: the study of Chinese History as a continuous whole, an orthodox historical perspective, and a Han-centred cultural view. The picture of the Chinese History curriculum that emerges is of a subject that began with a very traditional, academic emphasis, and over the course of time became ever more entrenched in its academic orientation. This trend differs from the patterns of curriculum change suggested by Goodson (1988) and Kliebard (1992), who tend to see the process of the development of school subjects as a move from either an academic to a utilitarian tradition or vice versa.

The next section discusses briefly the major types of forces that have been influential in curriculum change. In order to explain why a particular pattern of content knowledge has emerged, three levels of influences are taken into account: first, influences arising from micro-level educational interest groups; second, locally driven meso-level socio-political and socio-economic forces; and third, external factors viewed from the macro-level of colonialism/decolonisation. Although these three levels are analysed separately to enhance clarity, it is recognised that they are not mutually exclusive but are intertwined and have combined to bring about changes (or in some cases inertia) in the development of the curriculum for Chinese History. Later chapters (Chapters 2–5) attempt to analyse the complex interactions of these different forces and the varying degrees to which they have affected Chinese History in Hong Kong.

This is followed by a section which gives a brief review of philosophical approaches to the study of history in China, focusing primarily on a discussion of historiography, supplemented with references to epistemology and pedagogy. The discussion of these issues provides a background for the analysis in later chapters of the development of Chinese History in Hong Kong by placing it in a broader historical and philosophical context.

FORCES INFLUENCING CURRICULUM CHANGE

Micro-level Influences: Educational Interest Groups

Micro-level influences refer to the way in which subject communities may affect curriculum change. The term 'subject community' is used here to refer to individuals and groups associated in various ways with the same school subject, who work together to safeguard the status of that subject and their own interests as stakeholders. This community usually consists of government subject officers, academics, teachers and textbook writers who operate either as insiders (e.g. as curriculum developers) or outsiders (e.g. as a pressure group) in influencing policy- making with respect to their subjects. Members of the subject community may either organise themselves collectively to protect or promote their subject or work as individuals voicing their opinions through the media. According to Bucher and Strauss (1976), the interests that a subject community strive to protect typically include curricular 'territory' (in the form of space in school timetables), resources, recruitment and training. In the United Kingdom, for example, teachers, as a well-organised and professional group with professional codes governing membership, are particularly prominent members of their subject communities and are thus able to exert some influence on defining what is to be taught, and how. There are also members of the community who are accredited with the power to make 'official statements' — for instance, editors of journals, chief examiners and inspectors.

Some researchers, however, point out that subject communities are seldom homogenous groupings, with patterns of curriculum development frequently reflecting power struggles among rival members. For example, Goodson (1987b: 26–27) asserts that:

> The subject community [in the UK] should not be viewed as a homogeneous group whose members share similar values and definition of role, common interests and identity. Rather the subject community could be seen as comprising a range of conflicting groups, segments or factions.

Hong Kong

Unlike the situation in the UK, in Hong Kong there is no officially authorised teachers' council; and, worse still, anyone who possesses a university qualification, or an even lower qualification, can become a teacher as long as they register and obtain approval from the Education and Manpower Bureau (EMB, which before restructuring was known as the Education Department [ED]). Because they are not required to have a minimum level of professional preparation, teachers in Hong Kong are not recognised as professionals, nor do they become members of professional bodies, unlike the case with lawyers and doctors. However, a few teacher unions have been established which play an active role in the education sector, including the Professional Teachers' Union (PTU) and the Hong Kong Federation of Education Workers, which are affiliated to different political parties. Also, there are several teacher associations which aim at enhancing the teaching and learning of a specific subject or group of subjects, such as the Science and Mathematics Education Association, the Economics Education Association and the Geography Education Association. For Chinese History, however, it was not until 2000 that two formal teacher associations were set up in response to perceived threats to the subject. Before that, no organised efforts were made to advance the interests of Chinese History, and the only way in which its subject community was able to have any effect on the development of the subject was through various influential individuals, in particular academics and teachers, making their views known through the media.

Meso-level Influences: Socio-political and Socio-economic Forces

'Meso-level' influences are those socio-political and socio-economic forces that influence curriculum change — for instance, they may affect curriculum planning where the school curriculum is seen as an instrument of social control, and as reflecting the values of the dominant classes in a society. Young (1998) exemplifies this by distinguishing between high-status and low-status knowledge with respect to a subject's academic orientation, and argues that over time the school curriculum in the UK has become legitimised as high-status by the dominant groups who have the authority and/or power to determine its nature. He characterises an academic, high-status curriculum as one which emphasises the written word, individualism (that is, an avoidance of group work and cooperative learning) and abstract knowledge; in short, a curriculum which is often unrelated to daily life. A non-academic, low-status curriculum, in contrast, stresses the spoken word, group work and concrete knowledge, and is related to the outside world. Young argues that whether a high-status or low-status curriculum persists does not depend on pedagogical effectiveness, but rather on 'the conscious or unconscious cultural choices which accord with the values, beliefs and interests of dominant groups at a particular time' (ibid.: 20). As a result, attempts at curriculum change which could undermine the status quo might be doomed to failure.

A different view of the effect of meso-level influences is taken by Skilbeck (1992) who explains curriculum change in terms of four dimensions of socio-economic forces: economic forces, population shifts, changing socio-cultural values, and nation-building. Skilbeck argues that the curriculum either is, or can be made, directly responsive to forces and trends in the economy, as in the case of a government using the curriculum as part of a wider strategy of economic restructuring and development, a practice he sees as common in developing countries. Population shifts such as ageing, and the movement of ethnic and cultural groups across national boundaries, may also lead to a change of curriculum focus, such as an emphasis on lifelong education, mother-tongue teaching and multiculturalism across the curriculum. Changing socio-cultural values (e.g. the popularity of electronic media and the drive towards vocational, trade and practical skills training) can give rise to an increasing challenge to the dominance of the academic curriculum, and in particular to its relevance for mass education. Finally, Skilbeck notes that it is particularly common in developing countries and former colonies for the curriculum to be reconstructed for the purposes of nation-building.

Yet another way in which meso-level forces may be instrumental in curriculum development can be seen in Fagerlind and Saha's (1989) 'social system', in which the economic, social and political dimensions interact dialectically with one another, and together interact with education. In the process, education is both an agent of change and is itself changed by society. This can be seen, for example, in the arguments of political leaders in various countries in recent years that an overhaul of the existing education system is needed if the state is to maintain its international competitiveness through economic and social changes.

As well as being subject to social, cultural and political influences, education itself has the power to shape social and political attitudes, in that it can socialise people into accepting or reconstructing the existing socio-political/socio-economic status quo. According to Sweeting (1995: 75) 'the relationship between the socio-political and socio-economic forces, and the curriculum is symbiotic and mutually supportive, but they are not uni-linear'.

Hong Kong

In Hong Kong, various social, political and economic forces have influenced education. One example of the effect of political forces on the school curriculum was the concern of successive colonial governments to prevent unrest in Hong Kong and to avoid upsetting the PRC government by ensuring that the curriculum was apolitical. Sweeting and Morris (1993: 214), writing during the colonial era, argue that 'education is highly sensitive to, and influenced by, the changing political realities which have affected Hong Kong. While the overriding motive of the government has been to minimise any threat to its status, this has operated in parallel with the attempt to avoid offending the sensibilities of political leaders in the PRC'. The same authors (1995) identify two periods in which the school curriculum was modified to meet the political needs of a particular time. According to them, from 1945–82 the government was determined to avoid political issues in the curriculum, and no attempt was made to develop a sense of Chinese national identity. In contrast, during the decolonisation period, there was a rapid rehabilitation of politics and school curricula were amended to include political concerns and to develop a sense of Chinese identity in students. However, it has been suggested (e.g. Morris and Chan, 1997) that, in reality, the effect of the government's attempt at re-politicisation of the school curriculum as a result of the transition of sovereignty had little impact at the school level because schools continued to be more concerned with competing for academically able students than with integrating political issues into the curriculum.

Economic and social forces are also seen to have had an effect on education in Hong Kong, with Sweeting and Morris pointing out that 'educational change has followed rather than preceded major structural changes in the economy' (1993: 213). For example, during the 1950s and 1960s, manufacturing was the chief source of employment for most people, and consequently schools were mainly concerned with teaching students basic literacy and numeracy skills. This changed during the 1970s, when the decline of manufacturing and the rise of a service-based economy (e.g. banking and communications) led to revisions in the school curriculum, and schools were required to produce a more sophisticated workforce with ability in English and expertise in areas such as computer studies, accounting, commerce and business studies. There was also an emphasis on creativity and problem-solving skills.

Regarding the influence of social factors on the curriculum, Morris (1995a) points out that the existence of an ethnically and culturally homogeneous population in Hong Kong has given rise to a curriculum that has minimal emphasis on social efficiency and reconstruction.

As for the impact of socio-political-economic forces on school subjects, two Hong Kong studies have examined the development of Social Studies and History. The emergence of Social Studies was identified by Wong (1992: 318) as 'resulting from the socio-economic changes in Hong Kong in the 1970s which created the need and the condition for its emergence, and the prevailing political culture determined the means and processes by which it emerged'. In the case of History, Vickers (2000) explained that the subject's culture was influenced by social and political changes as well as by overseas curricular models.

These studies have discussed the varying degrees of influence that meso-level forces have had on the school curriculum in general, but none deals specifically with Chinese subjects such as Chinese Language, Chinese Literature and Chinese History. In fact, in contrast to some other subjects, Chinese History has only experienced minor changes over the last 60 years.

Macro-level Influences: Colonialism and Decolonisation

Colonialism and education

Perhaps the most negative view of colonialism is one of economic exploitation and cultural imperialism, as an inevitable consequence of both Western technological and economic dominance, and a product of 'immoral' policies pursued by Western governments or 'dominant classes' (Altbach and Kelly, 1978). According to this view, education is one means by which colonising governments gain and maintain economic and political control:

> Western formal education came to most countries as part of imperialist domination. It was consistent with the goals of imperialism: the economic and political control of the people in one country by the dominant class of another. (Carnoy, 1974: 3)

The teaching of history in particular has been singled out as an example of how education has been used to promote the interests of colonisers. Altbach and Kelly (1978), for example, claim that local history covers only the colonial period, and the little pre-colonial history taught shows the history of the colonised in a bad light in order to contrast it with the more favourable way of life under colonial rule. Also, at the same time as devaluing the culture of the indigenous peoples, colonial governments make every effort to promote their own cultures in order to socialise the colonised into the culture of the colonisers (Said, 1994), in this way preventing the development of local culture. This cultural dependence of the colonised on the coloniser was a way of reinforcing colonial control of the indigenous people, both economically and politically.

Invariably, according to the supporters of this cultural imperialism view of colonialism, the policies and practices of colonial education have been designed to bring about the following outcomes. First, in terms of the provision of education, schooling is unevenly distributed, and aimed at cultivating an elite group to help administer the colony, while mass education is neglected. Second, the curriculum intentionally devalues the indigenous culture, promotes the colonisers' culture, and aims at assimilating the indigenous people into a foreign culture. Third, as a result of colonial rule, problems such as the language of instruction and elitist education are left to be solved after independence because of what 'those who ran the schools wished to have them accomplish — which, put quite simply, was to assist in the consolidation of foreign rule' (Altbach and Kelly, 1984: 1).

However, the belief that colonialism has had a universally negative impact on the colonised is an overgeneralisation about colonial educational policies, and is not supported by extensive studies across a variety of colonies and at different periods in history. For example, Watson (1993: 147) cautions against such simplistic assertions:

> In the British context, at least, there was no universal policy. This [colonial education] varied between, and even within, individual colonial territories either according to the educational and social background of individual administrators, who frequently developed their own policy on the spot or according to the racial and ethnic composition of the territory concerned.

This contrasting view of colonial policy as improvisation rather than planned exploitation is held by other commentators such as Whitehead (1988) and Fieldhouse (1983) who cast serious doubts on the idea that cultural imperialism was 'a conscious and deliberate imposition of alien cultural values and beliefs on hapless indigenous peoples', and that 'education was deliberately used as a means of enforcing British cultural hegemony in the colonies' (Whitehead, 1988: 211). In many cases, they contend, educational planning was carried out in response to the specific social, cultural and economic needs of a particular society, and with the interests of the local people in mind, rather than from pure self-interest on the part of the government; and it was often characterised by 'confused goals arising out of benevolent intentions' (Fieldhouse, 1983). Whitehead argues that 'most colonial schooling certainly mirrored schooling in Britain, but there is ample evidence to suggest that this was more a reflection of local demand on the part of indigenous people themselves than an indication of any deliberate British policy to colonise the indigenous intellect' (1988: 215). In view of the complex nature and purposes of colonial rule, there is a need for a fuller, more sophisticated assessment of colonial education, rather than simply assuming that colonialism is a good or a bad thing. 'Altruism as well as exploitation had a part to play in the westernisation of colonial youth' (Mangan, 1988: 16–17).

A conception of colonialism which contrasts even more with the classic view than the one above, and which is little developed in studies of colonial education, is Robinson's (1986) 'collaborative contract', in which colonial administrations are seen as collaborating with the indigenous people. Robinson argues that for colonialism to be viable, the colonial administration cannot be solely dependent on the coloniser, but must enlist the support of the local people. In this way, colonialism usually proceeds 'by combining with local interests and affiliating with local institutions' (p. 270), so that 'the true metropolis appears neither at the centre nor on the periphery, but in their changing relativities' (p. 271).

One thing is certain: colonialism can take different forms, and caution should be exercised in order to avoid overgeneralising from one or other of the theories discussed above. It should also be recognised that perceptions of colonialism change over time, and colonial policies tend to alter accordingly; for instance, the perception of colonialism in the nineteenth century differed from that after World War II, when Britain was more inclined to allow a greater degree of autonomy in its colonies. Fan (1995: 233) suggests that when analysing the curriculum under British rule, the following aspects should be noted: the view of the sovereign state on colonialism; the international situation that might affect views on colonialism; the ethnic composition of the colonised state; and the consciousness of nationalism amongst the indigenous people.

Hong Kong

There are various interpretations of the effect of colonialism on education in Hong Kong. For instance, it has been seen as an example of cultural imperialism, with the government manipulating and controlling education. Proponents of this argument describe the main aims of colonial education as producing an educated, English-speaking elite to work with the colonial administration, while largely ignoring education for the majority and promoting British culture at the expense of Chinese culture. This rather one-sided view of colonial education in Hong Kong is exemplified in Tse's (1984: 47–51) claim that the colonial government '... suppresses mass education, and develops a group of elites to help with its administration ...' and '... in enforcing the use of English as the medium of instruction in secondary schools aims at separating Chinese students from learning Chinese culture, and instead nourishing them with English culture'. Other writers take a similar position; for example, Wong (1996: 328) asserts that 'All along, Hong Kong's Chinese education existed in a situation where the road was rough, and there was suppression from the (colonial) government'.

A more moderate view of the nature of colonial education in Hong Kong argues that, although the colonial government did influence the school curriculum by causing it to be depoliticised, it was because of the government's concern to minimise threats to its status and to avoid upsetting China, and not because of any desire to devalue Chinese culture: 'As reflected in the History syllabuses, textbooks, and public examinations, cultural imperialism was neither explicit nor strong. It had to do with Hong Kong's peculiar situation; for example, before the 1970s the government was intentionally trying to bring about the political apathy of the people and hence nothing was done to arouse peoples' national sentiments' (Cheung, 1987: 207). The conclusion that concern for the political stability of Hong Kong, rather than cultural imperialism, motivated the colonial government is also held by Morris and Sweeting (1995) who assert that depoliticisation was promoted for explicitly political motives. According to this view, the government did nothing to prevent the teaching of Chinese culture; in fact, '... far from "devaluing indigenous culture", colonial curriculum policy in Hong Kong had the opposite effect of creating a school subject (Chinese History) that presented a totalising, homogenous, quasi-religious vision of the Chinese past ...' (Vickers et al., 2003: 109).

These two interpretations of colonial policy in Hong Kong are inadequate, however, as each limits itself to one motivating factor in determining the curriculum: in the first case, cultural imperialism, and in the second, political considerations. In neither case is the viewpoint backed up by studies which investigate other factors (social and economic) which may have played a part in determining the nature of the Chinese History curriculum.

In complete contrast to the 'cultural imperialism' school of thought is the idea of collaboration between the government and various interest groups in Hong Kong. According to this view, collaboration in education took the form of a tacit agreement between the government and the subject community, made possible by the fact that their interests coincided, particularly in terms of avoiding contemporary political issues. According to Choi (1987: 146), although the government deliberately deleted the politically sensitive issues in school subjects in order to minimise confrontation between the Kuomintang (KMT) and the Chinese Communist Party (CCP) in Hong Kong, there was little opposition because:

> Post-war teachers were genuine Chinese. Since they had suffered from political hardships in China, they tried, as far as possible, to avoid talking about modern Chinese history. Moreover, many considered Hong Kong as a 'temporary shelter' and so were cautious not to get involved in politics. In their teaching they either consciously or unconsciously imparted Chinese culture to students.

Choi describes Chinese teachers at that time as practising 'self discipline', and argues that it was teachers themselves who avoided talking about modern Chinese history, leading to a sort of 'unconscious collaboration'.

Decolonisation and education

Following the universal process of decolonisation during the last century, the priority for most newly independent states was to begin a series of reforms, among the most important of which was a reorientation of the education system to reflect more strongly their specific cultures and social conditions. Although theories of colonialism diverge, commentators generally agree on the usual pattern of events in a decolonised country: first, reform of school curricula so as to portray the emergent nation and its new rulers in a different and better light, and to prepare students for nationhood; second, more prominence given to local languages as the media of instruction; and third, revision of subjects such as History and Geography to include much more local content (Morrisey, 1990; Altbach, 1992; Bray, 1997b).

Hong Kong

During the years leading up to the return of Hong Kong to China there were already signs that post-colonial education would follow the usual practices of decolonised countries. Policies were introduced to allow students to take examinations in Chinese at all levels, without any indication given on the certificates as to the language used, and additional Chinese language teachers were appointed — measures which are seen by Leung (1992) as examples of decolonisation or 'domestication' to encourage a smooth integration with the 'mother culture'. Also, speaking of education generally, Morris (1995b: 131–32) observed that the impending return of Hong Kong to China was having a marked effect on the formal curriculum of secondary schools in ways that appeared to indicate substantial collaboration between the outgoing British administration and the incoming Chinese authority: '… it [the impending retrocession to China] has influenced both the content and treatment of topics within the existing secondary school curriculum. The two specific influences identified were a distinct Sino-centrification and/or politicisation of some subjects [and] an attempt to try and ensure a smooth and trouble free period of transition prior to 1997.'

Similarly, Bray (1997a: 10) argues that: '… much of the emphasis of the added content was not so much on the Hong Kong identity as on the ways that Hong Kong students should see themselves as part of the larger country of which they were becoming part'.

The first few measures after the handover were also characteristic of a decolonised country. In the previous 60 years, the number of Anglo-Chinese (English-medium) schools far exceeded that of Chinese middle schools, even though Cantonese had been an official language since 1974, because of the perception that parents favoured English-medium education for their children. However, in 1998, the SAR government introduced a policy whereby all but 114 schools — about 1/4 of schools — were required to use Cantonese as the medium of instruction. In addition, from 1998, Putonghua, the official language of Beijing, became a core subject in both primary and secondary schools.

However, there are indications that some aspects of the school curriculum are not typical of post-colonial education. For instance, it is frequently the practice in decolonised states to use civic and political education as a means of promoting national identity but, as various commentators have pointed out, this has not been the case in Hong Kong where the curriculum has continued to be depoliticised. For example, Tse (1999) noted that in most schools, political education, in terms of nationalistic and democratic education, was basically absent. Instead, the dominant orientation of civic education was still concerned with developing the moral virtues of good citizens and promoting a cooperative relationship with the government. Moreover, in commenting on post-1997 civic education, Morris et al. (2000: 259) argue that 'the loyalty being promoted is not to the state per se, but to a sense of national identity based upon a homogeneous and totalising sense of Chinese culture, morality and values'.

HISTORICAL STUDY IN CHINA

Historiography in China

The Imperial Period (Pre-1912): The work and influence of Confucius

In China, as early as about the sixteenth century BC, there were official historians who kept records of state affairs. For instance, in the *Book of Odes*, there was the famous saying 'lessons from the Shang dynasty were not far off' (*yin jian bu yuan*), and this kind of record aimed at giving the emperor examples of actions to emulate or avoid. The *Spring and Autumn Annals*,[1] attributed to Confucius (approximately 551–479 BC), are seen by many historians as the founding work of China's historiographical tradition (Tu, 1998: 84). The purposes of writing history, according to Confucius, were to 'punish the bad and advise the good'; to 'unite the Han people and differentiate them from the barbarians'; to 'enhance the principles established by the emperors of the Xia, Shang and Zhou dynasties'; to 'examine the principles of personal matters'; and to 'distinguish between right and wrong deeds' (ibid.: 90–92). The narratives of Confucius in the *Spring and Autumn Annals* portrayed key historical actors as a gallery of moral exemplars for the instruction of future generations of Chinese rulers and their ministers. Personal deeds and individual events were narrated in great detail, and emphasis was placed on moral judgements about whether the actions of certain people were right or wrong, loyal or disloyal, ethical or unethical.

Another feature of the Confucian doctrine was its specification of the 'five relationships', establishing the hierarchical order of relationships between individuals — emperor and minister, father and son, brother and brother, husband and wife, and friend and friend; thus every individual had a proper position to observe, be it in the family, society or state. The doctrine was based on loyalty (to the emperor) and filial piety (individuals were bound by the patriarchal clan system); and it could serve both the political needs of the state and the social needs of a conservative agrarian economy, the basic unit of which was the patriarchal clan. In other words, the Confucian doctrines helped to maintain a stable social order (Liang, 1999: 80; Zhang, 1993: 92). Confucianism was the official philosophy of imperial China for more than 2,000 years — from the Han dynasty (206 BC) to the end of the Qing dynasty (1911). The Confucian classics formed the core of the traditional curriculum followed by scholars aspiring to official careers, and the influence of Confucian doctrines permeated Chinese society and culture (Liu and Wu, 1992: 218).[2]

It is worth noting here that Confucius' ideas were elaborated in the context of the socio-political situation in the Spring and Autumn, and Warring States Period (770–221 BC). As a living tradition of scholarship, in which the classic texts and the commentaries on them were constantly reexamined and reinterpreted in a fashion similar to that of Biblical exegesis in the Christian West, Confucianism was intimately bound up with the development of China's society and her political institutions throughout the imperial period. However, over the past century, Chinese societies have developed in ways radically divergent from the Confucian tradition; for example, the development of commerce and industry has given rise to individuals seeking opportunities in cities, rather than binding themselves to the traditional patriarchal clans of an agrarian economy. While some scholars, such as Tu (1989)[3] and He et al. (1998)[4] strive to re-interpret Confucian thought to make it relevant to the problems of modern China, contemporary Chinese politicians of an authoritarian inclination tend to appeal to a stereotyped, homogenised and anachronistic version of Confucianism, sometimes labelled 'Chinese values' or 'Asian values' (in Singapore) (Tu, 1999: 21).[5]

The work of Sima Qian, Liu Zhiji, Sima Guang and Zhang Xuecheng

In ancient China, historians, often working in an official capacity on the various dynastic histories, inherited and enhanced Confucius' ideas when writing history. Their work comprised bald narratives of events, focusing on the deeds of heroes and villains and praising or condemning their good or bad behaviour. History in ancient China was above all a vehicle for promoting the core doctrines of the Confucian orthodoxy, especially the virtue of loyalty to the Chinese state as personified by the emperor. Historical study was geared primarily towards expounding these doctrines rather than critically investigating the causes of events or the roles of individuals. The following examples taken from the work of renowned historians in different periods reveal the characteristics of historiography in China after Confucius.

Sima Qian's (145–87 BC) *Records of History* (*Shi Ji*) was the first orthodox history[6] in China. He stated explicitly that the aim of his book was 'to find out the reasons for the changes between the past and the present, and to explore what has happened between nature and men' (*tong gu jin zhi bian, jiu tian ren zhi ji*), so that emperors could understand the reasons for success and failure, prosperity and decline. His interpretation of orthodoxy — the imperial authority of the Han race — was later taken as the 'blueprint' when justifying the succession of thrones (Tu, 1998: 286). After Sima Qian, each imperial dynasty sponsored the compilation of the official 'dynastic history' of its predecessor. Hence, when the last dynasty, the Qing, collapsed, there were '24 Dynastic Histories'[7] which, taken together, constituted the orthodox account of the Chinese past from the Han dynasty to the Ming dynasty. Sima Qian's work was held in high regard in historical study in China and had a very significant impact on the later development of Chinese historiography.

In his famous book *Critique of Historical Work* (*Shi Tong*), Liu Zhiji (661–721) highlighted the three most important qualities for historians: talent, knowledge, and insight. All these qualities were aimed at determining whether people's deeds were good or bad so that the work of historians could put pressure on the emperors and courtiers to correct their improper behaviour.

Sima Guang's (1019–86) book *History as a Mirror* (*Zi Zhi Tong Jian*) reflected his belief that the role of history was to show examples of good and bad behaviour for emperors and courtiers to follow or avoid. In his view, a country's stability depended on the extent to which the emperors and courtiers adhered to the set of behavioural criteria delineated in historical texts.

Finally, in his book *The General Meaning of Literature and History* (*Wen Shi Tong Yi*), Zhang Xuecheng (1738–1801) said that the function of history was to elucidate the 'principle' (*dao*) which was embedded in the Six Classics (*Liu Jing*).[8] Hence the framework of criteria set by the Six Classics could be employed to scrutinise present behaviour, rites, ethics and systems. In this way, for many traditional Chinese scholars history took on something of the role sometimes fulfilled by Biblical scripture in Christian Europe — that of a resource with which to exhort or admonish rulers or ministers who appeared to be straying from the 'correct' path.

Chinese historiography has thus been characterised by its moralising, exhortatory function, originating with the Confucian classics and later prescribed in 'the 24 Dynastic Histories'. However, it is worth noting that this type of history functions best in a static society, or one where changes are minimal, so that the moral exemplars can be applied as a set of reasonable criteria for people to follow.

The 'official' historians and criticisms of their work

Two types of authors wrote orthodox history, the first being private individuals who were not official historians, and for whom writing history was a private business. Sima Qian was an example of this kind of historian as he wrote *The Records of History* in a private capacity, hoping that his work would be recognised by the state. The second type included official historians who worked in the State History Department, which was established in the Tang dynasty (618) and lasted until the end of the Qing dynasty (1911), when history writing was a national enterprise and a collective work. 'The 24 Dynastic Histories', which were orthodox histories, were mostly written by official historians. The approach to historical study fostered by this practice of 'official' history writing has been criticised by modern Chinese and Western scholars, e.g.

> They were historians who only knew the dynasty exists but not the nation … , only knew individuals but not a collective group … only knew the past but not present affairs … , only knew facts but did not have any ideals. (Liang Qichao, quoted in Lam, 1980: 5–6)

> Considerable studies have been made of the extraordinary development of textual criticism in China from the second century BC … The development of textual criticism did not bring with it any great advance in the higher forms of what we should call 'criticism' — namely, the scientific assessment of the value of evidence, and there has been considerable study of … one of the main reasons for the peculiar character of Chinese historiography — namely, the remarkable organisation that lay behind the historical writing. … The decisive element was the fact that historical writing was so much an official affair, and was bureaucratically organised. History came to be regarded as a useful guide for governors of states, and on the whole it was written by officials, for officials. It had the peculiar characteristics of what I should call 'civil service history'. (Butterfield, 1961, quoted in Tu, 1981: 34–35)

This review of Chinese historiography points to a situation where, before 1911, the central function of orthodox history was to provide moral exemplars for the emperors and their officials. In addition, history was written to serve the interests of the state — for example, loyalty was defined in terms of the current interests of the state; and Chinese historiography focused on the political elite, the imperial court and individuals, rather than on broader socio-economic or cultural themes. Commenting on the characteristics of traditional historiography in China, Plumb (1969: 12–13) wrote:

> The Chinese pursued erudition, but they never developed the critical historiography which is the signal achievement of Western historiography over the last two hundred years. They never attempted, let alone succeeded, in treating history as objective understanding.

Plumb's criticism may rather overstate the case as there were historians (not official historians) like Zhang Xuecheng (1738–1801) who did take a more critical approach to their work. In the process of historical investigation, he took note of the following concerns: 'record actual events' (*ji shi*), 'discard doubtful materials' (*que yi*), 'find out the truth' (*qiu zhen*) and 'be sceptical' (*huai yi*). Yet, as far as the orthodox history is concerned, Plumb's comments about the lack of critical historiography are valid.

The Republican Period

An impediment to modernisation or a vehicle for rejuvenation? Hu Shih versus Qian Mu

In the republican period (1912–49), intellectuals such as Hu Shih and Chen Duxiu proposed abandoning traditional classical studies and replacing them with Western learning. This is referred to as the May Fourth Movement, sometimes called the May Fourth New Cultural Movement, in which scholars and students advocated the introduction of science and democracy as measures to reform China in the face of foreign threats. During this period, Confucian classics were denounced as impeding the Westernisation of the state. In the 1930s, there were disputes in academic circles as to whether Confucian classics should be incorporated into the primary and secondary school curriculum.[9] At that time, the essence of Confucian classics, which included moralism, cultural values and didacticism, was integrated into the subjects of Chinese Language, Literature and History. However, in the late 1930s and mid-1940s, when China was invaded by Japan, history in general and Confucian classics in particular were regarded as an important means of stimulating patriotic sentiments.[10] Among a number of competing approaches to history were those of Hu Shih and Qian Mu. Hu favoured a complete Westernisation of China and regarded China's classical studies, especially Confucian studies, as discredited and irrelevant to the problems China faced in the modern world, and therefore to be discarded (Hu, 1935: 39). Qian Mu, however, saw history, and particularly Confucian studies, as a source for revitalising the spirit of the Chinese people in the face of adversity.

The work and influence of Qian Mu

Qian Mu's classic work *The General History of China* (1947)[11] shows his belief in the practical functions of history. Yet, unlike the traditional historians who, through writing about the deeds of historical figures, set up a framework of behavioural criteria for people to emulate or avoid, Qian Mu sought to adapt the Chinese historiographical tradition to serve the purpose of bolstering Chinese national and cultural identity. Thus, in Qian's work, culture becomes an identifiable past, as he views it as a source of life-force for the Chinese people;

and it is this cultural identity that revives their confidence and vitality in times of crisis, such as foreign threats and the spread of communism. In the introduction to *The General History of China*, Qian (1947: 7) wrote:

> National history requires two conditions: first, the true cultural evolution of the nation has to be revealed. This serves as the essential knowledge for those who want to understand China's political, social, and cultural development. Second, it should categorise the problems appearing in history for people's reference. The former aims at identifying the sources of our national life and the driving force of our whole history; the latter points out the symptoms of the disease from which our nation is suffering, hence finding ways to improve the situation.

In his narrative, Qian made use of historical events, people and systems to reflect on China's current situation and support his own political views. For instance, in the 1930s, in response to the influence of ideas about representative government and proletariat dictatorship, Qian referred to the government institutions of the Tang dynasty, where he claimed checks and balance already existed to limit the power of the emperor, and the official system as recorded in history demonstrated its effectiveness in administering the state. As a result, according to Qian, representative government modelled on that of the West was unnecessary (ibid.: 13). In the same vein, he argued that capitalist and proletariat classes did not exist as, in traditional Chinese society, commercial activities were not popular and merchants were not powerful enough to exploit the poor. Hence, for Qian, the Marxist idea of revolution provoked by workers and peasants to realise the dictatorship of the proletariat was not applicable to China (ibid.: 19).

Qian emphasised the unique features of Chinese culture in order to counteract what he regarded as the improper influence of non-Chinese ideas. He intentionally focused on those parts of history which he thought could assist in promoting nationalism and patriotism, and at the same time reinforced a sense of cultural identity among the Chinese in the face of the Japanese invasion and the spread of communism. His ideas were influential in the 1930s and 1940s and, according to Hu (1988: 144), Qian's *The General History of China* had a significant effect on history students in Taiwan.

Qian fled to Hong Kong after the communist takeover in 1949, and in 1950 set up New Asia College,[12] which became one of the colleges of the Chinese University of Hong Kong in 1963. He was the Dean of the College for 15 years (1950–65), and his book *The General History of China* became, and still is, one of the most popular references for Chinese History students in Hong Kong. Some of Qian's students, including K. T. Sun and F. L. Wong, taught Chinese History in the Chinese University of Hong Kong (CUHK) and were authors of some of the earliest local Chinese History textbooks.

Post-1949 China

After the communists set up their regime in 1949, official historiography in China was initially based on Marxist-Leninism, and historical developments were ascribed to the operation of dialectic materialism and the class struggle. Plumb (1969: 87–88) criticises Chinese historians of this period for their undiscriminating application of generalisations drawn from Western experience:

> Chinese historians, aided and abetted by Western students of their country, snatched at Western generalizations, particularly Marxist ones, and applied them to Chinese data. But this was rather as if the detailed concepts of advanced chemistry were used on a large quantity of freshly discovered biological facts. … To apply these in any meaningful way to China on the data available was well-nigh impracticable. Once the traditional generalizations were removed, Chinese history collapsed into fragments. The narrative of dynasties remained, of course, but explanation vanished.

However, after the Cultural Revolution, China was more inclined to the cultivation of patriotism, nationalism and the market economy, and hence historiography became less concerned with tracing the operations of the 'laws' of Marxist-Leninist historical theory.[13] Since the 1980s, Qian Mu's work has been rehabilitated in historical studies in universities.

HISTORICAL EPISTEMOLOGY IN CHINA

The Nature of Historical Knowledge: Political and Ethical Issues in Confucian Doctrine and Innate Reflection as a Method of Explanation

In imperial China, the main concern of intellectuals was the contemplation of political-ethical issues, such as loyalty and filial piety, and any interests beyond that were considered subsidiary. In politics, the emphasis was on the affirmation of political ideals and principles, while in ethics it was on the issue of self-reflection in order to achieve high moral standards. The nature of reasoning about political-ethical issues was considered to be basically innate, and the innate understanding of individuals was the origin of all knowledge (Chiang, 1924: 53) — that is, epistemologically, the experiential world was interpreted through the Confucian doctrines. The spirit of positivism was largely ignored and, instead, intuition, imagination and empathy were used to acquire knowledge of historical events and the deeds of individuals. Consequently, in terms of epistemology, it was the 'idealist' school (Chou, 1993: 64–65), operating through narratives, which characterised Chinese historical study.

This view of historical knowledge leads to a method of explanation which is rigid and formulaic. For example, for individuals who want to achieve perfection in political-ethical issues, the following steps should be taken: investigate things (*ge wu*); extend knowledge (*zhi zhi*); be sincere in thoughts (*cheng yi*); and rectify the heart (*zheng xin*). In this way one can achieve the following ideals: cultivate individuals (*xiu shen*); regulate families (*qi jia*); administer the state (*zhi guo*); and stabilise the world (*ping tian xia*) (Chiang, 1924: 80–81). This kind of innate reflection implies that historical knowledge involves a subjective, spiritual or even transcendental state, based on insight of a unique and essentially personal nature (Feng and Chou, 1996: 79).

The Concept of 'Holism' in Knowledge and the Use of Narratives as a Method of Explanation

Since Chinese scholars in the imperial period considered it important to inherit and preserve Confucian doctrines, knowledge was conceived of as the comprehension and enhancement of the ideology of the sage, rather than as the generation of new, personal views. 'Narrating but not interpreting history' (*shu er bu zuo*) reflected Chinese historians' perceptions of epistemology. As a result, traditional historians contributed little, if anything, to new knowledge. In this respect, the Chinese Studies Committee[14] in Hong Kong, in reviewing the history of Chinese studies in China, commented on classical studies:

> The person who could readily point his finger at the place in the Classics where a particular gem of knowledge was hidden was considered learned and well-informed. Thus, many Chinese scholars of the old school tended to regard perfection as residing in the past, and all they could hope for was to reach some degree of emulation. To them, therefore, the western idea of progress was a foreign conception; they were quite content with looking back to the glorious past. (Report of the Chinese Studies Committee, 1953: 2)

The features of epistemology in historical study in China were, therefore, manifested in the detailed narrative of events and individual actions. The decline and fall of a dynasty, for example, would be explained in terms of the incompetence of individuals such as emperors and courtiers. Structural, macroscopic perspectives — including such aspects as economic changes, social structure, and the interactive relationship between politics and the economy — were given little, if any, emphasis. In short, the characteristics of epistemology in traditional China were an individual's innate understanding of issues, of which political-ethical issues were the main concern, and a concept of holistic knowledge, where Confucian doctrines were used to expound rather than to re-interpret.

HISTORY PEDAGOGY IN CHINA

The Imperial Period (Pre-1912)

In the mid-nineteenth century, a classical education based on the literary studies of the 'Four Books' (*Si Shu*) and 'Five Classics' (*Wu Jing*) was regarded as the key to achieving ethical refinement and to solving the practical problems of life. Moreover, as the main subject for the State Examinations, Confucian classics played a dominant role in education in imperial China. Hong Kong's Chinese Studies Committee made the following remarks about the pedagogy of classical education:

> As passages of the Classics had often to be reproduced during State Examinations, children were taught to *memorise* them as soon as they began their schooling — whether or not they could puzzle out their meaning did not matter at this stage. *This largely accounted for the centuries-old Chinese method of teaching — memorisation and recitation before excogitation — which served its purpose in the day when winning distinction in the State Examinations was the aim and ambition of most scholars.* (italics added) (Report of the Chinese Studies Committee: 1)

Of course, learning by memorisation and recitation was not conducive to free expression and original thinking. Also, the situation became even worse in the Ming dynasty (1368–1644), when the standardisation of the public State Examinations ('*Eight-leg system*') led to an emphasis on the refinement of language rather than on originality of thought and content. In pedagogy, therefore, the emphasis was:

> ... in a piece of well-known Chinese literature — with harmonious rhythm, poetic phrases and many classical allusions and quotations, the very last word in beauty and elegance — often lacking in sincerity and at times amounting to very little, as 'matter has become the slave of manner'. (ibid.: 2)

During the Qing dynasty, this kind of literary study continued until the mid-nineteenth century, when some Chinese scholars began to be concerned about its deficiencies and sought to find ways to enhance learning. In the late nineteenth century, for example, Zhang Zhidong advocated: 'Let Chinese learning be the essence, and Western learning provide material efficiency' (*zhong xue wei ti, xi xue wei yong*), and this principle became the basic educational policy of the time. 'Let Chinese learning be the essence' implied that, in pedagogy, the main concern was still the indoctrination of students in the Confucian classics. Hence memorisation and recitation of the 'Four Books' and 'Five Classics' continued to be predominant until the end of the Qing dynasty in 1911.

The Republican Period (1912–49)

The May Fourth Movement of 1919 promoted the use of colloquial style Chinese (*baihua*) to replace classical style Chinese (*wen yan*)[15] as the medium of expression. At the same time, with the introduction of science and technology in the 1920s and 1930s, scholars such as Hu Shih began to challenge the didactics of classical Chinese. Although Hu's proposal 'I write what I speak' (*wo shou xie wo kou*) did facilitate the free expression of ideas, Confucian classics still played a major part in the curriculum, and straightforward indoctrination remained the dominant style of pedagogy. For example, during the republican period (1912–1949), the teaching of Chinese history was mostly confined to the understanding of orthodox history rather than its interpretation. When writing *The General History of China*, Qian Mu compared his work with that of 'the 24 Dynastic Histories',[16] which reflects the high regard still given to orthodox history in general and the status of Confucian classics in particular. In brief, the major characteristics of the teaching of history in China were: the indoctrination of orthodox history in general and Confucian doctrines in particular.

Historiographical study in China is better understood in the context of its socio-political system and related cultural beliefs. Confucianism and imperial politics in China led historians to see history as a doctrine whereby views on individual events and important people were firmly established, and the function of history was thus geared towards providing exemplars to guide the behaviour of individuals. As the doctrines were generated from individual events and people, and each was narrated in great detail, positivist inquiry did not take root in traditional China. Correspondingly, pedagogy manifested itself in the transmission and memorisation of established knowledge rather than in interpretation based on evidence.

THE PRESENT STUDY

Following the analysis in this chapter of the major forces which have been seen to be influential in curriculum change, and the review of historiography in China, Chapters 2, 3, 4 and 5 discuss the findings of the study. The study covers the period from 1945 to 2005, and the evolution of Chinese History has been divided into three conceptual phases related to its status within the school curriculum: emergence, consolidation, and crisis and opportunity. The first phase traces its emergence as an independent subject from 1945 until 1974, when Anglo-Chinese schools and Chinese middle schools followed the same CEE syllabus. The second phase, from 1974 to 1997 (the end of the colonial rule), was a period of consolidation for the subject, during which time it was not only able to secure its independent status against attempts to incorporate it into a new Social Studies subject, but also to become a common core subject for Form 1–3 (F1–3). In the third phase, from 1997 up to 2005, Chinese History faced a period of crisis in which its independent status was threatened by the SAR government's proposed reforms to the curriculum, but successful attempts were made by the subject community to resecure its place as a separate subject in the school curricula.

Chapter 2 provides a context for the detailed discussion of the development of the Chinese History curriculum in subsequent chapters with a brief review of politics, society and education in Hong Kong, from its beginnings as a British colony up to the present. The chapter also traces the way in which Chinese History emerged as a separate subject and consolidated its independent status at all levels in both Chinese middle and Anglo-Chinese secondary schools, and discusses the part played by political and social forces. Chapters 3, 4 and 5 each focus on one phase of the development of Chinese History, and analyse three aspects of the curriculum: the curriculum development process, the curriculum aims and content, and the impact of the curriculum on teaching, learning and assessment. The decision-making processes of the respective subject committees are analysed, and the relative roles and degrees of influence of the government subject officers, academics and schoolteachers who made up the subject committees are identified in order to determine the dominant force(s) in the decision-making process, and whether the approach to curriculum development was centralised or decentralised. The material for the analysis of the curriculum development process was obtained from interviews with members of the subject committees, minutes of meetings and other primary and secondary documents.

The curriculum aims and content are examined in order to determine how and to what extent they reflect the views of officialdom and the socio-political background of the time. The main issues considered are: whether Chinese History was intended to give students a cultural or a national identity; whether it was to be a vehicle for developing critical thinking or for the inculcation of orthodoxy; whether the emphasis was on interpretation of events based on source material and reasoned argument, or on memorisation of factual accounts; and finally, how it might contribute to civic, moral, national and ethnic education. It should be noted that in the early phase (1945–74) the curriculum was mainly set out in the lists of topics contained in the examination syllabuses and textbooks, and the content of the curriculum and the scope of study reflected the parameters defined by curriculum developers. Following the issuing of teaching syllabuses from 1975 onwards, however, the aims, content, methods and assessment were more clearly delineated for teachers' reference.

The impact of the curriculum on teaching, learning and examinations is looked at in order to assess in what ways and how far the official curriculum was actually realised at the classroom level. This is done through an analysis of examination questions, marking schemes, examination reports and textbooks, as well as the perceptions of teachers and officials as recorded in committee meetings and interviews.

Finally, Chapter 6 summarises the findings of Chapters 2 to 5, and identifies the pattern of change in the development of Chinese History, as well as the various kinds of forces which have been instrumental in determining the nature and scope of the subject. The relative impact of each of these forces is assessed, and the findings are then discussed within the wider theoretical context established in Chapter 1.

Terminology[17]

This study uses the following terms:
- **'Chinese History'** refers to the school subject devoted to the study of the history of China — as distinct from the separate subject 'History'. Chinese is used as the medium of instruction and assessment.
- **'History'** refers to the school subject that comprises topics from both Western and Asian history, and is studied and assessed through either English or Chinese.
- **'history'** refers to the discipline of 'history', or 'history in general', rather than a school subject.
- **'Anglo-Chinese schools'** are schools using English or a mixture of English and Chinese as the medium of instruction, while using English for assessment. Since 1998, with the enforcement of the new medium of instruction policy, the 114 remaining Anglo-Chinese schools have had to adhere to using English as the medium of instruction and assessment for all subjects other than Chinese and Chinese History.
- **'Chinese middle schools'** are schools using Chinese as the medium of instruction and assessment for all subjects other than English.
- **'Marking schemes'** are the point-reward-basis marking criteria used for CEE Chinese History.
- **'Orthodoxy'** refers to the historical views prescribed in the official dynastic history: 'the 24 Dynastic Histories'. The views were Han-centred, moralistic and geared to consolidating the rule of the current dynasty. 'The 24 Dynastic Histories' was later taken as the 'blueprint' for the interpretation of dynastic histories.
- **'Cultural History'** as specified in the Chinese History curriculum includes the following aspects: institutions, economic development, intellectual thoughts, examination systems and external relations. 'Traditional Chinese culture' specified in the aims of the curriculum refers to a homogenous vision of the culture of China's majority Han nationality.
- **'Political History'** is synonymous with dynastic history in that the history of the imperial courts, in particular the deeds of emperors and other key persons, is the main focus of study. It is not political history in its Western sense. The historical views of the dynasties are based on the state orthodoxy compiled in 'the 24 Dynastic Histories'.

2

Politics, Society and Education in Hong Kong: A Brief Historical Overview

Since, as seen in Chapter 1, the development of the Chinese History curriculum has been so greatly influenced by social and political factors, the following brief historical review of politics, society and education in Hong Kong may be helpful as a context for understanding the later discussion of the development of the Chinese History curriculum in the last 60 years.

POLITICS

The 1950s to the 1970s

When the British first came to Hong Kong, it was with the intention of setting up a post for trade with China. At that time, there were very few indigenous people in Hong Kong, the majority arriving only after it had become a colony. The first huge influx of people came at the end of the 1940s, continuing on into the 1950s, and consisted of refugees from Southern China and Shanghai who were fleeing from the civil war and the political turmoil in China. For them, colonial Hong Kong was preferable to communist rule; and they would stay as long as they were allowed to get on with their lives with minimal interference from the Hong Kong government. It is important to emphasise this unusual aspect of Hong Kong's early years as a British colony as it helps in understanding the socio-economic-political and educational changes that have occurred in its history. It explains why, for example, successive colonial governments have used two guiding principles in their policy-making: to prevent anti-British sentiment in Hong Kong, and to avoid upsetting China. This has been reflected in the emphasis the government has placed on stability and prosperity throughout colonial — and, indeed, post-colonial — times to avoid discontent among the local inhabitants or interference from China. As long as there were economic benefits, China would not interfere.

Although the colonial government was generally very strict in establishing order, it realised that to maintain stability and prosperity, and thereby gain the acquiescence of the populace in colonial rule, it needed a certain degree of cooperation from the local inhabitants. This it did by cultivating the local elite —businessmen and prominent figures in Hong Kong — and involving them increasingly in the administration of the colony. As noted earlier, this association between the colonial government and leading members of society has been called a 'collaborative contract' (Robinson, 1986). According to King (1973: 130), 'From the 1950s, the government of Hong Kong began to cultivate local elite so as to enlist them in the administration of the colony'; and he refers to this involvement of the local elite in policy-making in order to form an administrative partnership as 'administrative absorption of politics'. The colonial government was also aware that it needed to maintain an apolitical policy and restrict political discussion, especially after the arrival of large numbers of immigrants in the late 1940s and 1950s with affiliations to the two rival groups on the Mainland, the KMT and the CCP, which later culminated in disturbances in 1956.[1] In 1950, the Governor, Alexander Grantham, stated this clearly: 'We cannot permit Hong Kong to be the battleground for contending parties or ideologies'.[2] The association with the local elite and the maintenance of an apolitical society were to be the basis for colonial rule in Hong Kong.

After the riots of 1966 and 1967,[3] the government realised that steps had to be taken to prevent further unrest and to maintain an environment in which the colony could prosper. It therefore introduced a series of reforms in the areas of housing, health and education, and began to target the grassroots by listening to their concerns. These measures continued into the 1970s. For instance, the MacLehose government: greatly expanded housing, school and health reforms; absorbed anti-government figures and the elite into the administrative machinery and consultation bodies (King, 1981); increased public consultation and the mechanisms for doing so; established the Independent Commission Against Corruption (ICAC), and other anti-corruption measures; and generally attempted to build a more cohesive society — a 'Hong Kong identity' — particularly through a series of government-sponsored advertisements. At this time, the government adopted a policy of 'positive non-interference', whereby low tax, free currency exchange and free trade were implemented in order to promote a laissez-faire economy. Mindful of the concerns of both business interests in Hong Kong and the PRC, it was also careful not to upset either. For example, it resisted any demands for democratic reform, the result of which was that power in Hong Kong, was, in effect, in the hands of the civil service and business interests.

The 1980s to 1997

Particularly after the Sino-British Joint Declaration in 1984, there was increasing unease in Hong Kong over the prospects for the colony with the return of its sovereignty to China in 1997, in spite of the promise of 'one country, two systems' by the Chinese government. The Hong Kong government enacted a range of administrative reforms from the mid-1980s, such as more localisation and expanding the consultation process, but it carried out only minimal measures for enhancing democracy for fear of 'rocking the boat' by upsetting either business interests in Hong Kong or the PRC. The government's overriding concern continued to be to avoid antagonising China, while maintaining confidence and stability in Hong Kong. However, it was becoming increasingly difficult to preserve the delicate balance between the demands of the Hong Kong people for greater democracy and the interests of those groups, particularly from the business sector, which had previously supported the colonial government but were now already looking ahead to Chinese rule, and the PRC.

During these years, an increasing number of Hong Kong people were beginning to take an interest in political issues — at least in those issues which affected their way of life. Their fears for the future were heightened in 1989 by the June Fourth Incident in Tiananmen Square, and there were massive street demonstrations in sympathy for, and support of, the students in Beijing. Relations with China worsened as a result of this very strong display of feeling by Hong Kong people, coupled with the rise of various pro-democracy parties during the previous years, who, encouraged by their success in the first direct elections for the Legislative Council in 1991, were putting increased pressure on the Hong Kong government for democratic reforms. Relations between Hong Kong and China continued to deteriorate during the 1990s, especially when the last colonial government under Governor Patten began to institute reforms for greater democracy. The years leading up to 1997 saw an increasing division between the Patten government and the pro-democracy parties on the one hand, and the pro-China parties, business interests and the PRC on the other.

1997 and Beyond

In 1997, Tung Chee Hwa became the first Chief Executive of the SAR, through a selection process undertaken by a mostly appointed selection committee of 800 pro-Beijing members. There was an atmosphere of optimism for the future of Hong Kong, with political leaders in China affirming their commitment to the 'one country, two systems' policy, and promising a 'hands-off' approach to Hong Kong. The Chief Executive began by forming his administration and removing the traces of Patten's reforms, for example by curtailing the power of the civil service. He signalled his centralised and paternalistic style of government by setting up a 'ministerial' system in which civil service secretaries were appointed as ministers to take charge of the various policy-making branches, and by appointing members of the business and professional elites as consultants in various administrative bodies such as the Executive Council, the Education

Commission and the Housing Committee. Tension soon surfaced, however, as senior civil servants appointed by the Chief Executive competed with the various advisory committees to define and protect their territorial boundaries.

A key priority of the SAR government was to improve the economy, which had suffered badly as a result of the Asian financial crisis of 1997, and Tung's first real challenge was to counter the attack on the currency by speculators in October 1997. While this was successful, it was followed by a fall in stock prices and property markets. In order to stimulate the economy, the government made massive investments in rail, road, port and airport projects, and introduced various schemes such as the Cyberport (to make Hong Kong the technology hub of Asia), the Science Park and the Chinese Medicine Port. At the same time, measures were taken to boost tourist numbers, which had been steadily falling, such as a $50 million tourism fund, a proposed Disneyworld on Lantau Island, and a cable car to connect Tung Chung with the Lantau 'Buddha'. Another of Tung's major aims was to increase home ownership by reducing the cost, and increasing the supply, of public housing. Among the measures taken were: continuing the Home Ownership Scheme (HOS) begun in 1978, which involved the sale of subsidised flats; and introducing the Tenant Purchasing Scheme (TPS) in 1998, in which people were able to purchase the public housing flats they were renting. Another aim of the SAR government was to improve educational standards through reform of the education system.

However, Tung's popularity started to decline quite early for a variety of reasons. His aloof manner and autocratic style of governing meant that he was unwilling to involve the Legislative Council (Legco) more fully in consultations, or to explain his policies to the public. The abrupt way in which his administration introduced and implemented policies without proper or adequate public consultation added to the general feeling of dissatisfaction and frustration in Hong Kong. Another real cause for concern was the perception that he favoured business interests in Hong Kong, one example being the Cyberport, for which the development of the entire project was awarded without tender to Richard Li, the son of the business tycoon Li Ka Shing. Another illustration was the government's 'repositioning' of its housing policy, whereby HOS flats were transferred from sale to rental in 2000, a moratorium was placed on the sale of HOS flats in 2001 and the TPS scheme was ended in 2002 — measures which deprived those on lower incomes of the chance to own their homes. Although the government claimed that the reason for these reversals to public housing policy was to avoid competing with the private sector, many people thought that it was another example of favouring business interests, in particular property developers. Yet another factor contributing to public dissatisfaction with Tung was that his policy-making appeared to be more concerned with the interests of China than those of the people of Hong Kong. While the Basic Law had guaranteed 'one country, two systems', it seemed that there was a strong emphasis on the 'one country' at the expense of the 'two systems'. For example, he even went as far as asking the Standing Committee of the National People's Congress in May 1999, April 2004 and April 2005 for interpretations of the Basic Law, thus circumventing the Court of Final Appeal in Hong Kong and causing considerable consternation and fear for Hong Kong's autonomy.

Eventually, in response to the frustration that people felt and showed at not being able to effect any change — or even to have their dissatisfaction listened to, let alone acted upon — Tung set up the principal officials accountability system in July, 2002, by which 11 directors of bureaux appointed from both the business sector and the civil service, were made accountable to him. These principal officials were also appointed to the Executive Council. However, without any democratic checks, this had little meaning or provided little reassurance for Hong Kong people since the accountability would be solely to the Chief Executive and not to them.

Dissatisfaction with Tung's administration continued, if not increased, particularly as a result of a series of unfortunate incidents such as: the government's handling of the SARS outbreak in 2003; a high unemployment rate; negative equity for homeowners; the evident lack of collaboration among the three main administrative bodies, Legco, Exco and the civil service; the refusal of the Chief Executive to entertain any thought of democratic reform; and his seeming inability, or unwillingness, to improve the lives of the ordinary people. This dissatisfaction came to a head in July 2003, when half a million people took part in a march through the streets of Hong Kong in protest against the draconian anti-subversion bill (Article 23) that Tung was proposing to introduce. The Chief Executive withdrew the bill, but his administration continued to be beset by a range of ill-conceived and unpopular policies — such as reclaiming land from the Victoria Harbour; the improper decision of the government to give the American Chamber of Commerce HK$100 million in sponsorship to underwrite losses in hosting a series of concerts; and the government's decision to sell several blocks of HOS flats in Hunghom, originally intended for sale but left unoccupied for some time, to private developers at a considerable loss. (In the last case, the developers actually decided to demolish these new blocks of flats to build much larger, more luxurious ones, but this created so much public discontent that they eventually withdrew their plan.) Yet another source of contention was the West Kowloon Cultural District Project, which the government seemed determined to award to just one developer. It appears that, unlike colonial governments in the past, Tung's government was unable to balance the interests of the people of Hong Kong with those of the PRC. Finally, on 12 March 2005, with two years of his second term to run, he resigned. At the time there was speculation that the PRC, exasperated with his inability to maintain a stable, prosperous and harmonious society, had asked him to step down; and that his 'nomination', and subsequent 'election' as the vice-chairman of the Chinese People's Political Consultative Conference (CPPCC), a purely consultative body with no powers, was a 'face-saving measure'.

SOCIETY

Hong Kong has undergone distinct social and economic changes since its beginnings as a trading port with a comparatively small indigenous population dependent upon fishing and farming. The first changes came in the late 1940s and the 1950s as a result of the influx of refugees from the Mainland — mostly from Guangdong — who were fleeing from the domestic upheaval in China, and the ending of the Korean war in 1953, when the UN placed an embargo on trade with China, marking the end of Hong Kong's position as a major entrepôt for trade between China and the West. Manufacturing industries began to emerge, based on the plentiful supply of cheap labour among the newly arrived immigrants from Guangdong and financed by the entrepreneurs who had fled from Shanghai. By the 1960s, manufacturing had expanded from its origins in cotton textiles and woollens to become a major exporter of all sorts of manufactured goods such as clothing and electronic products. Encouraged by the efforts of the MacLehose government to increase public services and make Hong Kong a more cohesive society, Hong Kong people began to see Hong Kong as a permanent home, rather than just a temporary refuge from the troubles in China.

By the late 1970s, manufacturing began to give way to service and financial industries (e.g. communications, banking and insurance), partly because many manufacturers were moving their factories across the border in order to cut costs. This was soon to turn Hong Kong into the major world financial centre it is today. With increasing prosperity during this time, there emerged an affluent, more sophisticated and politically conscious middle class. Hong Kong was also becoming less of an immigrant city as a result of tougher immigration laws, including the end of the 'touch base' policy (by which 'illegal' immigrants had been able in the past to obtain legal residence if they managed to reach the urban area without being apprehended). The second and third generation Hong Kong people, who now saw the colony as their home and not just as a 'safe haven', identified nationally and patriotically with China in terms of culture and ethnicity, but they felt alienated from the communist regime on the Mainland and began to differentiate themselves as 'Hong Kong' Chinese.

Many of these middle class people emigrated during the 1980s and 1990s because of their forebodings about what would happen in 1997, fears which were exacerbated by the June Fourth Incident in 1989. This massive 'brain drain', mostly of professionals, including many teachers, reached 60,000 a year at one stage, and although many did return once they had gained the security of a foreign passport, it put a strain on the economy.

The economic recession of 1998 was another unsettling affair after the years of affluence and has continued, even up to 2005, to have an adverse effect on various sectors of society, who have in one way or another expressed their dissatisfaction with the government's seeming inability to improve the state of the economy or their standard of living.

EDUCATION

Administration and Policy-Making

The colonial era

Immediately after World War II, the large influx of refugees from the Mainland prompted the Hong Kong government to begin a massive expansion of education. At the same time, mindful of the political conflict on the Mainland, and its own vulnerable status as a colonial ruler of Hong Kong, it was determined to exercise strict control over all aspects of education and to pursue an apolitical school curriculum. This was to lead to centralised educational administration and policy-making and a depoliticised curriculum which were to last throughout the colonial era. The centralised and depoliticised nature of the colonial government's educational policy-making can be seen in the measures it took, after the establishment of the PRC in 1949, to control education and to avoid disputes between rival KMT and CCP supporters who had newly arrived from the Mainland (including schools with affiliations to the two political parties). Measures aimed at countering communist activities included, for instance, the establishment of the 'Special Bureau' within the ED in 1949, the amendment of the Education Ordinance in 1948 and the introduction of a new Education Ordinance in 1952. In 1952, the government also set up the Syllabuses and Textbooks Committee (STC) which had a three-fold remit: to draw up model syllabuses for schools; to advise the Director of Education on textbooks and other teaching aids; and to stimulate the writing and publication of teaching notes and textbooks suitable for the model syllabuses. In 1972, the STC was replaced by the Curriculum Development Committee (CDC) (renamed the Curriculum Development Council in the 1990s), which was an advisory body giving recommendations to the ED on all matters related to curriculum development, while the inspection of textbooks was carried out by the Advisory Inspectorate (AI) of the ED. The CDC comprised various subject committees made up of subject officers from the ED, particularly from the AI and the Examinations section, academics and teachers nominated by their principals. (The examination work was taken over by the Hong Kong Examinations Authority in 1978, which was renamed the Hong Kong Examinations and Assessment Authority [HKEAA] in 2002.)

In 1982, the government appointed the Llewellyn Commission to recommend educational improvements, which led to the formation of the Education Commission in 1984. The task of the Commission was to advise the Governor on educational issues, coordinate policy and produce planning reports. Between 1984 and 1997, it produced seven reports covering a wide range of issues such as: the problem of heavy homework demands; the inordinate number of subjects that students had to study; intense examination pressure and too much testing; an overemphasis on rote learning; and the decline in language proficiency. These issues were reiterated in the Education Commission's policy paper *Education Blueprint for the 21st Century* in 1999, which also summarised the essential qualities required for the future of society as creativity, imagination, self-learning ability and language proficiency. However, as it was only an advisory body, the Commission did not have the power to ensure the implementation of its proposals, and many of its recommendations were simply shelved.

In an effort to address these concerns, the colonial government tried to decentralise certain areas of education in order to allow schools to take more initiatives. For example, in 1988 the School Based Curriculum Development Scheme (SBCDS) was launched in order to encourage schools to be more innovative in curriculum planning. Also, the Direct Subsidy Scheme (DSS), begun in 1990, aimed at giving schools more financial autonomy. Finally, the School Management Initiative (SMI) was introduced in 1991 to give more responsibility to schools for their management. Unfortunately, the results of these initiatives have not been very promising; for example, only a small proportion of schools have joined the SMI and DSS, while the SBCDS has turned out to be more an exercise in designing classroom materials than in creating new curricula to suit the specific needs of students.

Post-1997

> The education system of old can no longer meet the challenges of the new age. Embracing the knowledge-based New Economy requires a large pool of talent equipped with the right skills and creativity. Rapid advances in science and technology have unleashed a series of perplexing social and ethical issues, which demand more critical and analytical thinking by our young people. Following our reunification, the need to groom a new generation of leaders has become ever more pressing. Therefore, without sweeping reforms of our education system, the quality of our education would not be able to meet the requirements for social development and the community's expectations. (Tung Chee Hwa, Chief Executive, HKSAR, Policy Address, 11 October 2000: 18)

The two main educational aims of the first post-colonial government under Tung Chee Hwa were to reform the school curriculum in order to meet the needs of this 'new age', and to unite students with the motherland and instil in them a sense of Chinese identity and belonging to China. In order to achieve the first of these aims, the government introduced a number of reforms which included: issuing firm guidelines on the medium of instruction, in which only 1/4 of the schools were allowed to be English-medium schools, with checks on their ability to be so; making Putonghua a core subject in primary and secondary schools; allowing students to take public examinations in Chinese at all levels, with no indication of the language used; appointing additional Chinese language teachers; providing IT resources for both primary and secondary schools; introducing benchmark language tests for teachers; and integrating the curriculum. However, some of these reforms ran into difficulties. For example, the question of which schools should be English Medium of Instruction (EMI) and which Chinese Medium of Instruction (CMI) remains a problematic issue with regard to the distinguishing criteria and implementation. Schools which wish to be EMI schools are supposed to demonstrate to the EMB that the ability of their students and teachers, and the accompanying strategies and facilities, are all conducive to the effective use of EMI; and they also have to be regularly inspected by the EMB to ensure that they meet the criteria. However, it is clear that the whole exercise was not very well thought out, and has not been implemented very effectively or fairly since some so-called EMI schools were obviously not suited to English-medium education, while others with better English language environments were forced to become CMI schools. Moreover, some of the schools which had previously used English as the medium found great difficulty in changing to Chinese, for example because their teachers were accustomed to teaching in English and there was a lack of Chinese language teaching resources. The problem has been accentuated by the fact that most parents wish their children to study in English-medium schools, believing it to be the key to their future success. Also, teachers protested against the compulsory language tests, with many of them fearing they would lose their jobs. The proposal to merge History with Chinese History also caused much controversy, particularly in the media, and many Chinese History teachers were unhappy, feeling that after the handover there was even more reason for the subject to remain independent in order to encourage students to develop a national identity. However, with the introduction of the new HKCEE Chinese History curriculum in 2004, and the proposed New Senior Secondary curriculum to be introduced in 2009, the independent status of Chinese History in the school curriculum seems to have been securely anchored (see subsequent chapters for details).

The second major aim of the SAR government, in contrast to the previous colonial government, was to use the school curriculum to promote national sentiment and to develop in students a feeling of Chinese identity. In order to achieve this, the humanities curriculum in general, and History and Chinese History in particular, were revised to include more about modern China, and to encourage discussion of political issues, something that had been taboo in the 1950s and 1960s. The Chief Executive's determination to bring home the need for Hong Kong people to leave behind their colonial past and be united with China can be seen in the phrases he often used in his policy addresses, such as 'our Chinese values' and 'reunite with the motherland'. He was supported in this by popular comments from various sectors of society such as 'Chinese in charge of our own households' and 'Correct the malpractice of the colonial government'. In his 1998 Policy Address, he also stated his aim of strengthening 'Hong Kong's own unique culture'. The 1999 Education Commission report, which detailed the major issues which needed to be addressed, recommended that students should learn more about modern China, to feel more a part of it, and that they should also be aware of the history and culture of Hong Kong — so that they had a sense of Hong Kong as a meeting place for the best of the East and the West. In general, in contrast to colonial times, when the curriculum was apolitical and aimed at developing a cultural, not a national, identity with China, the post-colonial SAR curriculum has been revised to include political issues and aims to develop an identity with China.

It was in the context of these striking political, social, economic and educational changes in Hong Kong through its colonial and post-colonial years that Chinese History has emerged as a subject in the school curriculum and consolidated its independent status. The next section reviews the development of the subject in terms of its nature and scope of study.

Chinese History: Emergence and Consolidation as an Independent Subject

Background: A brief history to 1945

During the first half of the twentieth century, in spite of the turbulent times in China, the colony was kept relatively stable, and the British authorities in Hong Kong avoided as far as possible getting involved in China's internal politics. It was felt by some that one way of minimising the destabilising influence of China's politics within Hong Kong was to reduce or even eliminate coverage of Chinese history in the local schools. In fact, as early as 1904, George Bateson Wright, principal of the Central School, was aware of the political sensitivity of having Chinese history taught to local students, expressing the following concern:

> On political grounds I am strongly averse to any instruction in Chinese History which would expose us to the charge of being the nursery for Revolutionists on the [Chinese] continent. (quoted in Sweeting, 1990: 198)

In 1925–26, there was a general strike and boycott of British goods in Guangzhou and Hong Kong, which led to serious anti-British feelings among the populace. According to Luk (1991: 658), 'the British in Hong Kong felt greatly threatened and adopted a cultural policy that deeply affected the Chinese culture component of the curriculum'. It was in these circumstances that Cecil Clementi, a Sinologist, was appointed governor in 1925. In the following year, he established the first government Chinese middle school, which adopted its syllabuses, textbooks and subjects from China — and at that time, its graduates could continue their studies in universities in China. In contrast, the so-called 'Anglo-Chinese schools', in which English was used as the medium of instruction, emphasised the learning of English as a second language and general (world) knowledge (history, geography and natural science), while classical Chinese was included only as a supplementary course; and distinguished graduates of these schools were encouraged to enter the University of Hong Kong for further study. Luk (1991) considers that Clementi's cultural policies aimed at balancing Chinese cultural tradition and contemporary Chinese nationalism in an attempt to avoid any threat to the stability of the colonial government.

In the 1930s, the British authorities were very concerned about the knowledge acquired by students in Anglo-Chinese schools, and so carefully selected the content of school subjects. The following statement made by a senior official at the Colonial Office reflects the nature of the school curriculum at that time:

> ... special local conditions justified more attention being paid to ancient civilisations than to current events. It is not considered desirable to interest Hong Kong students too much in political and administrative questions. (quoted in Sweeting, 1990: 198)

Consequently, in European history, only the earlier, more remote periods were included, while in Chinese history, which was part of a subject called Chinese Studies, the emphasis in the contemporary periods was on cultural, economic and intellectual history; political history was to be avoided.

1945–1974: The emergence of Chinese History as an independent subject

In the early part of this period, there was no independent Chinese History subject. In 1945, history teaching in government vernacular schools (later known as Chinese middle schools) was divided into 'China' and 'foreign'; Chinese history was taught in F1, F2, F4 (one semester) and F5, while foreign history was taught in F3 and F4 (one semester). In government schools (later known as Anglo-Chinese schools) only one subject, History (foreign), was offered. Chinese History as a subject first appeared in the 1948 ED Annual Report, which stated that the Hong Kong Certificate of Education Examination (HKCEE) for Anglo-Chinese schools would be revised to include Chinese Literature and Chinese History as one subject in order to give candidates a wider choice. Thus, in 1950 a new subject called 'Chinese Literature and Chinese History' was included in the CEE for the first time; and, in 1952, when the six-year Chinese School Certificate course was introduced, Chinese History and History were combined in one subject in Chinese middle schools. During the 1950s Chinese History was, therefore, combined with either Chinese Literature or History.

The next stage in the evolution of the status of Chinese History as a separate subject in the curriculum was in 1952, when the ED Annual Report revealed the government's concerns about the quality of textbooks, especially those for Chinese, history and geography. As regards Chinese History, the Report highlighted the fact that the textbooks in Chinese middle schools were not only educationally and politically unsatisfactory, but were predominantly concerned with Chinese history at the expense of world history. As a result of this, a Chinese Studies Committee was set up in the same year to review the aims of, and the setting of parameters for, the future development of Chinese subjects, including Chinese History. In 1953, the Committee issued a report in which it criticised the xenophobic nature of textbooks published in China, and recommended that Hong Kong should produce its own textbooks with an unbiased view of China and the rest of the world:

> The attitude so often derived from the learning of Chinese History, e.g. to look upon the Chinese Empire as the only empire of importance underneath the sky, and China as the Middle Kingdom, etc., is not educationally sound or desirable, and should be rectified. (Report of the Chinese Studies Committee: 14–15)

The Report further commented that:

> ... History textbooks published in China usually contain anti-foreign allusions, comments and propaganda, and are, therefore, not quite suitable for use in Hong Kong ... There is indeed an urgent need to produce History textbooks with an unbiased international goodwill and understanding rather than hatred and misunderstanding ... and only important historical movements be included. Hong Kong is contiguous to China. It is not only the show-window of World democracy in the East, but also the meeting-place and melting-pot of Eastern and World cultures. Here, Chinese students cannot (*sic*) only retain and cherish what is best in their own culture, but learn of what is best in British and World thought ... In these textbooks, the emphasis should be on Social and Cultural History rather than Political History ... Objectivity in treatment is, of course, to be strictly observed, especially in connection with such topics as the Boxer Uprising and the so-called Opium War. (ibid.)

The Report also stated that it would be inappropriate to include modern history in either Anglo-Chinese or Chinese middle schools, and that only cultural and social history should be taught:

> ... the two sections, one on Modern Chinese History (1644 AD – 1945 AD) and one on Modern World History (1789 to present), both sections are predominantly political, and so not quite in line with the general principles which, in the opinion of this committee, should govern the study of History. (ibid.)

Another recommendation was that Chinese History should be taught through the medium of Chinese, which meant, of course, that it would be difficult to merge it with History, especially in Anglo-Chinese schools where History was taught in English. This marked the gradual separation of Chinese History from History and

Chinese Literature (beginning in 1956), which culminated in its independence as a subject at all levels in both Anglo-Chinese and Chinese middle schools in 1967.[4] By emphasising the cultural and imperial court history of China (without nationalistic and racialist overtones) to the exclusion of modern Chinese politics, the report shows the Committee's view of Chinese History in Hong Kong as a cultural rather than a political subject, and this stance has been adhered to in the development of the Chinese History curriculum ever since. The sensitive nature of Chinese History at the time, and the government's determination to maintain firm control over all aspects of education, particularly in view of the disputes between rival KMT and CCP groups in Hong Kong, is also reflected in the setting up of the Syllabus and Textbook Committee (STC) in 1952, and its issuing of teaching guidelines for Chinese History. In 1962, the STC issued 'Recommended Guidelines for 5-year Chinese Middle Schools', and in 1970, 'Recommended Guidelines for Anglo-Chinese and Chinese Middle Schools'. Publishers followed these guidelines and produced textbooks accordingly, which were then examined by the STC before being included in the list of recommended textbooks.

Before 1958, Chinese History's period of study in both types of schools covered up to 1945 (the end of World War II). However, after the riots of 1956, which made the government even more aware of the possible destabilising effects of the rivalries in modern Chinese politics, both Anglo-Chinese and Chinese middle school syllabuses were amended in 1958 to remove modern history, with the end-date becoming 1911 (the end of the Qing dynasty). The curriculum emphasis thereafter was on the history of the Sui, Tang, Song, Yuan, Ming and Qing dynasties (581–1911), which are regarded by Chinese historians as the golden periods of Chinese cultural and imperial history. Subsequent revisions of the CEE (Anglo-Chinese schools) in 1972 restored the end-date to 1945 as it was thought that the politically sensitive period was after 1945. This can be seen in the response of A. G. Brown (a senior official in the ED) to a query by the press regarding Chinese History's period of study: 'History is history, we have to wait for a time when subjective political factors and military conflicts are resolved … Therefore in order to avoid getting bogged down in political conflicts, history has to stop in 1945'.[5] Hence there was no coverage of history after the middle of the twentieth century, which meant that students did not study the civil war (1945–49) and the establishment of the PRC. During the 1970s, there were criticisms in the press from supporters of the KMT and the CCP about the scope and nature of the Chinese History curriculum:

> Of textbooks on Chinese History — the leftwing groups criticised the 'time period' covered by the textbooks, which did not mention the emergence of the present communist government in China. (*South China Morning Post*, 30 September 1973)

> Chinese History textbooks in China give a chronological narration of the Opium War up to the Cultural Revolution, but no reference is made concerning the Republic of China. (ibid.)

> The textbooks are outdated ... they still use 'Peiping' instead of 'Beijing.[6]

However, it is important to note that the emphasis on cultural and imperial court history and avoidance of contemporary issues was not due solely to the government's determination during the 1970s to exclude political issues from the curriculum. There was a very influential group of scholars and teachers who had come from China in 1949 to take refuge in Hong Kong, whose preference was for, and expertise was in, dynastic history, and who held orthodox views of Chinese historiography which they strove to promote in the curriculum. They had no interest in modern history and felt that the proper study of Chinese History should be concerned only with cultural and imperial court history. Their views were reflected in the textbooks they produced, which were described by academics as lacking in analysis, reflecting history in a straightforward way, and extremely conservative and pro-Nationalist. It was in this way that the nature of the Chinese History curriculum was defined, and would remain practically the same for the rest of the period (see subsequent chapters for details).

1974–97: Consolidation of Chinese History as an independent subject

In 1974, the status of Chinese History was reinforced when the Anglo-Chinese and Chinese middle schools' curricula were merged and the two types of schools followed the same CEE Chinese History syllabus. This was followed a year later by the two junior level syllabuses being made uniform, and in 1992, the F6 syllabuses. In this period, despite a number of threats to its status, it remained an independent subject. One such threat came in 1975 when the government tried to restructure the curriculum in order to meet the needs of less academically oriented students. Following the 1974 White Paper outlining the expansion of education, the CDC began to revise the school curriculum and in 1975, A. G. Brown, Chairman of the CDC, put forward a proposal to integrate Economic and Public Affairs, Geography, History and Chinese History to form a new subject, Social Studies. When the plan was announced in March, there was an uproar in the Chinese History community: the government was accused of trying to weaken Chinese 'national sentiment' by integrating Chinese History into Social Studies, thereby depriving it of its independence as a school subject. On 7 March 1975, the *Oriental Daily* protested against the government's intentions. Academics, union leaders and teachers expressed the following views:[7]

Chinese University professors:

- This policy has something to do with more people discarding their Chinese identity and naturalising as British. (H. S. Chuen)
- Conspiracy of the coloniser to carry out colonial education — this integration will weaken students' Chinese awareness and national conception. Social Studies aims at enhancing students' sense of belonging to HK. This action is in itself incorrect; being HK Chinese we should not only have HK in our minds. (K. T. Sun)

Union leaders:

- The integration will add much burden to teachers and students [and] this is another form of colonial education. In weakening students' knowledge and sentiment of China, the government aims at transforming Chinese into Hongkongese. (Szeto Wah, Chairman, Professional Teachers' Union)
- The integration will lessen the number of lessons for Chinese History, and this will make the situation worse, given that the 5,000 years of Chinese History cannot be completely taught at present. (W. S. Lam, Chairman, government school non-degree teacher union)

A school teacher:

- It will be difficult to implement. We have 31–32 lesson/weeks [so] how can we have time to plan the lessons; there are not adequate facilities to support teaching.

In response to this public outburst, senior government officials[8] attempted to clarify the situation by saying that a working group had been formed, with only one representative from the ED, and that the outcome would be the result of 'collective views'.[9] It seems, however, that the proposal was not even welcomed by some of the subject officers, such as C. S. Lam and D. L. Luk.

> I was the Chinese History officer in the examinations section. I remember very well that I discussed the issue with Y. K. Kow, the Chinese History inspector. We were against the proposal made by A. G. Brown. Obviously if Chinese History was integrated in Social Studies, the teaching of it would be reduced to a great extent. From the perspective of teaching and examinations, we considered the proposal very improper. At that time members of the subject committee were against it … together with pressure from the media, A. G. Brown, of course, could no longer insist. (C. S. Lam)

> Before I joined the Education Department in 1975, I was upset about merging Chinese History with History, Geography and EPA to form the Social Studies subject. This reorganisation would reduce the time for our students to learn Chinese culture. It is important to let our students

> understand more of our 5,000 years [of] glorious culture. Chinese
> culture is the source of our nation's unity. (D. L. Luk)

The outcome of this dispute was that Social Studies was introduced, but
without Chinese History, which continued as an independent subject. Also, the
CDC recommended that it should become one of the common core subjects.

In the same year, 1975, the first Chinese History syllabus for junior secondary
schools was issued. While it emphasised dynastic history, cultural history was
organised thematically, with selected themes being studied from a developmental
point of view, and formed a separate part of the curriculum. In a manner atypical
of colonial education, the teaching syllabus aimed to encourage an identification
with the indigenous culture.

> Chinese culture has a long history. ... In five thousand years, the
> Chinese nation has produced great achievements in intellectual
> thinking and technology. Moreover, there are special characteristics in
> the way of life and social organization of the Chinese nation. Hence
> the first most important aim of teaching Chinese History is to guide
> students to appreciate the long-existing Chinese cultural tradition and
> the characteristics of the way of life of the people. (Chinese History
> syllabus, F1–3, CDC, 1975: 3)

The introduction of the new syllabus meant that there were now syllabuses
for all levels (junior level, senior level and Higher and Advanced level), and thus
the status of Chinese History was consolidated. However, in the new syllabus, the
use of the term 'Contemporary China' in place of 'Republic of China' was
criticised by a right-wing newspaper, the *Popular Daily*, as an attempt by the
government to please communist China:

> What is more difficult to understand is whether or not the Education
> Department has been under pressure from communist China or the
> Department itself wants to make use of this opportunity to please the
> communist government. People can't simply kick the Republic of China
> (Taiwan) out because there are no diplomatic relations between the
> Republic of China and the British government. ... The British people
> have been enjoying democracy and freedom. How can they, just for the
> sake of pleasing communist China, assist the communists to proceed
> with this policy of hoodwinking the people. (Front page, *Popular Daily*,
> 7 July 1975)

The newspaper also reported identical views from two academics who were critical
of the ED's concern with pleasing the PRC.[10]

Another source of public concern during the 1970s and 1980s was the
absence of contemporary history. This was particularly the case whenever issues
arose about Japanese textbooks' treatment of the Sino-Japanese War and Japan's
ambitions in Diao Yu Island. Local politicians and other public figures blamed

the government for de-emphasising contemporary history so that students had become apathetic regarding affairs of 'national' importance'.[11] In 1975, in response to the leftist newspaper *Wen Wei Bao*'s querying the government's attitude towards the teaching of the recent past, P. S. Chan, senior inspector of History, told the press that if teachers were able to get hold of suitable materials, they were free to teach history up to the present.[12] However, he added that the government had not yet decided whether the CEE would extend the end-date, which meant, of course, that teachers would not bother to teach contemporary history if it were not in the public examination. In fact, in 1982 the CDC extended the scope of study at junior level to the contemporary period, but without setting an end-date, and the syllabus explained that it was more appropriate for teachers to introduce the contemporary part by means of a type of current affairs discussion,[13] implying that, unlike dynastic history, students could view contemporary issues from different perspectives. The reasons given for de-emphasising post-1949 history are reflected in the following comments:

> Concerning the extension of the scope of studies to 1976, the major problem is on setting the marking scheme, in particular [on] the Cultural Revolution when there are not yet any official views established in China. (D. L. Luk)

> In the 1970s, even the scope of studies in Mainland China was only up to 1949. There have not yet been any concluding remarks made about the Cultural Revolution. But the most important concern is the political stance of textbooks. (C. N. Leung)

The minutes of meetings on 28 May 1984 and 28 January 1986 identified the following as the reasons for not extending the range of study beyond 1949:

> ... because of the problem of source materials, students' skills in analysing contemporary history, setting and marking examination papers.[14]

It was only in the 1990 (CEE) and 1994 (AS-L and A-L) syllabuses that the end-date was extended to 1976 (the downfall of the Gang of Four), the reasons being:

> The scope of study should be extended beyond 1949 ... only a general idea of post-1949 history is required, value judgements are not needed, ... enough materials and official publications are available in the market.[15]

According to the main decision-makers, C. N. Leung and H. C. Wong:

> The downfall of the Gang of Four signifies the end of the Cultural Revolution. Therefore 1976 can be regarded as a landmark of contemporary Chinese history. (C. N. Leung)

> In the late 1980s public opinion on the inclusion of contemporary Chinese History put pressure on the subject committee to review the syllabus. (H. C. Wong)

Newspaper reports also reflected these views:

> Many historians feel the syllabus can be extended to around 1976 because 'the dust has settled' for the period and reference books on the matter are easily available on the market. (*South China Morning Post*, 10 July 1989)

However, the chairman of the Hong Kong Federation of Education Workers, K. N. Cheng reminded teachers of the following point when teaching post-1949 history:

> The history between 1949–76 is more sensitive. Since it is now offered, training on the *attitudes* and *principles* in teaching this part of history is needed. (italics added) (*Sun Pao*, 14 July 1989)

However, Chinese History went no further than 1976; and in this, the government of the PRC played an indirect role in affecting the history curriculum in Hong Kong. In a document entitled 'Draft prepared for DCI (CD) for press interview' (with a reporter from Canada) on the question 'To what extent has curriculum development relating to History and Chinese History taken into account Beijing's view?', the reply from the ED was illuminating:

> While the need to equip our students with knowledge of the latest developments in China is appreciated, one must guard against the danger of including the events of the last 20 or 30 years for study, the reason being that such events cannot be interpreted historically, as public and government records which are essential sources for historical study are normally withheld for a period of 30 years, thereby making any contemporary studies superficial and unscholarly ... the issue of whether or not Beijing's views are taken into consideration in curriculum planning and development relating to History/Chinese History does not really exist. This, however, does not preclude the caution one has to exercise in dealing with contemporary China or current Sino-Hong Kong relations. While there is neither the need nor the ground to 'please' Beijing in that specific context, one has to be discreet not to provoke her unnecessarily nor to sow the seeds of discord through reckless handling of subject-matter, e.g. the inclusion of biased views or unwarranted comments etc.[16]

It is worth noting that this draft was prepared in 1990, soon after the June Fourth Incident, which might have prompted the ED to be careful in dealing with Beijing. The document reveals concern on the part of the ED not to provoke China, and in order not to do so, they used spurious reasons for not including events in the last 20–30 years. The China factor thus implicitly restricted key government officials, such as the Director of Education, to a set of norms acceptable to the PRC.

Another potential cause of friction between the subject community and the government occurred in 1993, when the CDC prepared a curriculum guide to restructure the curriculum in which Chinese History was no longer a common-core subject, but an optional subject under Humanities. The Guide argued that the common-core curriculum was overcrowded and should be reduced, with schools being given the flexibility to select subjects from defined subject groups. Interestingly, unlike the controversy over the omission of contemporary history in the curriculum, there was no reaction to this recommendation, although it might have seemed to diminish the status of Chinese History. This was probably because it was already an optional subject in senior forms in most schools, and a compulsory subject only at the junior secondary level.

However, there was a minor stir when, on 27 June 1994, it was reported in the press that the June Fourth Incident would be included in the junior level Chinese History textbooks in the coming academic year. On the following day, the Director of Education, Dominic Wong, denied this and stated that 20 years should lapse before an event could be included in the curriculum. On 29 June 1994, he told the press that after a meeting with the publishers, they had agreed to delete the part concerning the June Fourth Incident; and he also stated that the ED was planning to issue a circular to publishers stipulating that only those events which had happened at least 20 years previously could be included in school history textbooks. This provoked an outcry against what was seen as an attempt at censorship on the part of the government;[17] even the last colonial Governor, Chris Patten, responded by saying, 'We can't set 20 years as a criterion to determine that only events that happened 20 years ago can be included in the textbooks'.[18] This implies that Wong's view did not represent that of the colonial government, and there was speculation that Wong was trying to please the Beijing government, which would become the new sovereign state in four years' time.

A much more serious issue arose in 1995. Concerns over 1997 had served to intensify the political sensitivity of Chinese History, especially on the part of the pro-Beijing group, who used it to attack the Governor's authority. An example of this was when the History subject committee (as distinct from the Chinese History committee) produced a revised junior secondary History curriculum in which the history of Hong Kong was to be included, and recommended it for use in 1998. The recommendation implied that the history of Hong Kong would not be included in the formal Chinese History curriculum, and this generated controversy in the press as the ED's motives were seen in some quarters as part of the colonial government's desire to dilute the 'nationalistic sentiment' of students by internationalising and creating a more independent Hong Kong after

1997. W. Y. Wu, the group leader of the Cultural sub-group of the Preliminary Working Committee for the SAR, told the press[19] that, while Chinese History as a subject should promote 'national sentiment' and become a compulsory subject after the handover, Hong Kong history should be incorporated into Chinese History instead of into History as Hong Kong is a part of Chinese territory. Following his recommendation, different views were expressed in the media about what was seen as interference in educational matters in Hong Kong.

1997–2005: A period of crisis and opportunity for Chinese History as an independent subject

1997 marked the end of the colonial era, when Hong Kong became a Special Administrative Region of the People's Republic of China, and the Chief Executive, Tung Chee Hwa, immediately set out his plan to promote Chinese Studies in general, and the history, culture and values of China in particular:

> We will incorporate the teaching of Chinese values in the school curriculum and provide more opportunities for students to learn about *Chinese history and culture.* This will foster a stronger sense of Chinese identity in our students. (italics added) (Tung Chee Hwa, Chief Executive, HKSAR, Policy Address, 8 October 1997)

In fact, the first few reforms of the Chinese History curriculum did seem to reflect this aim, and to conform to the usual practice in other decolonised countries. For example, in 1997, the F1–3 syllabus was revised to stress the importance of arousing national sentiments through studying Chinese History, and the aim of 'cultivating a sense of belonging to the nation and its people'[20] was added. Also, Hong Kong history was included in the syllabus for the first time with the aims of 'enhancing students' interest in studying this subject and establishing local and national sentiments'.[21] In the following year, the CEE syllabus was also revised, but with only one change being made: the statement 'The People's Republic of China was set up and the Nationalist government moved to Taiwan' was changed to 'The People's Republic of China was set up'. According to H. C. Wong, the Senior Curriculum Development Officer, 'this is to comply with the One China policy'. The decision was made in the subject committee meeting held on 11 October 1996, which stated that 'post-1949 Chinese History has to be based on "One China policy" and hence the F4–5 syllabus has to be revised accordingly'.

However, Tung's other aim of reforming the curriculum in order to meet the challenges of the 'new age' involved a holistic approach to curriculum reform, which threatened the status of Chinese History as a separate subject. In an attempt to protect this status, the local subject community played an increasingly assertive part in defining the nature and role of the subject in the school curriculum. Following the Education Commission's review of the education system in Hong Kong, in its proposed reforms, the CDC suggested eight Key Learning Areas

(KLAs) for the new curriculum, with Chinese History to be included in the 'Personal, Social and Humanities Education' (PSHE) KLA. In response to this proposal, an article[22] entitled 'Curriculum reform cannot wipe away the colour of colonial education: the crisis of Chinese History under curriculum integration' appeared the following January in a local newspaper, which sparked off another dispute (which continues today) between the government and the Chinese History community. As a result, the CDC announced on 7 April 2000 that there would be four options for schools to choose from concerning the place of Chinese History in the curriculum: (1) as an independent subject; (2) as one of the subjects in the KLA 'Personal, Social, and Humanities Education'; (3) tailoring the subject to meet their needs; and (4) the merging of Chinese History and History to form a new subject called 'New History'.

However, it was generally believed that the last option, merging Chinese History and History, was the real goal, and the campaign to keep Chinese History as a separate subject continued to be strong and forceful. The resulting controversy in the media lasted from April to July 2000, with a large number of parties involved. The views on the proposal of the key parties are summarised below:

Teachers' Associations and Unions:

- 'With a view to uniting Chinese History teachers and protecting the interest of the subject, a Chinese History Educators' Society Preparatory Committee is set up on 15 May 2000.'
- 'The 'new history' will kill Chinese History. Chinese History is not a general subject; it is for the education of national sentiment.' (Education Convergence [a teacher association])
- 'Under colonial rule, students developed a weak sentiment to China; they had little knowledge about Chinese History and culture. Now we should strengthen Chinese History instead of weakening the subject.' (Hong Kong Federation of Education Workers [a leftist teacher association])
- 'More options are now opening up for schools. It is not a matter of killing Chinese History.' (The Professional Teachers' Union [Hong Kong's largest teacher union])

Academics:

- 'National history is a unique thing to a country. Chinese History can be expanded to cover world history, but not the other way round. It is essential to teach the subject in an ethno-centric manner.' (S. T. Kwok)
- 'Curriculum integration is a trend; history education can remain the core in the humanities.' (W. O. Lee)
- 'Chinese History as a national history has a special role to play. Other than understanding China in the past, there is an implicit national responsibility

put on students ... But in Hong Kong the content and methods have to change.' (K. M. Cheng)

School teachers:

- 'I hope officials will rethink the merger. They should not just be concerned with curriculum concepts and ignore the special meaning embedded in Chinese History.'
- 'The merger can broaden students' perspective on history.'

Opinion polls:

- '90% of teachers felt Chinese History should become a compulsory subject.' (Hong Kong Federation of Education Workers)
- '60% aged 15–29 objected to the merger.' (The Hong Kong Youth Association)

The press:

- 'Chinese History should be strengthened not weakened.' (Editorial, *Ming Pao*, 7 April 2000)
- 'Education Department merges the two histories and is bombarded for ignoring national sentiments.' (Front page, *Oriental Daily*, 8 April 2000)
- 'The Education Department has evil intentions in merging the two histories.' (Editorial, *The Sun*, 23 April 2000)

A District Council member:

- 'There is nothing wrong with the curriculum. We just need to change the methods and examination. I'll collect people's signatures, and these will be forwarded to the Chief Executive.' (L. L. Fung)

Response from the government and committee representatives:

- 'After the handover, we all have a sentiment towards Chinese History ... Chinese History should aim at promoting students' sense of belonging to, and identification with, the nation and its people ... Chinese History will not be cancelled but will be strengthened.' (Fanny Law, Director of Education).
- 'The merger is to let students view the world from the Chinese History perspective and vice versa. We do not intend to weaken Chinese History, but on the contrary, the new curriculum will develop students' national identity.' (W. N. Bau, Chief Curriculum Development Officer, CDI).
- 'We have no intention to kill Chinese History. Chinese History will be the core of the content after merging with History.' (S. F. Au-yeung, Chairman, Personal, Social and Humanities Education, CDC).

The PRC government also involved itself in this issue when Beijing's top education official, Chen Zhili, told *The Sunday Morning Post* on 28 May 2000 that:

> Chinese History is part of world history but as Chinese, we should learn Chinese History thoroughly. The subject should be introduced to students in a very comprehensive and scientific way. There needs to be more academic discussion on whether it should be merged into world history as a small part.

The various views can be categorised according to three perspectives, two against the merger and one in favour: (1) the merger signified the extension of colonial influence as its aim was to reduce the study of national history; (2) Chinese History education symbolised national pride, and so it should remain as an independent subject; and (3) the merger should be viewed as a curriculum integration which would help to enhance students' global perspectives.

A second wave of opposition to the proposal, mainly from members of the Chinese History teacher associations, was triggered off in November 2000, when the CDC published the consultation document *Learning to Learn: The Way Forward in Curriculum Development*, which proposed to incorporate Chinese History into the PSHE KLA. Although the principal figures involved in the reform repeatedly emphasised the importance of Chinese History education in the consultation document in an attempt to pacify the Chinese History community,[23] the fear that 'the study of Chinese History as a continuous whole' was likely to be non-existent in the PSHE KLA provoked them into launching another media battle against the government, which lasted from November 2000 to February 2001. Their views expressed in the press are summarised below:

Opposition to integrating Chinese History into PSHE

- 'Killing Chinese History has been decided; consultation is only a rubber stamp.' (K. L. Wong, Chinese History teacher)
- 'The revised curriculum can only give students a general idea of Chinese History. It can hardly develop students' understanding of our country. For example, in the junior secondary curriculum, topics relating to Chinese History only amount to 1/30. In doing this, our students will become "rootless" persons.' (Hong Kong Teachers' Association of Chinese History Education)
- 'Chinese History education will become bits and pieces. Without adequate knowledge of national history, our next generation will have no consciousness of searching for their "roots", and there is no way for them to confirm their national identity.' (P. W. Leung, Chairman, The Chinese History Educators' Society)
- 'The pre-condition of merging: the time allocated to Chinese History education cannot be reduced. The teaching of Chinese History is equivalent

to national sentiment education.' (K. K. Siu, Head, Department of Chinese, Chu Hoi College)

- 'Our students have to be immersed in Chinese History education, otherwise they will become "money minded" and "rootless" persons.' (C. L. Hui, Chairman, Hong Kong Teachers' Association of Chinese History Education)
- 'Chinese History should be studied as a continuous whole. Integrating it with other subjects will destroy the holistic nature of Chinese history.' (C. W. Chan, Chinese History teacher)
- 'This is the beginning of the handover. The reconstruction on the part of our next generation, of the sense of belonging to our country is very important. The Chief Executive, Tung Chee Hwa has repeatedly emphasised the importance of Chinese History education. Yet regrettably, Chinese History now appears to be becoming a non-independent subject.' (C. W. Chan, Chinese History teacher)
- 'Chinese History education has to be properly positioned.' (C. T. Hung, University of Science and Technology)

School-based tailoring:

- 'In the name of school-based curriculum development, the government is trying to kill Chinese History. How can a school-based curriculum development be successfully implemented without support from experts.' (Hong Kong Federation of Education Workers)

As an independent subject:

- 'The government has stressed that schools can opt for an independent Chinese History. Yet the whole document has not given any concrete planning and arrangement for its mode of teaching if it is to exist as an independent subject. It is doubtful whether the government will give enough support and assistance, or leave Chinese History to survive on its own.' (K. L. Wong, member, Hong Kong Teachers' Association of Chinese History Education and Chinese History teacher)

As the ninth Key Learning Area:

- 'Chinese nation, history and culture can be added as an independent KLA.' (C. L. Hui, Chairman, Hong Kong Teachers' Association of Chinese History Education)
- 'Chinese history and national condition as an additional KLA.' (Hong Kong Teachers' Association of Chinese History Education)

Never before had the subject community expressed such powerful opposition to the government and, as a result of such strong feelings, the first teacher organisation was formed specifically to represent Chinese History. In June 2000, the Hong Kong Teachers' Association of Chinese History Education was set up with the aims of 'protecting and enhancing national history education at the level of basic education ... and of enabling teachers, through national history education, to develop students' patriotic thoughts and affection for the people. In doing this it is hoped that students can become citizens who care about the country's past and future'.[24] Then, on 7 July 2000, another teacher association called 'The Chinese History Educators' Society', was formed',[25] whose aims included 'to strengthen the power of the profession', and 'to show concern and respond to political and social issues relating to Chinese History education'. The active role played by these two teacher associations was unparalleled in the past and included: interviewing the Secretary of the HKEA about the continuous decline of Chinese History's results in the CEE and A-level; organising seminars for teachers and students; collecting data on the discrepancy between students' mock examination results and A-level examination results; and holding press conferences on the results of surveys on teachers' views on the integration of History and Chinese History and the eight KLAs.[26] According to K. F. Fung, the executive officer of the Chinese History Educators' Society:

> We aim at guarding the independent status of Chinese History. We take the initiative in enhancing teachers' professional knowledge and keeping them informed of those policies affecting Chinese History. In the past there was no Chinese History association established to look after the interest of the subject, and we think it is time that the subject community has to adopt an active role. We'll enlist the support of teachers from schools and tertiary institutions, as well as scholars from abroad. In the long run, we aim at occupying seats in the decision-making process.

The high profile adopted by the two teacher associations did exert pressure on the government, as shown in the subsequent consultation document *Learning to Learn*, which emphasised that 'the strengthening of the understanding of Chinese history is essential for helping young people to enhance their national identity'.[27] As a result of all this opposition, the government has not rushed into introducing 'New History'; instead, great care has been taken in handling this new subject in order not to infuriate the Chinese History subject community. While constructing New History's curriculum (later renamed 'History and Culture'), the CDI carried out a pilot scheme in a few schools to evaluate it in F1 to F3. Throughout the three years of the pilot scheme (2000–03), the government adopted a low profile, and has never released the results to the public, or to the schools which have been recommended to adopt the new subject; and since then there has been no follow-up work. It has been speculated that History and Culture was shelved because of political pressure. In 2000, the CDC and the HKEA jointly prepared a new CEE curriculum, and in 2005 a new Senior Secondary Chinese History curriculum, to be introduced in schools in 2004 and 2009 respectively. In contrast to the previous curriculum, these new curricula have the following characteristics: they are aimed at enhancing students' recognition of, and sense of belonging to, the nation and the race; they focus on modern history, with less emphasis on ancient history; and they adopt an enquiry approach in both learning and assessment. Thus, since the handover, although Chinese History has experienced a period of crisis, because of its politically privileged position and the tactics adopted by the two teacher associations, it may have an opportunity to survive in the secondary school curriculum.

As regards the role played by the PRC government, Beijing's top education officer Chen Zhili's statement in the press referred to earlier ('... as Chinese, we should learn Chinese History thoroughly. The subject should be introduced to students in a very comprehensive and scientific way ...') did draw the PRC government into the power struggle between the SAR government and the subject community. For the PRC government, Chinese History symbolises the revival of national education after the colonial rule, and it is also a means of cultivating national identity. Any attempt to weaken the subject's status in the school curriculum would put the PRC government in an embarrassing position, especially in the face of the accusation that 'the SAR government is heading for the restoration of colonialism',[28] and/or 'the SAR government is undermining national pride'.[29]

CONCLUSION

During the first period, from 1945–1974, Hong Kong experienced dramatic social and economic changes, beginning with a massive increase in its population as a result of the influx of people fleeing from the troubles in China. The government adopted the twin policies of avoiding involvement in affairs on the Mainland and preventing unrest among the people in Hong Kong as it was conscious of its rather weak status as a colonial power and possible threats to the stability of Hong Kong from various disputes and riots. One of the ways in which the government sought to achieve these aims was through education, by ensuring that the school curriculum remained apolitical and that students did not develop a sense of identification with China. The major changes in society and the economy over the years did not alter this aspect of education, but they did affect education in other ways, such as the avoidance of the study of contemporary China in the humanities subjects and the centralisation of the curriculum development process. It was during these eventful times that Chinese History emerged as a separate subject in its own right, and from the start it was characterised by an overwhelming concern with dynastic history — particularly imperial court history. Because of the political sensitivity of the subject, Chinese History was even more affected by the apolitical policy of the government than were other school subjects.

The period from 1974 to 1997 also saw marked social, economic and even political change in Hong Kong, particularly during the years leading up to the transfer of sovereignty to China. This was a time when Hong Kong began to find itself a stable, more prosperous and cohesive society, especially as a result of the government's laissez-faire economic policy, its measures to improve social services and housing, the introduction of universal free compulsory junior secondary education, and because people were beginning to feel a sense of belonging to the territory. The emergence of a middle class and the rise of a service economy had their effects on education. For example, in order to meet the needs of the new economy, and to satisfy the ambitions of the more prosperous middle class with regard to their children, the school curriculum was broadened to include more emphasis on language ability and the teaching of subjects such as economics, business studies and computer studies. During the transition period, attempts were made to introduce political issues into the curriculum and to develop national sentiments among schoolchildren. However, despite the restructuring of the secondary school curriculum and the broader curriculum reforms taking place during these years, apart from one or two threats, the independent status of Chinese History was consolidated. It remained basically the same throughout the period, with just minor additions to and deletions from its content.

After the handover of Hong Kong to China in 1997, a major concern of the SAR government was to try to improve the economy, which was depressed as a result of the Asian economic crisis; and various measures were introduced and projects set up to stimulate it, particularly concerning infrastructure and tourism, but without much success. Other policies undertaken by the SAR government since then have not been very successful either, and have added to the general feeling of dissatisfaction on the part of the people of Hong Kong. Particular causes for complaint have been the repeated refusals of the government to entertain any thought of democratisation; the apparently increasing involvement of the PRC in the affairs of Hong Kong; and the inability of the government to improve the lives of the ordinary people.

The SAR government has also aimed to reform the education system in general and school curricula in particular to meet the needs of a knowledge-based society, and to instil in the young a feeling of belonging and identity with China, and give them a sense of national pride. Unfortunately, not all the measures introduced have been successful, and the series of reforms in education have been severely criticised. As regards Chinese History, the SAR government's curriculum reform has not strengthened its status, as has been the practice in other decolonised states. On the contrary, its status seems to have been weakened, or at least been threatened, and this has led to a power struggle between the subject community and Beijing officials on one side, and the SAR government and curriculum reformers on the other. The concessions made by the SAR government in restoring the independent status of Chinese History reflect the influence of politics on education in general, and on curriculum reform in particular.

3

The Emergence of Chinese History
as an Independent Subject (1945–74)

Chapter 2 gave an overview of politics and society in Hong Kong from 1945–2005, and of how political and socio-economic forces affected education in general, and Chinese History in particular. This chapter analyses the development of Chinese History in depth from 1945 until 1974, when Chinese middle schools and Anglo-Chinese schools finally adopted the same Chinese History syllabus. It was during this period that Chinese History emerged, and consolidated its status, as an independent subject. The analysis is concerned specifically with: the curriculum development process for Chinese History; the aims and content of the curriculum, which were formulated during this process; and the impact of the curriculum on teaching, learning and examinations. This analysis can enhance our understanding of the influence of the local subject community on the making of the Chinese History curriculum during this initial phase.

THE CURRICULUM FOR F1–5

The Curriculum Development Process (F1–5)

During the 1960s, Chinese History emerged as a separate school subject, firstly at junior secondary level, and later also at senior secondary level. At that time, the Advisory Inspectorate of the ED was responsible for administering all subjects, and there were subject inspectors for different subject groups. Chinese History was combined with History to form the 'History Section' but, as there was no senior inspector post for Chinese History, the senior inspector heading the 'History Section' was a History specialist, which meant in reality that Chinese History was subordinated to History. In terms of the allocation of resources and curriculum change, therefore, this organisational set-up was bound to affect the development of Chinese History. The colonial government's bureaucratic culture had a far-reaching impact on the subject, as D. C. Lam, the head of the History Section, recalls in describing his experience of working in the government:

> It is important that we were not held responsible for any trouble that occurred. Although not all officers worked for money, the restrictions and *bureaucratic culture* obviously hindered the motivation of staff. Between 1968 and 1975, there were lots of problems in Chinese History. Every now and then, feature articles relating to Chinese History appeared in the newspapers. The issues related to textbooks, examinations, and political factors. Once the issues were made known to the public, the senior officers, who were mostly British, would require a full English translation of the coverage of the incident. Under such circumstances, how could we work things through? Therefore, officers would try to avoid being caught in any issues. And hence a mentality of 'no work no fault' was common amongst civil servants.

It is therefore not surprising that when Chinese History became an independent subject the few changes made were confined to minor issues such as dividing the examination syllabus into sections, and introducing multiple-choice questions to replace fill-in-the-blanks and short questions. To a large extent, this inertia reflected the mentality of the officials — 'nothing ventured, nothing lost'.

During this phase, the composition of the CEE Chinese History Committee was approximately 15% AI subject officers, 60% schoolteachers and principals, and 25% academics.[1] The minutes of meetings of the Chinese History subject committee (CEE) on 18 March and 24 April 1969, and 31 March 1970, indicate that the officials took most of the initiatives — for example, dividing history into four sections, splitting multiple-choice questions into five sections from which students were to choose three, combining the CEE (English and Chinese) Chinese History syllabuses, and proposals for the Chinese History common-core syllabus. However, although the CEE Chinese History subject committee was largely dominated by government officials who initiated the revision of the curriculum, university teachers were able to find ways to influence decision-making in order to protect their interests (and those of their specific university departments) through their approval or otherwise of new initiatives. For example, during the debate on the scope of study (see Chapter 2), T. W. Lin the HKU representative, proposed that 'the period for study should be extended to include the Modern history of China',[2] and his proposal was later taken into consideration by the senior official A. G. Brown (again, see Chapter 2). Lin's concern to protect HKU's interests was explicit:

> The Chinese History syllabus for the HKCEE must be drawn in accordance with that of the Advanced Level examination. In the circumstances, I am afraid that I cannot give you any comment on this draft until after a discussion has been held in the Department of Chinese.[3]

In fact, the examination syllabuses issued in 1958 (CEE English) and 1960 (CEE Chinese) stated clearly that 'the syllabus was to meet HKU's entrance requirements'. In contrast to the dominant role of the government officials in curriculum planning, the part played by the schoolteachers on the subject committee was minimal as they seldom expressed views in the meetings; for example, the minutes of meetings held between 1969 and 1971 show that they made no proposals or recommendations. Part of the reason for this could be that, as the head of the History section explained, the teachers on the committee were often friends of the government officials and had been nominated by them.

The centralised, top-down approach to curriculum development for F1–5 can be illustrated in the way that syllabuses were produced in 1962 and 1970. In the Preface to the *Recommended History Guidelines for 5-year Chinese Middle Schools* (1962), it was stated:

> This recommended syllabus is produced by a committee comprising the ED inspectors, lecturers of the Colleges of Education and teachers of government and non-government schools. It is suitable for use in government secondary schools. Yet there is no stipulation that this syllabus be adopted. Schools can adopt other syllabuses approved by the ED if they deem it necessary.

The syllabus was produced by a designated committee composed predominantly of government subject officers, and although it stated that the committee included schoolteachers, they played practically no part in the decision-making. Moreover, no mention was made in the syllabus that teachers generally had been consulted in its production, nor were any supporting materials provided for them. Publishers wrote textbooks according to the syllabus, and these textbooks were then sent to the Syllabus and Textbook Committee for approval. Similarly, for the syllabus issued in 1970, teachers were advised 'to use audio-visual aids, such as wall-maps, models, slides, tape recorders, and movies to enhance teaching', but there was no specific advice to them on how they were to obtain such materials. Teachers were expected to implement the teaching guidelines and this implementation was seen as unproblematic.

The following incidents also help to illustrate the highly centralised approach to Chinese History's curriculum development. When Y. T. Li, secretary of the HKCEE Board, requested that the Chinese History subject committee consider reducing the time required for answering the long questions, the subject committee made no attempt to consult schoolteachers about the appropriate number of questions for students to answer, or the corresponding time required. Committee members deemed that 110 minutes was appropriate to answer four long questions, and the following letter was written by S. Y. Li, chairman of the Chinese History subject committee, to Y. T. Li on 30 September 1970, specifying members' views:

> I regret that my committee does not favour reducing the time for answering the long question. The present allocated time of 110 minutes is hardly sufficient for 4 answers. Any reduction will result in unnecessary hurry on the part of the candidates and hence deterioration in the quality of the answer.

Similarly, the division of Chinese History into four sections, of which students chose three was a decision made at the meeting on 15 September 1970. There was neither consultation on the periodisation of Chinese History, nor on the arrangement concerning the choice of sections. As always, officials played a dominant role in the decision-making process, with no opportunities for teachers to have their say.

Curriculum Aims and Content: Before Chinese History Became an Independent Subject

Before Chinese History became an independent subject, the Director of Education, Douglas Crozier, appointed the Chinese Studies Committee with the following aims:

> ... to consider the position and aims of Chinese Studies (Chinese Language, Literature and History) in the educational system of the Colony and to make recommendations, in the light of the present-day needs, as to the general principles which should govern Chinese Studies, [and] the content of the courses ... . (Preface, Report of the Chinese Studies Committee)

At that time, the subject 'History' in Chinese middle schools was inclusive of Chinese history and world history and was taught in Chinese; and its curriculum was based on the Nationalist government's curricula issued in 1941 and 1948. At the same time, in the Anglo-Chinese Schools, Chinese History and Chinese Literature formed one subject, and the Chinese History curriculum was adopted from the last two sections of the Nationalist government's curriculum. There was also another subject 'History' (including British Commonwealth History), which was taught through the medium of English. It was because both the Chinese middle schools and Anglo-Chinese schools had adopted the Nationalist government's Chinese History curriculum that the Chinese Studies Committee considered it necessary to issue reminders governing Chinese History education in Hong Kong for fear that the political overtones in this curriculum might have an adverse effect. Therefore the report (p. 21) emphasised, instead, the appreciation of Chinese thought, literature and traditions:

> To the modern Chinese, the problem [the collapse of traditional beliefs] is even more realistic, for many of them have lost respect for most of the long-established Chinese virtues, but have not been able

to assimilate the best of the Western virtues. This is indeed a vital need: to have all the sound and healthy elements in the fabric of the Chinese social life and culture to be revived. ... *The study of History has a high moral and social value,* for it can not only provide standards of reference by which to criticise our own age, but also give one the ability to get outside oneself. (italics added to show the Committee's perception of the value of Chinese History).

On curriculum content, the report recommended that in the Chinese middle schools, 'Chinese History should be learnt before World History', and that the Chinese History syllabus for the Hong Kong Chinese School Certificate Examination should be revised: 'the emphasis of the new syllabus should be social and cultural rather than political'.

In short, the views expressed in the report confirmed the value of Chinese thought, literature and tradition, and viewed Chinese History as having distinctive cultural, moral and social values and exemplars that could guide students towards correct attitudes. However, the report avoided mentioning 'national identity' and/ or 'national sentiment' and, instead, emphasised the fostering of cultural bonding through the study of Chinese History.

The Curriculum for F1–3

From 1945 to 1974, no teaching syllabuses were issued. In 1962 and 1970, the ED published two sets of guidelines for Chinese middle schools and Anglo-Chinese schools respectively, which mainly contained a list of teaching topics for F1–5 and a brief mention of the aims and methods of teaching, which gave some idea of the nature of the Chinese History curriculum. The curriculum had three distinguishable features throughout the three phases: (1) the study of Chinese History as a continuous whole; (2) an orthodox historical perspective; and (3) a Han-centred cultural viewpoint. (A more detailed analysis of these three aspects can be made in the second phase [1974–97] and the third phase [1997–2005] as during these periods teaching syllabuses were issued in which official views on Chinese History were clearly presented.)

Table 3.1 is an overview of the development of junior level Chinese History in the first phase (1945–74) (see p. 58).

The study of Chinese History as a continuous whole

When the junior level Chinese History curriculum was formulated (and the Nationalist government's curriculum was abandoned) in the 1960s, the Anglo-Chinese schools and Chinese middle schools both emphasised the dynastic-based, chronological development of Chinese History. The curriculum covered more

Table 3.1 Development of the F1–3 Chinese History curriculum 1945–74

	Anglo-Chinese schools		Chinese middle schools	
Year	1945–59	1960–74	1945–61	1962–74
Key curriculum document	Nationalist government's curriculum	Chinese History guidelines	Nationalist government's curriculum	Chinese History guidelines
Genesis	F1–4 adopted the Nationalist government's curriculum	in 1960,[4] F1 Chinese History was made an independent subject; guidelines were issued for the three-year and five-year secondary curriculum	followed the syllabus of the Nationalist government issued in 1941	in 1962, F1 Chinese History was made an independent subject; in the same year, the five-year Chinese middle schools guidelines were issued
Aim	strong nationalistic sentiment	a general understanding of the chronological development of Chinese history	same as the Anglo-Chinese schools	same as the Anglo-Chinese schools
Content arrangement	chronological arrangement, from pre-history (~2100 BC) to 1945			
Curriculum emphasis	dynastic history as the framework supplemented with cultural history			

than 4,000 years of history (from ~2100 BC to 1945), but with a heavy emphasis on the earlier periods. It should be noted here that dynastic history was mostly concerned with the history of emperors, key persons and imperial court events, and thus should not be understood as 'political history' in its Western sense. According to the *Recommended Chinese History Guidelines for Anglo-Chinese Schools and Chinese Middle Schools* (1970: 4) produced by the ED:

> Chinese History is organised as a complete unit for F1–3. It traces history from pre-historic times to the Qing dynasty and the modern period. The rise and fall of dynasties, important events, their changes and impacts are outlined. It is hoped that in these 3 years students can gain a basic knowledge of the development of Chinese History.

The curriculum developers' insistence on the study of Chinese History in its entirety was reflected in the way that the curriculum was arranged — a chronological account of dynastic history. Their perception of the nature of Chinese History's content was revealed even more clearly in the F4–5 curriculum, which is discussed later.

An orthodox historical perspective

As reflected in the 1962 curriculum guideline, individual topics embodied value judgements which reflected the traditional, orthodox view of Chinese History. Some examples of these are:

- 'Wang Meng *usurped* the Han throne': Because Wang Meng was a brother of the empress rather than of the emperor, he was traditionally judged by historians as being a usurper to the throne.
- 'The *prosperity* of the reign of Li Shimin': This is an orthodox view recorded in 'the 24 Dynastic Histories', despite the fact that there were also records made by non-official historians that during Li Shimin's reign the living conditions outside the capital were poor.
- 'The *disorder* created by Empress Wu and Wei': Women were regarded as inferior to men, and whenever women had political power they were seen as creating disorder.
- 'Emperor Qin Shihuang's *tyrannical* rule': Qin Shihuang was labelled a despot, despite the contributions he made to unify the nation.

The same topics were listed in the 1970 Chinese History guidelines for Anglo-Chinese schools and Chinese middle schools.

A Han-centred viewpoint

The third characteristic of Chinese History was the way in which it distinguished the Hans from the non-Han races. The examples below illustrate this point:

- 'The five *barbarian* tribes invaded the Han territory': The non-Han races were called 'barbarians', and 'invasion' was used to describe their deeds — in contrast to the Han Emperor Han Wu Di's conquest of the territory of the non-Han races which was referred to as *territorial expansion.*
- 'The An Shi *uprising*': The non-Han generals An and Shi revolted against the rule of the Tang emperor Xuan Zong, and traditionally historians regarded their actions as an uprising.
- 'Mongols became the *masters* of China', and 'Manchurians became the *masters* of China': It is only in describing the rule of these two non-Han races that the word 'masters' is used, underlining the distinction between the Han and non-Han 'races'.[5]

Hence, although the guidelines specified the importance of arousing students' interest in history, and encouraged teachers to use questioning techniques and audio-visual aids, all these means were directed towards the prescribed ends of traditional orthodoxy — that is, the orthodoxy inherited from 'the 24 Dynastic Histories', which was state-centred and moralistic in nature (see Chapter 1, 'Historiography in China', p. 13).

The Curriculum for F4–5

The F4–5 curriculum had similar characteristics to the F1–3 curriculum, in that the Nationalist government's curriculum was abandoned in 1960, and it was arranged chronologically with dynastic history predominating. However, with regard to the aims and scope of study, the F4–5 curriculum was different from F1–3 curriculum, as can be seen in Tables 3.2 and 3.3.

Anglo-Chinese schools

Table 3.2 Development of the F4–5 Chinese History curriculum: Anglo-Chinese schools, 1945–74

Year	1950–57	1958–64	1965–71	1972–73
Key curriculum document	Nationalist government's curriculum	examination syllabus and guidelines	examination syllabus and guidelines	examination syllabus and guidelines
Genesis	followed the Nationalist government's curriculum; Chinese History and Chinese Literature formed one subject in the CEE	the riots in 1956 gave rise to a new curriculum in which coverage of contemporary history was reduced	for the purpose of widening students' subject choice, it was made an independent subject in the CEE	to lessen students' burden, the whole of history was divided into four periods from which students were to choose three to study
Aim	nil	to match A-level requirements, and to develop students' comprehensive understanding of Chinese History	nil	nil
Content arrangement	Ming (1368) to contemporary period	chronological development – 1958: Song (960) to 1911 – 1959: Sui (581) to 1911	chronological development; Xia (~2100 BC) to 1911	four periods, to choose three: – Xia (~2100 BC) to Han (AD 220) – Three Kingdoms (220) to the Five Dynasties (960) – Song (960) to Ming (1368) – Qing (1644) to 1945
Curriculum emphasis	cultural history	dynastic history, supplemented with cultural history		

Table 3.3   Development of the F4–5 Chinese History curriculum: Chinese middle schools, 1945–74

Year	1952–59	1960–62	1963–64	1965–66	1967–71	1972–73
Key curriculum documents	Nationalist government's curriculum	examination syllabus and guidelines	examination syllabus and guidelines	examination syllabus and guidelines	examination syllabus and guidelines	examination syllabus and guidelines
Genesis	H-level examination, introduced in 1952, adopted the 1941 Nationalist government's curriculum	by the 1960s, the syllabus no longer followed the Nationalist government's curriculum	the whole of history was divided into two periods; students were to answer questions from both periods	in 1965, a five-year curriculum was set up; same examination paper was used as the six-year H-level	independent subject in the CEE (Chinese)	the whole of history was divided into two periods; students were to answer questions from both periods
Aim	strong national sentiment	to meet A-level requirements, and develop students' comprehensive understanding of Chinese History	same as 1960–62	same as 1960–62	same as 1960–62	nil
Content arrangement	Qing (1644) to 1912	chronological, Xia (~2100 BC) to 1911	chronological, Zhou (~1122 BC) to 1793	same as 1963–64	same as 1963–64	chronological, Xia (~2100 BC) to 1911
Curriculum emphasis	dynastic history; contemporary history only dealt with the Nationalist government, with nothing on the development of the CCP	dynastic history, supplemented with cultural history				

The study of Chinese History as a continuous whole

When Hong Kong stopped using the Nationalist government's Chinese History curriculum and began to devise its own curriculum in the 1960s, both Anglo-Chinese schools and Chinese middle schools emphasised that their F4–5 curricula were aimed at 'meeting the university entrance requirements and developing students' comprehensive understanding of Chinese History'.[6] For this reason, the curriculum had to be academically oriented, and the chronological scope stretched from the Xia dynasty (~2100 BC) to 1945. In the CEE (English), however, students were allowed to choose specific periods to study within the 4000-year historical time-frame. The curriculum emphasis of both types of schools was basically dynastic history, integrated with cultural history, and so the curriculum was characteristically decontextualised and depoliticised.

How members of the subject committee perceived the nature of Chinese History can be seen in their response to requests by Y. T. Li, Secretary of the HKCEE Board, to reduce the time for answering questions (During this period, the time allocated to Chinese History's conventional questions was 110 minutes [to answer four questions], compared with 75 minutes for History [to answer two questions], 90 minutes for Economic and Public Affairs, and 75 minutes each for Physics, Chemistry and Biology). At its meeting on 5 January 1970, the committee decided not to make any amendments to the time allocation of the examination, on the following grounds:

> (i) The study of Chinese History requires considerable understanding and knowledge and the syllabus cannot be reduced. Besides, Chinese History should be studied with a sense of *continuity* and is quite different from European History which can be studied as separate units. (ii) Chinese History as an independent subject in the HKCEE (which is not the usual practice in foreign countries) should be made as *dignified* as possible. (iii) Candidates will not be able to finish answering both conventional and multiple choice type questions if the time is reduced in the examinations. (italics added) (Minutes of meeting)

Another illustration of the key curriculum developers' insistence that Chinese History should be studied in its entirety can be seen when, on 2 September 1970, the Principal of St Paul's Co-educational College wrote a letter to the committee requesting them to consider reducing the length of the syllabus, by giving candidates a choice of selecting two, instead of three sections out of four. In its meeting on 15 September 1970, the subject committee stated:

> Chinese history should be studied as *a continuous whole*. To select three sections out of four is already not desirable. To take two sections out of four is downright degrading. (italics added) (Minutes of meeting)

Apparently, the subject committee had developed a clear concept of the nature of Chinese History, and this was translated into the official curriculum. Chinese History was seen as a 'knowledge-focused' subject: it could not be compartmentalised, and should be studied in its entirety, chronologically, from pre-history to the contemporary period (ending either at 1911 or 1945, to avoid getting involved in modern Chinese politics).

In an interview, D. C. Lam,[7] the head of the History section at that time and not a specialist in Chinese History, again highlighted the Chinese History inspectors' insistence on treating Chinese history as a continuous whole:

> Before the introduction of the 1975 Chinese History syllabus for F1–3, I was thinking of confining Section A [dynastic history] to 30%. A simple narrative of the chronological development of the whole of Chinese history would suffice. Whereas for Section B [cultural history], I intended to include more relevant topics so as to arouse students' interest — for example, examination systems, external communication, and commercial development. Yet my colleagues [Chinese History inspectors] did not agree with me, nor did members of the subject committee. They regarded it as important to study in depth *the entirety of individual dynasties, for fear that otherwise our students would forget their own origins.* I found the reaction to be too strong and hence I abandoned my proposal. (italics added)

As a result, in the teaching syllabus introduced in 1975 (F1–3) dynastic history was predominant and occupied 60% of the content.

An orthodox historical perspective

Established views were clearly presented in the examination syllabus, which specified the focus to be on 'historical personages in China and their respective contributions, with an emphasis upon biography'.[8] Hence, there was a list of names of those officially recognised as important people, such as 'Zhou Gong, Dong Zhongshu, and Zheng Chenggong',[9] and their 'contributions' were defined in the marking schemes. Just as with the F1–3 guidelines, topics such as 'The *prosperity* of the reign of Li Shimin', 'The *disorder* caused by empress Wu and Wei', and 'Wang Mang *usurped* the Han throne' already expressed value judgements concerning individual events and people. By the same token, the Chinese History guidelines for the Anglo-Chinese Schools and Chinese middle Schools (F4–5) issued in 1970 also listed topics which embodied established views such as: 'The *tyrannical* Qin government and its rapid downfall', and 'The *uprising* of Huang Chao'.

A Han-centred viewpoint

As with the F1–3 syllabus, some of the topics listed in the examination syllabuses during this period distinguished the non-Han races from the Han race. This feature can be illustrated best in the Yuan and Ming dynasties — for example, 'Emperor Ming Tai Zu expelled the Mongols and restored the rule of the Han race',[10] and 'The disintegration of the Yuan [Mongol] *empire*'.[11]

Overall, therefore, the curriculum for F1–5 which evolved and changed during the first phase, when Chinese History emerged as a separate subject, had two major characteristics: it focused on established knowledge, and it was examination-oriented. When Chinese History became an independent subject, the period covered eventually stretched from the Xia dynasty (~2100 BC) to 1949, and this was expected to be studied in its entirety. Later, in the CEE, this was divided into three periods, from which students were allowed to choose two to study. Nonetheless, even with this arrangement, students were still required to study either 1,300 years or 1,700 years of history which was heavily focused on imperial court events and personages, and which presented both an orthodox historical and a Han-centred view of Chinese history. The definition of the content of the Chinese History curriculum in this period was to have a significant impact on its development in the second (1974–97) and third (1997–2005) phases.

The Curriculum (F1–5): Impact on Teaching, Learning and Examinations

The study of Chinese History as a continuous whole

The nature of the teaching and learning of Chinese History at this time can be seen in the comments made by various members of the Chinese History community, reflecting on their experiences as students:

> In the 1950s my teachers had fled from Mainland China. They were full of national sentiments when they taught us Chinese History. They insisted that as Chinese we should gain *a comprehensive knowledge of Chinese History*. (italics added) (S. C. Koo)

> In the 1950s I studied in La Salle College. At that time teachers taught according to the textbook. There was no emphasis on interpretation of historical events. We recited the textbook which covered more than 3,000 years [of] dynastic history. The aim was to help us get good results in the public examination. Yet I know that there was a group of scholars from the Mainland, for example, Chan Hak Man, Ho Ka Yun, and Wu Tin Yum who published Chinese History textbooks which aimed at promulgating *the importance of having a comprehensive knowledge of Chinese History in a British colony*. (italics added) (C. Y. Wong)

In the 1950s I was a secondary student. My teachers were from the Mainland. Although they taught Chinese History, they were not Chinese History graduates. Teachers of other subjects, for example, Physics, Mathematics, and Chinese Language, had a strong passion in teaching Chinese History to Hong Kong students. Perhaps they took that as *a means to develop students' Chinese identity.* (italics added) (C. S. Lam)

C. S. Lam remembered his own experience as a Chinese History teacher:

From 1968 to 1973 I taught Chinese History in a government school. At that time we used F. L. Wong's textbook from which a full account of Chinese history from the Xia dynasty to 1911 was given. At that time there was no distinction between a syllabus and a textbook. We followed the textbook closely and taught according to questions set in the examination. For example, the examination put much emphasis on dynastic history, and we then traced the intentions of the questions and used it as our teaching guide. We did not care whether students could 'digest' [it] or not. After all, *it was impossible to go through every single event throughout more than 3,000 years.'* (italics added)

The above retrospective accounts suggest that these members of the subject community regarded the teaching and learning of Chinese History as a means to cultivate Chinese identity in Hong Kong. In terms of learning, this meant a comprehensive understanding of historical China was deemed necessary to develop a Chinese identity which was cultural rather than political.

With regard to examinations, the extensive scope of study in Chinese History was a major factor in the unsatisfactory performance of students in the CEE, and comments such as 'inaccurate facts'; 'blind guessing'; and 'unclear concepts'[12] were common in the Annual Reports of the ED Examinations section. In view of the very long period studied, students tended to focus more on some parts than others, and the examination reports revealed that the most popular topics were from dynastic history (especially the periods of Tang, Song, and Ming), with the best answers on questions related to the administrative achievements of individual dynasties and the reasons for their rise and downfall.[13] In contrast, modern history (1911–45) was the least chosen section, and the performance of students was also the poorer[14] than on dynastic history.

An orthodox historical perspective

An indication of the effect that the orthodox nature of the Chinese History curriculum had on teaching and learning can be seen in the comments of some of those who were teachers at the time:

In general, schools would employ Chinese Language teachers to teach Chinese History … [and] many teachers took Chinese History teaching as a perfunctory routine. Some even adopt the bookish learning approach, as if they were teaching Chinese Language, for example, reading aloud the text, and explaining new vocabulary. *Rarely did teachers challenge views presented in the textbook.* Teachers tended to use only one textbook to teach and assume that it could solve all the problems in history learning. (italics added) (Y. F. Wu, 1973: 172)

The following accounts are interviewees' recollections of their experiences as Chinese History teachers:

> I taught Chinese History in Kowloon Wah Yan from 1969 to 1979. In the 1960s there was no syllabus, and we relied on the textbook. I followed Ling Kee's textbook closely. I had no doubt about the textbook quality as all textbooks had to be approved by the ED. It was of course *safe to adopt established views.* (italics added) (S. T. Kong)

> In my teaching, examinations were my major concern. For those questions just set, I would pay less attention to them. Emphasis would then be put on those questions that might appear in the coming examination. We all followed the textbook. I believe many teachers adopted this approach to teach Chinese History. (D. L. Luk)

Since Chinese History involved the study of more than 3,000 years and the reciting of large quantities of 'hard' facts and orthodox views in the examinations, it tended to be an unpopular subject in schools. This can be seen in the findings from research carried out by Noah Fehl, Professor of History at CUHK. His study, 'History in Hong Kong middle and secondary schools', also addressed problems concerning Chinese History education generally. According to Fehl:

> Textbooks in world history have less acceptance than those in Chinese History in Chinese schools in FI and II. In FV the reverse is true. In English schools in FI, II, III and V Chinese History textbooks suffer in comparison with those in world history although in many of these schools in FI–III Chinese History textbooks are in the Chinese language. The comments of history masters [principals] and teachers constitute a substantial consensus that Chinese textbooks and most English school textbooks in Chinese History are definitely unsatisfactory. (1966: 22)

His report also highlighted the views of Chinese middle school principals concerning the inadequacy of Chinese History textbooks:

> The textbooks in Chinese History are too factual. Chinese History should be written from a wider knowledge of China in its world setting. The perspective of available textbooks is not clearly applicable to the contemporary Hong Kong situation. (ibid.: 24)

These unfavourable views of Chinese History may be attributed to the requirement that it was to be taught and studied as a continuous whole, and involved memorising a body of facts and orthodox views contained in the textbooks. As with other subjects, the implementation of Chinese History was to a large extent controlled by the requirements of the CEE. Fehl pointed explicitly to the seriousness of the matter:

> We are at the heart of the matter: the examination-oriented education in Hong Kong ... the pressure for passes exerted by parents ... A school is evaluated by the pass percentages of its students. Teachers are rated by the success of their students in the examinations. Students are diverted from a natural interest in subjects and a desire to learn and understand to a harsh and anxious competition for success in examinations ... the only way you can deal with *model answers*, as with a nonsense syllabus, if you must 'get' them is to *memorize* them. (italics added) (ibid.: 37)

Since the 'model' answers already specified the orthodox views, students had to memorise these 'answers'. Siu et al. (1975) came to a similar conclusion after analysing five years (1970–74) of CEE Chinese History essay questions:

> Dynastic development and historical figures' personality and achievement were the two most important foci of the CEE. Emphasis was on established knowledge and memorisation of this knowledge.
>
> Question distribution tended to focus on a few aspects. Over the years the intention and format of the questions were rather stable. With the flexible choice of questions, students could easily choose a particular type of question to answer. This helped to encourage the study of a particular type of knowledge. (Siu et al., 1975: 117–39)

Before 1969, the examination consisted of fill-in-the-blanks, true or false questions, short questions and essays, while after 1969, only multiple-choice questions and essays were set. K. Y. Tsun, secretary of the HKCEE (English) Chinese History subject committee, expressed his views on the nature of assessment for Chinese History, as follows:

> An ideal Chinese History examination paper should be set like this: recall (60%), comprehension (20%), thinking (20%). (Tsun, 1973: 31)

Since Tsun was a key decision-maker in the subject committee, his views to a large extent indicate that Chinese History was regarded as a subject in which the recall of factual accounts and orthodox views was far more important than the stimulation of students' capacity for critical thinking and reasoned argument.

These orthodox views were also seen in the marking schemes.[15] For example, in the examination syllabus, Zhou Gong was included as an important person who had made significant contributions, and the marking scheme specified the following views:

Contributions made by Zhou Gong: (1) assisting Emperor Cheng (2) setting up the feudal system (3) producing rituals and music (4) organising education (0.5 mark/point, total 2 marks)[16]

As another example, in the curriculum the deeds of the two generals An and Shih were viewed as an uprising, and the examination marking scheme specified:

Reasons for the uprising of An Shi: (1) the corrupted political culture — Emperor Xuan Zong did not attend the court [1 mark] but doted on his concubine Yang Gui Fei [1 mark] (2) treacherous court officials were in power — e.g. Li Linfu, Yang Guozhong [2 marks] (3) using non-Han generals and soldiers — the 'Hu' [a non-Han race] organisation was formed which threatened the Han rule [2 marks] (4) the destruction of the 'Fu Bing'[military] system [1 mark] — non-Han army led by An Shi began the invasion [1 mark][17]

Students gained marks only for citing these prescribed views, while other interpretations, even with supporting evidence and argument, were not given any credit.

A Han-centred viewpoint

The official syllabuses and guidelines reflected a very Han-centred view, with the non-Han races, the Mongols and the Manchus, being presented in a negative light. The extent to which this was implemented can be seen through a parallel analysis of the examination questions, marking schemes and textbooks. The following question was commonly found in the CEE:

Kublai Khan set up the Yuan dynasty, yet in less than 90 years, the Yuan dynasty collapsed. Explain.[18]

The corresponding marking scheme specified the following reasons:

(1) Mongols adopted the racial discrimination policy [it specified the Han people were badly discriminated against] (2) the problem of succession to the throne (3) chaotic politics and corruption (4) the economy collapsed (5) natural disaster (0.5 mark/point)

The topics in textbooks were also in line with the Han-centred historical view presented in the official guidelines — for instance, 'The five barbarian tribes invaded the Han territory',[19] and 'Emperor Wu Di's territorial expansion'. The following textbook narratives presented these established views:

The five barbarian tribes were less civilised and they had long been eager to invade the Han territory. They wanted to seize the rich natural resources of the Middle Kingdom.[20]

Externally, one of the most significant contributions of Emperor Wu Di was the conquest of the barbarian's territories.[21]

Textbooks presented a negative view of both the culture and the rule of the Mongols:

> The culture of the Mongols was superficial. They used force to make themselves the masters of China. Not only did they disregard Chinese traditional culture, they also devastated it. Therefore in Chinese history, the Yuan dynasty's cultural achievements were the worst ... They did not have any ideals in administering the country. The Mongols only knew how to suppress the Han people so that there was no chance for the Han race to revolt against the Mongols. They [the Mongols] were ignorant of political and ethical responsibilities ... With the decline of the Yuan dynasty, the Han race was able to restore the tradition of Chinese history.[22]

> The superficial cultural foundation of the Mongols resulted in their short-sighted administration. They ruled the country on the basis of immediate interest ... The Mongols introduced different religions to the country ... the aim was to 'paralyse' the national sentiment of the Han people and to prevent the possibility of revolt by them ...[23]

With respect to the rule of the Manchus, examination questions distinguished the non-Han race from the Han race:

> The Manchus, as an alien race, once they became the masters of China, adopted the policies of conciliation and suppression. As a result, the Manchus were able to rule China for 260 years. Give an account of the administrative policies of the Manchus.[24]

The marking scheme described the following policies of the Manchus:

> The conciliatory policy aimed at bribing the Han people, and the suppression policy was intended to threaten the Han people. The marking scheme specified five policies of conciliation and suppression and 2 marks were given for each policy.[25]

The textbooks contained similar views:

> The tactics adopted by the Manchus were pinpointed against the Han people. Emperor Tai Zu was extremely anti-Han. When emperor Tai Zong came to the throne, he adopted a conciliatory policy, and in particular, he made good use of the Han people to help administer the country.[26]

In brief, in terms of teaching and learning, and examinations, the Chinese History curriculum exhibited the following features: an emphasis on bookish learning and students' memorisation of orthodox views; unpopularity among teachers and students; a focus on decontextualised and depoliticised knowledge; and an explicit Han-centred interpretation of history.

THE CURRICULUM FOR H-LEVEL AND A-LEVEL

The Curriculum Development Process (H-Level and A-Level)

The A-level examination syllabus was set mainly for those who sought admission to HKU, and before the setting up of the Examinations Authority in 1978, it was administered by HKU's Matriculation Board. The examination syllabus, setting of questions and marking were all done by HKU's Chinese History teachers. According to the Chairman of the A-level Chinese History subject committee:

> A-level Chinese History was first devised by Law Heung Lam, and in the 1970s I took over the chairmanship. The staff at HKU were comparatively more familiar with the sophistication of A-level questions. There were, of course, individual staff who set questions badly, so that questions had to be set again. For example, how could a sixth-form student answer a question related to the staff's own expertise. Therefore, in the committee I assumed the role of a co-ordinator to make sure that the A-level questions were of high standard.[27]

Throughout this whole period (1945–74), members of the Chinese Department of HKU held the chairmanship of the A-level Chinese History subject, and their ideas about Chinese History directly affected the subject. The head of the ED's History section, D. C. Lam, verified this when he talked about university teachers' views on curriculum development:

> Before the setting up of the HKEA, the two universities (HKU and CUHK) manipulated the A-level and H-level respectively. Government officials had a lesser part to play in the respective committees.

In other words, A-level Chinese History was HKU's territory and the A-level curriculum matched the areas of expertise of HKU's staff.[28] From 1956, when A-level Chinese History was first offered as an independent subject, up to 1974, no major changes were made to the syllabus.

Similarly, the H-level examination catered mainly for candidates seeking entrance to CUHK, and during this period the examination was administered by the University. Teachers from its History Department — namely K. T. Sun, C. C. Lo and H. B. So — were mainly responsible for the development of the H-level examination curriculum, and consequently their views of Chinese History had a direct impact on the subject. Qian Mu, who had had taught K. T. Sun, wrote a foreword to Sun's Chinese History textbook and commended it thus: '[Sun's book] this textbook gives a detailed account of the success and failure of historical events. Attention is also given to commenting on the correct or incorrect behaviour of historical figures'.[29] Sun clearly considered it important for history to offer moral exemplars to students. S. T. Kong, a student in the early 1960s, recalled Sun's teaching: 'Sun is a typical Confucian follower, and Chinese History was a moralising agent in his teaching'. In the H-level examination topics, emphasis was given to the contributions and impact of individual historical figures.[30] It is interesting to note that, as revealed in the minutes of meetings from 1967 to 1974, no recommendations were made to revise the existing syllabus.

Overall, then, teachers at HKU and CUHK were in control of the development of the A-level and H-level curriculum respectively. According to the A-L subject committee chairperson, 'the A-level subject committee did the whole thing — from designing to producing the syllabus — and teachers were to teach according to the syllabus. The subject committee wrote to the schools annually informing schools of the changes made to the examination syllabus. Worthwhile issues would be brought up in the committee for discussion'.[31] The approach to curriculum development was highly centralised, and school teachers were neither involved nor consulted in the process. It is worth noting that during this phase (1945–74), university academics collaborated with the colonial government in producing and implementing the Chinese History curriculum.

The Curriculum: Aims and Content (H-level and A-level)

The H-level examination was created in 1965 for students seeking entrance to CUHK, which had been set up two years earlier. The A-level was already primarily an entrance examination for HKU, catering for F7 students, and the syllabuses of these two examinations were the key curriculum documents that defined Chinese History's content at this level. Table 3.4 (see p. 72) illustrates the development of the H-level and A-level Chinese History curriculum between 1956 and 1974.[32]

The study of Chinese History as a continuous whole

A-level and H-level examinations were intended to meet the entrance requirements of HKU and CUHK respectively. In terms of content, the two examinations were theme-based and, apart from dynastic history, supplementary themes to be studied were foreign relations, the Chinese race, institutions, scholarship and culture. For the A-level, for 13 years (1956–69), students had to study from the Zhou dynasty (~1122 BC) to the Ming dynasty (1643), and in 1970 the scope of study was further extended to include the Qing dynasty (ending in 1911). Similarly, from when the H-level was first introduced in 1965 until 1974, its period of study ran from the Zhou dynasty (~1122 BC) to the Qing dynasty

Table 3.4   Development of the H-level and A-level Chinese History curriculum (1956–74)

Level	A-level			H-level
Year	1956–62	1963–69	1970–75	1965–74
Key curriculum document	examination syllabus	examination syllabus	examination syllabus	examination syllabus
Genesis	independent subject, as the entrance examination for HKU	same as 1956–62	same as 1956–62	an independent subject in 1965 and entrance examination for CUHK
Aim	to assess students' general knowledge of Chinese History and advanced knowledge of four historical themes	same as 1956–62	same as 1956–62	nil
Content arrangement	theme-based, from the Zhou dynasty (~1122 BC) to the Ming dynasty (1643)	same as 1956–62	theme-based, from the Zhou dynasty (~1122 BC) to the Qing dynasty (1911)	theme-based, divided into 10 dynasties, from the Zhou dynasty (~1122 BC) to the Qing dynasty (1911)
Curriculum emphasis	politics, foreign relations, Chinese nation, institutions, scholarship and culture	one paper added: an in-depth study of a specific dynasty	the Qing dynasty was added as another specific dynasty.	dynasty-based, integrated with geography, institutions, intellectual thoughts, the Chinese nation and culture

(1911) — that is, the entire dynastic history of China.[33] The sixth-form curriculum was thus characterised by a heavy emphasis on content knowledge of more than 3,000 years of ancient and medieval history, and modern and contemporary history (from 1911 onwards) was ignored.

An orthodox historical perspective

Similar to the F1–5 syllabuses, the H-level[34] tended to promote traditional established views on historical events and personages — for example, 'Wang Mang *usurped* the Han throne', 'The *disorder* created by Empress Wu and Wei', 'An Shi *uprising*', 'The *territorial expansion* of the Han dynasty' and 'The *territorial expansion* of the Tang dynasty (in contrast to 'invasion').[35] Students were expected to present established views rather than offer interpretations.

A Han-centred viewpoint

The same Han-centred orientation as in the F1–5 syllabuses is revealed in the topics listed in the 1965 H-level examination syllabus: 'The *assimilation* of non-Han races'; 'Manchurians' *invasion*'; 'The five *barbarian* tribes invaded the Han territory'; 'The *Mongols* ruling policies'; and 'The *Manchus* ruling policies'. The above topics clearly distinguished the non-Han race from the Han race, and the interpretation was one based on a Han-centred viewpoint.

Overall, the H-level and A-level examination syllabuses were devised with a view to selecting the most able students for university entry, and the curriculum was therefore geared to individual rote learning rather than collaborative group work.

The Curriculum (H-level and A-level): Impact on Teaching, Learning and Examinations

The study of Chinese History as a continuous whole

The study by Fehl mentioned earlier showed the adverse effect of the H-level curriculum on sixth-form students in both Anglo-Chinese and Chinese middle schools. He found that Chinese History was the least popular subject among students,[36] and he inferred that this could be attributed to the massive volume of hard facts that had to be memorised. As it covered more than 3,000 years of history, an enormous number of events and important people had to be studied, so it was not surprising that students disliked the subject.

With regard to the effect of the A-level curriculum on examinations, the examination reports between 1960 and 1970 commented that candidates tended to memorise texts, and the reports abound with criticisms that students: 'cram their answers with disconnected and very often irrelevant historical facts'; 'stick to textbook narration and seldom refer to other materials'; 'demonstrate no critical thinking in their answers'; and give answers 'irrelevant to the questions'.

With such an extensive period to study, hardly any analysis could take place in the classroom, with the result that, in the examination, students tended to regurgitate 'model' answers that they had 'learned' in class.

An orthodox historical perspective

The following recollections give a glimpse of what it must have been like to study Chinese History in the sixth form at that time:

> I studied in a Chinese Middle School in the late 1950s and early 1960s. My teachers mainly came from Sun Yat-sen University. Studying was geared towards obtaining good results to enter the university. Memorisation of established views was inevitable. (H. C. Wong)

> In the late 1950s life was hard. We all studied hard to fight for a place in the university. We accepted that there were tons of facts to remember in Chinese History. No pain, no gain. This is studying. (D. L. Luk)

> In the 1960s when I was studying in F6 in the secondary school, my teachers were anti-communist. Since they were Qian Mu's students, their political stance was clearly pro-Nationalist. They referred to the capital of China as 'Peiping' instead of 'Beijing'. Rote learning was common. (F. S. Tsang)

The recollections of the above three government officials shows that they all had to rely on memorisation in studying Chinese History. It is interesting that, when they became teachers, they still emphasised the memorisation and recitation of established views and factual accounts, and orthodox views were thus passed on from one generation to another:

> When I taught Chinese History in 1974, public examination results were my most important concern. I spent most of the time drilling students in examination techniques. (F. S. Tsang)

> As a sixth-form teacher, I regarded [it] as my major responsibility to help students to obtain good results in the examination. If you analysed the past examination questions, you would know that similar questions had appeared over the last 30 years. Yet I also trained their analytical skills. In other words, students had to know how historians arrived at certain conclusions. (H. C. Wong)

> The most important thing was to drill their examination skills. The so-called higher order thinking was in fact a repetition of historians' conclusions. Students did not have the ability to make their own judgements. As teachers we had to teach students how to present the answers systematically. (D. L. Luk)

In terms of content knowledge, the teaching and learning of the F6–7 Chinese History curriculum was very much geared towards the two examinations, with a focus on decontextualised and depoliticised knowledge. This feature reflects the fact that the Chinese History curriculum, at both H-level and A-level, was specifically designed to meet the entrance examinations of the two universities.

The examinations were also very much concerned with traditional, orthodox views of Chinese History, as can be seen in the following question:

> What were the reasons leading to the *Taiping revolution*? Why did this revolution fail? (H-level examination, 1954)

The Taiping rebellion occurred in the mid-1800s, and aimed at overthrowing Manchurian rule. Here the examination question described it as a 'revolution', and students were confined to viewing it from this perspective in their answers, while ignoring the possibility of its being viewed as a rebellion. The following are other examples of orthodox historical viewpoints:

> The Song dynasty was weak in national power but strong in academic achievement. Explain. (H-level examination, 1966)

> The decline of the Ming dynasty was attributable to the eunuchs' interference in politics. Explain. (H-level examination, 1974)

The two questions above specified an orthodox view, which students had to accept, rather than interpret or criticise. Further examples include:

> The Eunuchs' control of power led to the collapse of the Ming dynasty. Explain the reasons. (H-level examination, 1974)

> What kind of organisation were the Boxers? How did they start their rebellion? What were the outcomes of this rebellion? (H-level examination, 1961)

Here, orthodox views were clearly presented, such as the idea that 'the eunuchs' control of power led to the collapse of the Ming dynasty', and that the Boxers' actions were a 'rebellion'. The students' task was to elaborate on these established views without criticism.

A Han-centred viewpoint

The following H-level and A-level examination questions distinguished the Han race from the non-Han race, and revealed a Han-centred cultural viewpoint:

> Examine the achievements made by the Han race in the anti-Manchurian struggles in the Qing dynasty. (H-level examination question, 1952)

> The invasion of Han territory by the barbarians (wu hu luan hua) affected the migration of Chinese. Explain. (A-level examination question, 1956)

> The Yuan dynasty and the Qing dynasty were non-Han races who administered China. They adopted different policies to rule Han people. Compare their policies. (H-level examination question, 1967)

In general, the nature of knowledge in the examination questions reflected an orthodox historical perspective and a Han-centred viewpoint, and was prescriptive, decontextualised and depoliticised. All these characteristics were also embodied in the official curriculum.

CONCLUSION

In the initial period of the first phase (1945–74), schools adopted the Nationalist government's Chinese History curriculum until the report of the Chinese Studies Committee in 1953 recommended that Hong Kong should devise its own curriculum emphasising social and cultural, rather than political, history. This shows that Chinese History was a sensitive subject from the beginning. At the same time, the Committee advised that this curriculum should aim at reinforcing Chinese moral and social values, but without going to the other extreme of fostering xenophobia. However, the subject which emerged did not conform completely to these aims. Social and cultural history were only supplementary to dynastic history (although the latter was not 'political history' in its Western sense, but was the history of emperors, key persons and imperial court events). In addition, the orthodox and Han-centred nature of the curriculum showed that the curriculum developers were more in agreement with the traditional view of Chinese History (as in 'the 24 Dynastic Histories') than that recommended by the Chinese Studies Committee. The moralising function of Chinese History, which was emphasised in the report and in line with 'the 24 Dynastic Histories', was not explicitly expressed in either the actual curriculum, or in the curriculum as realised at the level of teaching and learning, and examinations. It was also during this first phase (1945–74) that the notion of 'the study of Chinese History as a continuous whole' began to be established, and this was taken as the study of history from the pre-historic period to either 1911 or 1945.

At all levels (junior secondary, CEE and H-level/A-level), the Chinese History curriculum adopted the orthodox views enshrined in 'the 24 Dynastic Histories' and a Han-centred cultural viewpoint, and focused primarily on imperial court history, with cultural, social or economic history accorded a distinctly minor role. There was also a bias towards the study of the earlier periods of history, which further indicated that the curriculum was heavily content-oriented, taking no account of students' interests and experience.

Publishers followed the examination syllabuses closely to ensure that their textbooks would pass the official review, their safest option being to adopt a conservative approach. Textbook writers therefore adhered to traditional, orthodox views and Han-centred interpretations of history, for commercial as well as political and historiographical reasons (see Chapters 1 and 2). Government officials made no attempt to produce a detailed curriculum guide when Chinese History emerged as an independent subject, but only issued examination syllabuses that ensured that the content to be taught would be based on dynastic chronology. Traditional and Han-centred views of history were reflected in the syllabus topics, textbooks, examination questions and marking schemes; and, as teachers implemented them at the classroom level, Chinese History teaching remained almost exclusively concerned with the transmission of established knowledge. Students were simply expected to reproduce 'model answers' in the examinations, and so it is not at all surprising that Chinese History was an unpopular subject with them.

In terms of the curriculum development process, the CEE was controlled mainly by key personnel within the ED, who adopted a top-down approach to curriculum dissemination. The curricula for A-level and H-level were controlled by HKU and CUHK respectively, which aimed at selecting the 'best' candidates, and the content at these levels was based on themes which were also arranged chronologically. Teachers were neither consulted nor given support in their teaching. Although the emphasis on dynastic and cultural history (and the exclusion of contemporary history and Hong Kong history) reflected the colonial government's active role in defining the subject, it does not seem to conform to stereotypical ideas about colonial curricula. The development of Chinese History during this period shows the convergence of interests of the three key parties: the Hong Kong government allowed the study of indigenous culture and history as long as it remained depoliticised and decontextualised; the local subject community was willing to cooperate with the government about the nature of the curriculum since it coincided with the interests of influential members; and, indirectly, the PRC influenced the key people in their exercising of a form of self-regulation. As far as all three parties were concerned, Chinese History should encourage students to identify culturally with China but keep them away from modern Chinese politics. The impact of this curriculum on local students is described by Luk (1991: 668):

> Thus, generations of Hong Kong Chinese students grew up learning from subjects about Chinese culture to identify themselves as Chinese, but relating that Chineseness to neither contemporary China nor the local Hong Kong landscape. It was a Chinese identity in the abstract, a patriotism of the émigré, probably held all the more absolutely because it was not connected to tangible reality.

4

Consolidation of Chinese History as an Independent Subject (1974–97)

Chapter 3 examined the development of Chinese History from 1945–74 during which the vision of Chinese History took shape. The principal aim of this chapter is to explore the ways in which the subject community inherited the nature and role of Chinese History from the first phase and secured them in the school curriculum between 1974 and 1997. This analysis can help to explain how a strong subject culture was established that helped to shield the subject from the broader curriculum reform that took place in the 1990s.

THE CURRICULUM FOR F1–5

The Curriculum Development Process (F1–5)

In contrast to the previous phase, there is no evidence that the colonial government, for political reasons or otherwise, interfered with Chinese History during this period. The minimal changes that were made to the subject can be attributed more to the personal preferences of subject officers and committee members, and of the local subject community. Among the various groups that made up the Chinese History subject community — government officials, university lecturers and schoolteachers — those who exerted the most influence in the decision-making process during this period were again government officials. D. C. Lam, a graduate in History and Geography from HKU, was still the head of the History section of the Advisory Inspectorate, while D. L. Luk was the Chinese History inspector in 1975 until he retired in 1994. Both Lam and Luk were official members of the Chinese History subject committee. Although Chinese History was still subordinated to History, there not even being a senior inspector post for Chinese History until 1986, Luk managed to have virtually a free hand in deciding on issues regarding the Chinese History curriculum. As he explained in an interview:

I had been in the Education Department for 19 years (1975–94), responsible for the development of the Chinese History curriculum. The colonial government had never given me political pressure on what should be done with the curriculum. The initiatives had largely come either from me or from C. N. Leung in the HKEA, while decisions rested with the subject committee, which comprised members from tertiary institutions and secondary schools.

When asked who played the dominant role in shaping the curriculum, Luk said:

Members of the subject committee were predominant. There were about 10 members in the committee … In the meetings never once did we have to vote for a decision. We all had a consensus …

In reality, however, it was Luk who dominated the subject committee, and it was his preferences which carried the most weight, with the other members generally going along with his decisions. Moreover, although the CDC subject committee did have a representative from the tertiary sector, minutes of meetings show that HKU's representative was never present at any of the meetings between 1974 and 1997, and so university teachers exerted no direct influence on the F1–5 curriculum. In this way, Luk was able to resist major changes to the Chinese History curriculum, at least those changes which he thought would threaten his vision of how the subject should be taught and examined. In this, he was supported by C. N. Leung who headed the HKEA Chinese History committee until 1993, when he became the senior curriculum development officer in the CDI. He held similar views to Luk on the nature of Chinese History, and these two officials had the greatest influence in determining the nature of the curriculum during this phase.

An example of the authority enjoyed by Luk occurred in 1975, when D. C. Lam was considering reducing the weight of dynastic history in the F1–F3 syllabus:

In 1975, when I proposed to reduce dynastic history and introduce cultural history, I was accused of 'forgetting my own origins'. My Chinese History colleague did not agree with me, and nor did the members of the subject committee. They got hold of the 'Chinese History system' that the study had to start from the Yellow Emperor up to the Qing dynasty. (D. C. Lam)

On another occasion, it was because of Luk's opposition to the inclusion of Hong Kong history in Chinese History that those responsible for the 'History' subject took the initiative in including Hong Kong history in their syllabus. According to Lam, in 1988 he suggested including Hong Kong history in Chinese History:

I first asked Luk to consider incorporating Hong Kong history into Chinese History. However Luk turned down my proposal. I then turned to the History officer Jane Cheng and Cheng immediately took up the task.

The reasons that Luk gave for rejecting the proposal were:

> We have to learn Chinese History. Each dynasty has its own characteristics. Students should, as far as possible, learn these characteristics before they can come to appreciate the greatness of China. Given that time is insufficient to study Chinese History, how could we include Hong Kong history in the curriculum? At that time there was not even one member in the subject committee who had studied Hong Kong history, including the chairman. I objected to the inclusion of Hong Kong history in Chinese History.

The subsequent minutes of the Chinese History subject committee record that:

> Members felt that it would be more appropriate to implement Hong Kong history as a brand new individual subject or include it as a part of a Social Studies or World History syllabus. (Minutes of meeting, CEE Chinese History subject committee, 31 October 1989)

However, it was Luk who was responsible for Hong Kong history not being included in Chinese History.

During the whole of the second phase (1974–97), the F1–5 subject committee's minutes of meetings reveal that the issues discussed consisted mainly of: extending the end-date of the period of study for Chinese History; the use of block marking instead of point-reward-marking; and readjusting the weighting of ancient history and contemporary history (in favour of placing more emphasis on the latter). On all these issues, D. L. Luk, supported by his counterpart in the HKEA, C. N. Leung, was the one whose views dominated, and it was to a large extent because of these two officials that no major changes were made to the curriculum during this time: dynastic history remained the core content of the curriculum; Hong Kong history was excluded from it; the point-form examination marking scheme was maintained; and the end-date for Chinese History was only extended to 1976, when the final verdict on the Cultural Revolution was given by the PRC.

Luk's views on the nature of the subject to a large extent resembled the characteristics of the Chinese History curriculum between 1974–97:

> Section A (dynastic history) was more important. Each dynasty has its own characteristics. We stressed that all these characteristics had to be brought up in our teaching so that we could see the *greatness of Chinese History* … To promote moral education and civic education through teaching Chinese History was something required by the then Director of Education, M. K. Leung. At that time all subjects received the same instruction. My senior, P. S. Chan (History senior inspector) asked me to do this [a draft on how to incorporate civic and moral education into Chinese History teaching]. Hence I used one hour to complete a one-page table which incorporated *moral values* into specific events and

personages ... There was no way that *Hong Kong history* could be included in Chinese History. We did not have enough time to complete the existing syllabus. ... I objected to the introduction of *data-based questions* in Chinese History. I understood very well that students did not have the ability to answer data-based questions ... *Point-reward-marking* (in the marking scheme, students' answers were marked on the basis of a points score) was a must because students were poor in language. It was beyond their ability to write an essay ... *Memorisation* was a must in studying Chinese History. If we were too high sounding, sooner or later, no students would opt for studying Chinese History. (italics added)

The curriculum development for Chinese History was highly centralised. The ED was responsible for the revision of the junior level curriculum, and D. L. Luk was in charge of initiating change and the production of teaching materials. In the curriculum revision process, teachers were consulted, but more to ensure effective promotion and implementation of the curriculum than to influence decision-making. For example, when the junior level Provisional Syllabus was introduced, a two-day exhibition was held 'to solicit teachers' opinions' (reported in *Wah Kiu Yat Po*, 17 July 1980); and for the revised curriculum introduced in 1982, seminars were organised which aimed at 'familiarising teachers with the content and framework of the revised curriculum, collecting teachers' views, and discussing issues relating to the implementation of the curriculum' (reported in *Wah Kiu Yat Po*, 8 November 1982). In both cases, however, consultation was primarily a way of disseminating the revised curriculum, and teachers were simply issued with materials to help them to implement it. These took the form of: (1) samples of schemes of work; (2) reference materials; (3) seminars; and (4) worksheet examples.[1]

The HKEA and ED collaborated in the development of the CEE curriculum. According to D. L. Luk, 'the CEE Chinese History was taken care of by me in the ED, and C. N. Leung in the HKEA. Sometimes we did exchange our views concerning the revision of the curriculum'. When the CEE teaching syllabus was first introduced, a questionnaire survey was conducted to collect teachers' views on the revised curriculum. However, it was for the CEE subject committee (CDC and HKEA) to decide whether or not views were to be adopted, and there was no channel through which teachers could actively participate in the curriculum development process. The power of decision-making rested with the government officials. Once the syllabus was issued, publishers were to write textbooks in line with it, and these were reviewed by the Textbook Review Committee before they were allowed to be put in the market. In the process of textbook review, D. L. Luk was the final judge of what was the appropriate content for inclusion and he alone defined historical accuracy (see Chapter 2). According to Luk:

Ultimately all Chinese History textbooks had to come to me for final approval. I would check the factual accuracy, sentence structure, content, the phrases used, how well the content went with the curriculum etc. in very great detail. I had to make sure that things written down were *accurate*. When I was working in the Education Department, there were not any mistakes in the textbooks. (italics added).

Obviously the role played by Luk as the final decision-maker was not welcomed by the publishers. Their complaint about having to restrict textbook writing to a specific approach suggests that Luk's definition of historical 'accuracy' was not considered by them to be acceptable or authoritative. When he was asked why all Chinese History textbooks looked alike, he said 'history is history; it is all the same. The scope has been set by the curriculum. Therefore textbooks are very much alike'. This implies that Luk, a key figure in the construction of the Chinese History curriculum, viewed the subject as a body of facts rather than as an interpretive discipline.

According to H. C. Wong, a member of subject committees at different levels for more than 20 years: 'once the syllabus was adopted, there would not be any follow-up work to monitor its development'. Seminars were arranged for teachers, and they were provided with teaching materials, and it was assumed that implementation would not present any difficulties.

In the process of curriculum development, the subject community did play a reactive role on issues related to Chinese History, but there is no evidence that their reactions were organised by unions or community organisations. For example, in relation to matters such as the Social Studies incident in 1975, Dominic Wong's (Director of the Education) '20 year rule' statement in 1994, and the Hong Kong history controversy in 1995, the subject community confined its actions to expressing its views in the media. No further organised activities were conducted, and no groups organised themselves as a joint force to exert pressure on the government. In view of the dominant role played by government officials in the decision-making process, and the highly centralised approach to curriculum development, it is worth exploring how the content of Chinese History was defined by these officials in the official curriculum.

The Curriculum (F1–5): Aims and Content

The curriculum for F1–3

During the first phase (1945–74), the ED had only issued teaching guidelines consisting mainly of a list of content topics, but in 1975 the first junior level teaching syllabus was published, which expressed clearly the official views on Chinese History education. This document contained the aims, content, methods and assessment guidelines for Chinese History and included two syllabuses, namely the Temporary Syllabus (the old syllabus, to be phased out in 1977) and the Provisional Syllabus (the new syllabus, to be adopted in 1977). The major differences between the Temporary Syllabus and previous syllabuses were in two of its aims which emphasised cultural history and the development of analytical ability. The Provisional Syllabus went even further by giving cultural history its own, separate section, thus affording it equal status with dynastic history. Another teaching syllabus was issued in 1982, which was largely based on the Provisional Syllabus, but with a few changes, the most noticeable being an additional aim of developing good behaviour in students through studying the actions of historical figures. Table 4.1 illustrates the development of the F1–3 Chinese History curriculum between 1974 and 1997.

Table 4.1   Development of the F1–3 Chinese History curriculum (1974–97)

Year	1974–81	1982–97
Key curriculum document	• teaching syllabus	• teaching syllabus
Genesis	• Chinese middle schools and Anglo-Chinese schools adopted the same syllabus • the teaching syllabus issued in 1975 included (1) the Temporary Syllabus: the old syllabus used until 1977 and (2) the Provisional Syllabus: the new syllabus adopted in 1977	• the 1982 syllabus was based on the Provisional Syllabus with some minor changes
Aims	• emphasised the importance of Chinese culture, the understanding of the meaning of history as 'continuity' and 'evolution', and the development of analytical ability	• same as the Provisional Syllabus, with an additional aim: 'to develop students' good behaviour through studying the deeds of historical figures'
Content arrangement	• Temporary Syllabus: Xia (~2100 BC) to 1949 • Provisional Syllabus: Shang (~1600 BC) to contemporary China (end-date not specified)	• same as the Provisional Syllabus
Curriculum emphasis	• Temporary Syllabus: dynastic history integrated with cultural history • Provisional Syllabus: two sections, with equal emphasis A. dynastic history B. cultural history	• same as the Provisional Syllabus

The study of Chinese History as a continuous whole

The study of Chinese History as a continuous whole that had been a major feature of the syllabuses of the previous phase (1945–1974) remained prominent in the 1975 and 1982 syllabuses, with one of the aims being to help students to understand the meaning of 'continuity', and 'evolution' in Chinese History'.[2] The scope of studies in the Temporary Syllabus was the same as the 1945–1974 syllabuses, stretching from the Xia (~2100 BC) to 1949, but in the Provisional Syllabus (and the later 1982 syllabus) the period was extended right up to the contemporary period (but with no end-date). Consequently, as in the first phase, practically the whole of Chinese history had to be studied. According to D. C. Lam, his Chinese History colleagues believed that Chinese History should be treated as a continuous whole and they described it as an 'unshakable system'. Y. K. Kow, one of the main figures in the drafting of the syllabus, explained that 'the spirit of the new syllabus [Provisional Syllabus] was to study the uniqueness of each dynasty and its development'.[3] In other words, Chinese History was seen as a sacred and indivisible body of knowledge, and the sheer volume of content was thus inevitably large.

An orthodox historical perspective

As noted in Chapter 1, the orthodox historical views prescribed in 'the 24 Dynastic Histories' contained a moral agenda, and were originally used for the edification of emperors. The Chinese History curriculum from 1945 to 1974 had incorporated these orthodox views in ascribing judgements to individual events and people and this was again very evident during this second phase. Consequently, despite the expressed aim of the F1–3 syllabus 'to cultivate students' objectivity and analytical power',[4] there was actually little room for students to develop arguments and arrive at their own conclusions through analysis. In the 1982 syllabus, a new aim was included: 'to develop students' good behaviour through studying the deeds of historical personages'.[5] The following are examples of the orthodox views in this regard in the F1–3 teaching syllabus:

> After the unification of China, Qin Shihuang oppressed his people and levied heavy taxes on them. That was why the Qin dynasty only lasted for 15 years.[6]

> Emperor Wu Di's rule was the most glorious period of the Han dynasty. Teachers should explain how he extended Chinese territory [his military action was described as 'extended' rather than 'invaded'] and undertook many construction projects. In terms of military and cultural achievements he contributed to a prosperous period in the Han dynasty.[7]

> Ming Cheng Zu succeeded to the throne. He feared that Ming Hui Di had taken refuge overseas so he sent Zheng He to the South Sea to find Hui Di, but he made the excuse that he just wanted to enlist more tributary states.[8]

The above official prescriptions were established views concerning both the reasons for the rise and fall of individual dynasties, and the good or bad behaviour of individuals. To illustrate these views further, the CDI issued a curriculum circular in 1993 which emphasised 'the historical lessons to be learnt from the disasters caused by the factional conflict in the later Han period: this was a conflict between right and wrong, one that represented the state's interests (state university students and courtiers) versus private interests (eunuchs)'.[9] The official guide never failed to state which party was right and which was wrong, but seldom required teachers or students to provide proper arguments to support such claims, or to look for counter-arguments based on evidence. It is therefore doubtful whether such high-sounding aims as 'to cultivate students' objectivity and analytical power' were really valued highly by curriculum developers. Although the two syllabuses (1975 and 1982) suggested that teachers should adopt different methods in their teaching, such as story-telling, discussion, simulations and the study of source materials, the ultimate end was to teach their students the orthodox views as, according to the syllabuses, 'the advantage of studying history is: to understand that history's lessons can benefit our present lives'.[10] In this case, the curriculum was intended to shape students' thinking in ways that were deemed appropriate by the key decision-makers, especially with regard to their moral behaviour and value judgements. This indoctrination of students without providing supporting evidence was in itself problematic since they would be at a loss as to whom they should emulate or condemn, and on what basis they should make such judgements.

Cultural history and a Han-centred viewpoint

Unlike syllabuses in the past, the 1975 Temporary Syllabus stated explicitly the worth and eminence of Chinese culture:

> Chinese culture has a long history. In five thousand years, the Chinese nation has produced great achievements in intellectual thinking and technology. Moreover, there are special characteristics in the way of life and social organisation of the Chinese nation. Hence the first and the most important aim of teaching Chinese History is to guide students to appreciate the inherent Chinese cultural tradition and the characteristics of the way of life of the people.[11]

However, as with past syllabuses, cultural history was still integrated with dynastic history, and it was the Provisional Syllabus (and the later 1982 syllabus) which was to give greater prominence to Chinese culture by affording it a separate Section B. Moreover, the 1982 syllabus further explained the function of Chinese culture, and included it as an aim in the teaching syllabus:

> The survival and development of a nation depends on its racial unity. *Cultural tradition plays a crucial role in uniting all people together.* Hence

the first and the most important aim of teaching Chinese History is to guide students to appreciate the inherent Chinese cultural tradition and the characteristics of the way of life of the people.[12] (italics added)

This educational aim had not been explicit in the first phase (1945–74). As for the reasons for giving such prominence to Chinese culture, the key decision-makers expressed different views. D. C. Lam, one of the officials involved in the drafting of the syllabus, explained why he had proposed including Chinese culture as a separate part of the syllabus:

> I proposed to strengthen cultural history. I believed the focus should be on the romance of history. This could arouse students' interest in the subject. This was the most important aim of Chinese History education.

However, when recalling the most important change made to the Chinese History curriculum over the last 60 years, H. C. Wong, a member of the subject committee, considered that the separation of cultural history from dynastic history was of major importance:

> Previously the syllabus had a strong flavour of dynastic history. In each dynasty, cultural history was included as supplementary to the political development. In this way it would give an unclear delivery of the development of different aspects of culture. With cultural history separately included in Section B, a sense of continuity of the cultural development could be achieved.

Lam and Wong saw the study of Chinese culture as important for stimulating students' interest, and to foster pride in Chinese culture. The 1982 syllabus summarised some of the highlights of the culture of different dynasties:

> From aspects of socio-cultural, livelihood and customs we understand that in the Shang dynasty the standard of living was very high. At that time culture was already developed.[13]

> Teachers should point out in particular that during the Han dynasty intellectual thinking was so successful that the loss during the Qin dynasty [when scholarly books were destroyed] could be made up. The achievements of the Han dynasty are seen in its inheritance and glorification of the academic traditions. Students should take note of this point.[14]

> Concerning the Tang culture … teachers could list the following examples: Japan and Korea sent missions to China. Their students were sent to learn Chinese culture and imitate China's institutions and rituals.[15]

> The inventions made in the Song dynasty — printing, the compass and gunpowder — made significant contribution[s] to world civilisation.

> Students could compare the technological achievements during this period in China and with those in Europe.[16]

> Following the invasion by Mongols of West Asia and Eastern Europe ... merchants, missionaries, scholars, and artists from the West went to the East. Hence China's movable-type printing, gun-powder, firearms, and compass passed to Europe ... Europeans used the compass as a tool in sailing and [this] contributed to the discovery of new sea routes and the new continent. Gunpowder was used to produce weapons, which led to the collapse of the Western feudal system.[17]

It should be noted, however, that the 'glory' of Chinese culture continued to be very much Han-centred, referring to the culture of China's majority Han nationality, while the culture of the two non-Han ruling races, the Mongols and the Manchus, were portrayed in a negative light. In fact, both their culture and their ruling policies were denigrated. This can be illustrated in the case of the Mongols in the following extracts from the syllabuses:

> With regard to the culture of the *Yuan* dynasty, teachers can point out that in the history of China there is *nothing special* about the culture of the Yuan dynasty. There is one thing which teachers can highlight — literature. On the one hand, [Han race] intellectuals were grief-stricken at the fall of the Song dynasty, while on the other hand, under the administration of the Mongols, they did not have any channel to enter the officialdom.[18] Therefore they put their efforts into writing traditional operas ... Teachers can also point out and discuss with students why the Mongols did not *learn from the Han race* as there were no contributions made by them in the fields of cultural and institutional development.[19] (italics added)

> 'They [Mongols] were nomads when they set up their regime in China. They were good at battles, poor in organisation. Therefore during the Yuan reign, there was continual confusion and chaos in politics and customs. Teachers can discuss with students 'what was the impact of the low social status given to the Confucian scholars' ... Teachers can discuss with students the fact that in the Yuan dynasty, the emperors did not have any ideals in administering the country. Their ruling policy was segregation, suppression, and deprivation. Hence Yuan rule was bound to fail.[20]

Similar disparaging and dismissive views were expressed regarding the other non-Han dynasty, the Qing dynasty, with respect to its culture and rule:

> Students do not have much interest in the cultural systems of the Manchus. Hence a brief narration would suffice. There is no need to emphasise the evolution of culture during the Qing dynasty.[21]

> Students can be told that the Manchus were also an *alien* race who ruled over China ... Policies of oppression and conciliation were adopted so

that the Han people could not revolt against the Manchu rule. That was why the Qing dynasty was able to last for 260 years.[22] (italics added)

It is interesting to note that this bias towards the Han race was evident as early as the time of Confucian studies — 'unite the Han people and differentiate them from the barbarians' — and was later embedded in 'the 24 Dynastic Histories' (see Chapter 1). It might well be argued that curriculum developers in Hong Kong adopted the historical views of 'the 24 Dynastic Histories', which then became a 'tradition' to be maintained in the subsequent development of the subject.

The curriculum for F4–5

In 1974, Chinese middle schools and Anglo-Chinese schools adopted the same new Chinese History examination syllabus at senior secondary level, which differed little from previous F4–5 syllabuses, except that it contained three sections from which students could choose two, either A and B or B and C (see Table 4.1). However, in 1990, the first CEE teaching syllabus was issued, which differed greatly from previous ones. First, although students were still required to study the entire course of Chinese history, from the Shang (~1600 BC) to 1976,[23] it was now divided into two sections — dynastic history and cultural history — thus, as with the F1–F3 syllabus, giving equal status to the latter. There were also two new aims: cultivating students' analytical ability and encouraging good behaviour. Table 4.2 (see p. 90) illustrates the development of the F4–5 Chinese History curriculum between 1974 and 1997.

The study of Chinese History as a continuous whole

The attempt by the Chinese History subject committee to reduce the amount of history that students had to study in the 1974 syllabus, by allowing them to choose just two out of three sections, was criticised in various quarters. In 1983, the CDC Chinese History subject committee discussed the issue of dividing Chinese History into sections as in the syllabus introduced in 1974 and noted that:

> Committee members viewed that Chinese History should be taught as a continuous whole and should not be compartmentalised. The syllabus should start from the Shang dynasty (~1600 BC) and end in 1971. It was decided that this recommendation be made to the HKEA CEE subject committee to form a joint working group to discuss this issue.[24]

The decision-makers' firm belief in the indivisible nature of Chinese historical study finally gave rise to a revision of the syllabus in 1990, whereby the choice of two out of three sections was abandoned and the whole of Chinese History from ~1600 BC to 1976 was to be studied. The rationale for this was set out in one of

Table 4.2   Development of the F4–5 Chinese History curriculum (1974–97)

Year	1974–89	1990–97
Key curriculum document	examination syllabus	examination syllabus and teaching syllabus
Genesis	Chinese middle schools and Anglo-Chinese schools adopted the same examination syllabus	in 1990 the first teaching syllabus was issued
Aim	not stated	emphasise: (1) knowledge of Chinese culture; (2) knowledge of facts concerning the rise and fall of dynasties; (3) cultural history; (4) cultivating students' objectivity and analytical power; and (5) nurturing students' good behaviour
Content arrangement	three sections from which students were to choose two: A. Shang (~1600 BC) to Southern and Northern Dynasties (420–581) B. Sui (581) to Ming (1643) C. Qing (1644) to 1945 [in 1979 the end-date was extended to 1949]	the entire course of history was to be studied (from the Shang dynasty ~1600 BC to 1976), two sections: A. dynastic history B. themes in cultural history
Curriculum emphasis	dynastic history, integrated with cultural themes	equal emphasis on dynastic and cultural history

the aims of the new syllabus: 'to understand the basic facts of the rise and fall of the successive dynasties', and that 'dynastic history and cultural history were complementary to each other so as to strengthen students' holistic conception of the historical development of Chinese history'.[25] C. N. Leung the HKEA officer, told the *SCMP* that 'the [Examinations] authority hoped that the revised syllabus [1990] might enable students to acquire a more comprehensive and complete understanding of the history of China'.[26] This lengthening of the scope of study in the F4–5 syllabus brought it into line with the F1–3 curriculum, where students were required to study the same period of history, although in less detail. Nevertheless, the study of more than 3,000 years of history which mainly involved imperial court personages and events was both a heavy burden for teachers and students and irrelevant to the interests and day-to-day experience of students. In 1996, the CEE subject committee members did express their feeling that the 1990 syllabus was too 'heavy':

> … the 1990 syllabus was too heavy and that such a long time frame and so many events would be difficult to teach and could hardly be covered within the prescribed number of lessons. They suggested that the requirement be changed from answering one question from Shang to Ming, and another question from Qing to 1976, to answering two questions from the Shang to 1976.[27]

However, this proposal was eventually rejected by the majority of the subject committee 'on the grounds that: if this were done, students would just concentrate on studying a particular period, which would undermine the aim [to study Chinese History in its entirety] of this subject, and would be detrimental to the maintenance of standards'.

Hence, in terms of content, the 1990 syllabus was even more demanding than its predecessors. In studying the whole of Chinese history, students were now required to answer a total of four questions as opposed to three previously, and the examination time was lengthened to two hours, which was the longest among the humanities subjects. It is evident that the subject was becoming more academically oriented than in the first phase (1945–74). In addition, as noted in Chapter 2, once this extended period of study (from the Shang dynasty [~1600 BC] to 1976) was instituted in the official syllabus, anybody who attempted to reduce the scope (e.g. as in the third phase [1997–2005] with the options 'PSHE' and 'New History') would be accused of 'forgetting one's origin' or 'reviving colonialism'.

An orthodox historical perspective

The 1990 syllabus adopted the same traditional approach to history as all previous syllabuses, and while one of its aims was 'to cultivate students' objectivity and analytical power', any such analysis was only possible within the parameters of the orthodox prescriptions. The following extract from the minutes of a subject committee meeting reveals the members' perceptions of the 'real' intention behind the teaching and examination syllabuses; they considered it undesirable to set questions requiring critical thinking:

> All along, the ED syllabus and the HKEA syllabus only required students' general knowledge of Chinese History. Rarely are there questions set relating to critical thinking. Even if in the future there are questions requiring students to analyse and criticise, the proportion should *not* be high … If we ask students to give their own opinions it would be beyond their ability to answer.[28] (italics added)

This shows that the major decision-makers knew very well that students were used to repeating facts without challenging the verdicts given in the official syllabuses, and considered they would be unable to give their opinions if asked.

There was a new aim in this syllabus, 'to nurture students' good behaviour', which was to encourage students to emulate or condemn those historical figures about whom traditional moral judgements had been made in the syllabus or textbooks — such as 'Qin [Shihuang] created a *tyrannical* government; people were extremely discontented and this led to the downfall of the dynasty'[29] and 'Han Wu Di rewarded academic achievements and expanded the territory; he was to be applauded'.[30]

The views the main decision-makers expressed about the moralising function of Chinese History show the thinking behind this aspect of the curriculum:

> The value of Chinese History lies in its moral values. Let students learn the moral values. I believe men make history, and history repeats itself. There is a direction in history. Nothing changes except the names of people and places. That is why politicians must learn history. (D. L. Luk)

> It is inevitable that when we teach history we have to relate it to moral education. For example, Wen Tianxiang (a Han who resisted the rule of the Mongols) was a role model of Han loyalty. (C. S. Lam)

> History is a mirror, in which there is a paradigm of success, failure, gain and loss. If you want to teach students the meaning of life, there are lots of examples in [Chinese] history. From the past we understand the present. The greatest aim of studying [Chinese] history is to avoid making the same mistakes. (F. S. Tsang)

According to these individuals, students could simply emulate the behaviour of historical figures as stated in the syllabuses. History was seen largely as a gallery of moral exemplars, and analysis and argumentation based on evidence were not a major concern.

Cultural history and a Han-centred viewpoint

With regard to Chinese culture, as in the F4–5 syllabuses in the first phase (1945–74), the principal aim of the 1990 syllabus was 'to understand traditional Chinese culture'.[31] The intention was for students to establish a cultural identification (rather than a political one) with China (see Chapter 2 for a detailed analysis). However, unlike in previous syllabuses, cultural history now consisted of four cultural themes — institutions, economic development, foreign relations and intellectual thoughts and religion — which were studied chronologically, and which formed a separate section distinct from dynastic history. The 1990 syllabus contained the following guidelines relating to the 'greatness' of the Chinese culture:

> Teach students about the Shang society [~1600 BC] and culture so that they come to understand the long inherent tradition and culture of China.[32]

> In the Spring and Autumn, and Warring period, great schools of thought, namely, Confucianism, Taoism, the Mohist School and the Legalist School had a far-reaching impact … students should have an enhanced understanding [it should be noted that students were not expected to make interpretations] of the origins of traditional Chinese thought.[33]

The syllabus continued to reflect the same Han-centred view of history as the F1–3 syllabuses, explicitly highlighting the ways that the two non-Han races, the Mongols and Manchus, had governed the Han race badly.

> Teachers should guide students to discuss the administrative policies of the Mongols [referring to the oppressive polices against the Han race] and their impact on the decline of the dynasty.[34]

> Manchus adopted the policies of oppression and conciliation to rule the Han race, therefore their reign was longer than that of the Mongols. Teachers should discuss with students the ways that the Manchus administered the Han race.[35]

Therefore, in the second phase (1974–97) changes made to the intended Chinese History curriculum (F1–5) were minimal. The minor changes that were made had three characteristics. First, the time-frame covered a long period and was related to highly specialised content. The more than 3,000 years of history from the Zhou dynasty (~1122 BC) to 1976 was to be treated as a continuous whole and had to be studied in its entirety; and topics such as dynastic succession, socio-economic development, foreign relations, intellectual history and institutions were specialised themes included in the syllabus. Second, the inculcation of orthodoxy, as manifested by the moral exemplars which featured in syllabuses and textbooks, was regarded as an important aim. Third, a Han-centred viewpoint was embedded in the teaching syllabus. Therefore, in terms of learning, as in the first phase, individualised rote learning, rather than collaborative group work and critical thinking, could better meet the needs of the curriculum

The Curriculum (F1–5): Impact on Teaching, Learning and Examinations

In this section, the implemented curriculum is examined in terms of teaching and learning, and examinations, with the aim of revealing the extent to which the three aspects of Chinese History's content (the study of Chinese history as a continuous whole, an orthodox historical perspective, and a Han-centred viewpoint) as identified in the curriculum were manifested at the level of the classroom and examinations. Apart from published data and interviewees' personal accounts, there is also a parallel analysis of examination questions, marking schemes and textbooks in order to see how Chinese History's content was projected.

The study of Chinese History as a continuous whole

The overwhelming emphasis that the curriculum gave to dynastic history was reflected in Chinese History textbooks during this time. An analysis of textbooks by L.W. Pong identified the following features of their content: one-fifth concerned palace intrigues; one-quarter to one-third dealt with warfare; one-tenth was about rebellions and uprisings; 7 to 8% concerned literary achievements; and 5% artistic or cultural activities. For the historical figures who played dominant roles, one-quarter were emperors, one-third scholar-officials, one-eighth soldiers, and the others were eunuchs, women, monks, merchants and artisans. Pong concluded that the Chinese History curriculum helped to portray a flat, cartoon-like, shallow and non-transparent image of historical China (1987: 113–23). This analysis reveals two aspects of the Chinese History curriculum: that the content of dynastic history was irrelevant to the interests of students; and that in the official syllabus 'dynastic history' was also referred to as 'political history' (the two terms were used as synonyms), but in fact Chinese History's 'political history' (or dynastic history) took a very distinctive form, and was not 'political history' in its Western sense. It had more to do with the events and important people of the imperial court, and these characteristics of dynastic history were regarded as 'the basic facts of the rise and fall of dynasties',[36] the learning of which was stipulated as one of the aims of Chinese History teaching in the official syllabus. This implies that curriculum developers held the view that the rise and fall of dynasties were attributable to the deeds of emperors and other key persons, while macro and structural perspectives had no part to play in the analysis and explanation of these historical events. However, the narration of dynastic history in this way, with no 'analytical framework', gave rise to contradictory phenomena in history. One example of such an apparent contradiction was when students learned from their textbooks that in the Tang dynasty the troops stationed in the border areas outnumbered those stationed in the central areas which led to the downfall of the dynasty; but that in the Song dynasty, the troops stationed in the central areas far exceeded those stationed on the borders which was regarded as the main factor in the dynastic decline.[37] It was thus unfortunate that many teachers were over-reliant on the textbooks in their concern to cover the syllabus.

There was much criticism of the CEE syllabus in terms of the enormous amount of subject-matter to be covered and the fact that many students were inevitably forced to rely too much on memorisation. A report of an ED seminar for Chinese teachers in 1998 gave an indication of the concerns of teachers and the problems arising from the extensive scope of study: the main concerns were the length of the syllabus, the large number of things to be learned, the fact that the public examination questions were always very much the same, and that, partly as a consequence of these factors, students resorted to reciting model answers.[38]

In addition, from 1975 to 1997, many feature articles appeared in the newspapers criticising Chinese History's 'heavy' content knowledge, which resulted from the insistence of the curriculum planners on the need to study the whole of Chinese History. The comments revealed that both teachers and students raced from one dynasty to another; that teachers were over-dependent on the textbook in order to get through the syllabus, leading to boredom on the part of their students; and that students relied on rote-learning for examinations:

> It is a pity that I was not born thousands of years earlier — Chinese History is one of students' least liked subjects, and if it is not the least liked, it is the second or the third least liked subject. The biggest problem lies in the fact that there are *tons of material to be memorised.* Textbooks are written in accordance with the chronological development of events, not with students' ability ... *rote learning* for examination purposes.[39] (italics added)

> Chinese History is compulsory at the junior level. Yet the curriculum is *complicated.* Textbooks are dull; teaching is boring ... Chinese History is the least liked subject.[40] (italics added)

> I have been teaching Chinese History for almost 20 years. I once conducted a student survey on their interest in Chinese History. The result was: more than half students disliked the subject. Many teachers *read the textbook aloud* in class, and the textbook is boring and contains lots of *names of people and places.*[41] (italics added)

> We have conducted interviews with teachers concerning the new CEE Chinese History syllabus. They generally consider the syllabus too long and fragmented. There is a big jump from one event to another. Students have no option but to learn by rote.[42]

> Students are 'galloping' through events which are presented in bits and pieces. 5,000 years of history has to be gone through from F1–3, yet students are not even clear about the chronological arrangement of dynasties. In F4–5, they can choose to study ancient or modern history (sections A and B [~1600 BC–1643] or sections B and C [581–1945]), and to them the whole historical framework becomes a blur. Some better students can see both the forest and the trees, but they cannot tell the relationship between the two. *Historical facts completely fill up their minds* — causes, course, results and impacts of the rise and fall of dynasties. However, they know nothing about the characteristics of individual dynasties, and the whole picture of history.[43] (italics added)

Another aspect of teaching and learning resulting from the lengthy time-frame involved in the study of Chinese History was the tendency of teachers and students to avoid contemporary history. Many preferred to focus on ancient China since the CEE questions set for this period were stereotyped, which made question-spotting comparatively easy. As a result, the following outcomes were observed:

> Students are ignorant about modern China. Only 40 students (out of 1,000) know Sun Yat-sen's 'Three People's Principle.[44]

> Our students are indifferent to politics and contemporary China. Students regard contemporary China as something equivalent to party politics. Since politics is 'dirty', it is better to stay away from it. Students inherit the present anti-communist culture, and are ignorant of and unwilling to find out China's change and development in the last 30 years.[45]

> Students are not hearing about post-1949 events because there are no questions dealing with the period in HK examination papers (before 1995 only pre-1945 questions were asked in the CEE). A study conducted by Julian Leung revealed that most secondary schoolteachers do not go past World War II in their teaching of Chinese History.[46]

The CEE reports from 1980–97 confirm that students did not pay much attention to history from 1911 to 1976, there being relatively few attempts to answer these questions,[47] and tended to put most of their effort into studying dynastic history. Students were obviously concentrating on those periods in which they thought it easier to gain marks. The reports also commonly criticised students for their lack of skills of analysis and comparison, their over-reliance on textbooks and examination guides, and their dependence on rote learning and inability to reorganise materials.[48]

An orthodox historical perspective

Textbooks reflected the traditional, orthodox view of Chinese History set out in the syllabuses during this time, and certainly did nothing to encourage students to think analytically, supposedly one of the aims of the syllabus. They were generally seen as inadequate, particularly as regards their uncritical treatment of the historical narrative:

> The inadequacy of textbooks — (1) outdated materials, faulty arguments (2) boring layout (3) narratives broken into bits and pieces. On the whole textbooks deliberately *avoid criticising historical events*. Students are only led to recite facts. There is no development of students' national identity or views of history.[49] (italics added)

As a consequence of many teachers' over-dependence on textbooks, much of the teaching of Chinese History, far from encouraging original thought, was concerned with getting students to learn the traditional, established 'facts' of history:

> Only facts are taught, and no analysis or evaluation of these 'facts'.[50]

> Chinese History teachers very often deal with the subject as a body of facts rather than approaches to facts.[51]

Apart from textbooks, teachers also relied heavily on examination questions and marking schemes, using them as their teaching guide to prime their students, and trying to cram them with facts that frequently came up in examinations. In the words of S. C. Koo, a Chinese History teacher:

> To help students get good results in the CEE was the primary concern. Therefore teaching was done in accordance with examination questions and the requirement of the marking schemes. We understood very well the 'game' that *new interpretation will not gain any credit.* (italics added)

This practice did nothing to improve the situation since the marking schemes were also prescriptive and mirrored the orthodox views of history set out in the syllabus, particularly with regard to their condemnation/praise of historical figures, leaving little room for students to interpret historical personages or events. The following examples taken from the CEE marking scheme illustrate this:

> The downfall of the Qin dynasty was due to: (i) the imposition of heavy taxes and military service (ii) severe punishments to suppress the people (iii) old adherent[s] of previous dynasties plotting to revolt against the Qin (iv) the second emperor was a despot (3 marks for each point).[52]

> From the mid Qian Long period, the empire was declining. This was because: (i) officials were corrupted (ii) there were little reserves in the state treasury (iii) there was a socio-economic recession (iv) poor quality of the emperors (v) anti-Qing spirit was high (vi) poor military power (3 marks for each point).[53]

As might be expected, the major concern of students was to recite as many established 'points' as possible in order to gain high marks in the examinations. The following feature article in a newspaper aptly sums up the very detrimental influence of the prescriptive nature of the CEE questions, format and marking schemes on the teaching of Chinese History:

> The content and method of teaching (the CEE class) is based on the examination questions, format, and marking schemes. The CEE curriculum can be understood as a '*memorisation*' curriculum. For example, in the illustration given by the HKEA, the question '*describe the course of the Cultural Revolution*', reveals the examiners' intention — to encourage students to memorise dry facts, and nothing else. In the *marking scheme*, marks are given to correct points, disregarding faulty answers. Hence textbooks list masses of abstract, sweeping and unconnected statements. In the HKEA's examination reports, repeated statements are made year after year: 'We feel sorry for students' poor performance.' How should we teach Chinese History? What exactly do we want our students to learn?[54] (italics added)

It must be said that the whole educational culture of Hong Kong emphasised examination results in the fierce competition for university study. This, together with point-reward marking scheme, no doubt influenced the teaching and learning of Chinese History; and this explains to some extent why the curriculum aims — to 'cultivate students' objective attitudes and their skills of analysis',[55] and to 'understand the causal relationship between events so as to develop students' objectivity and skills of analysis'[56] — were not realised in practice. Nevertheless, it was also, for a large part, the view of history set out in the syllabus and reflected in textbooks, examination questions and marking schemes which led to teaching and learning being reduced to the reproduction of established knowledge in many classrooms.

Cultural history and a Han-centred viewpoint

Cultural history was not very popular with either teachers or students. Many teachers found it difficult and, being more familiar with dynastic history, tended to concentrate on that. The following comments give some indication of the difficulty and boredom associated with the teaching and learning of cultural history:

> I taught Chinese History from the 1940s. During this time the curriculum was difficult and boring. The 1975 syllabus (F1–3) included cultural history as Section B. However, topics in Section B were more suitable for sixth-form or university students, for example, the history of intellectual thought, foreign relations, and technology. Junior form students were not able to handle all these.[57]

> The new syllabus (CEE) included cultural history — specific topics included economics, religion, foreign relations, and institutions. This could hardly stimulate students' interest.[58]

The examination reports for this period confirm that the majority of students devoted most of their effort to studying dynastic history, and the most unpopular topics, and the ones which resulted in the poorest results, were from cultural history. Various factors could account for the lack of emphasis on cultural history, such as: teachers were more familiar with dynastic history; teachers and students found it a difficult and uninteresting subject; or the manner in which it was presented in textbooks and examinations. Whatever the reasons, cultural history was not properly recognised and emphasised in either teaching or in the examinations, and thus there was a gap between the official curriculum, which emphasised its importance, and its implementation.

Examination questions and marking schemes again reflected a Han-centred view of Chinese History with its assumed superiority of the Han race. For instance, a question which often came up in the CEE about the Yuan dynasty concerned the relationship between its downfall and its poor ruling policies (between 1970 to 2000, questions were set on the Yuan dynasty's downfall and its ruling policies in 11 years).[59] Also, marking schemes were explicitly disparaging about the Yuan in this respect, as can be seen in the following example:[60]

(1) The Yuan dynasty's racial discrimination policy:
    (a) Dividing the races into four classes; the Mongols were the superior class.
    (b) In the civil examinations Mongols were given preference.
    (c) The judiciary was partial to the Mongols.
(2) The dynasty's political measures
    (a) The problem of who should succeed to the throne led to conflict
    (b) The Mongols were good at military affairs, but poor at administration.
(3) Religious measures
    (a) The lamas were imperious and domineering.
    (b) Freedom of religion led to divergent thoughts, and it was difficult for religion and politics [combined together] to be put into effect.
(4) Economic measures
    (a) The chaotic financial situation
    (b) Corrupt officials.

Textbooks also portrayed the Mongols in a poor light, as can be seen in the following extracts from two of the most popular textbooks, published by Ling Kee and Everyman's Book Company:

> Since the Mongols were *weak in their cultural foundation*, they ruled for self-interest, rather than the long-term benefit of the country. The Mongol empire's ruthless ruling tactics were unprecedented:
> (1) They enforced a division of classes.
> (2) *Strict control of the Han people*
> (3) Made use of religion to eliminate opponents.

> The downfall of the Yuan dynasty was due to its lack of political ideals. They only enforced segregation, oppression, and deprivation in their rule. Hence politics remained chaotic.[61] (italics added)

> The Mongols administered China for less than one hundred years. Throughout their rule, *they did not accept the traditional civil administration which was inherited from the Qin-Han period*. Politically, the Mongols could be characterised as the ancient feudal aristocrats who settled in a new place by force. At that time, in Chinese society [this refers to Han Chinese society], the cultural and economic standards were one hundred times higher than during the Spring and Autumn feudal period. *The Mongols were backward in their politics*. They only knew military invasion, and personal interest. ... In terms of civil administration, there was no achievement. Therefore Mongol rule could be summarised in two phrases — oppression to prevent revolt, and abusing the people.[62] (italics added)

Other publishers, such as the Four Seas Publishing Company and Modern Education Publishing Company, gave similar accounts in their textbooks.

A similar negative approach towards the other non-Han dynasty, the Qing dynasty, was taken in examinations and textbooks. One of the most popular questions asked in the CEE asked about their ruling policy over the Han people,[63] and the question and marking scheme below show how the examiners differentiated the Han culture from that of the Qing, treating the Manchus in a very critical fashion:

> The power of the Qing was grounded in the policies of conciliation and oppression adopted in the earlier period. (1) What were the intentions of the policies of conciliation and oppression? (2) Give three examples to illustrate the two policies.
>
> (1) Conciliation policy — make use of the Han people to rule over Han [territory].
> (2) Oppression policy
>   — being aliens, Manchus' culture and economy were backward. Hence they needed to use force to maintain their rule.
>   — since anti-Manchu activities were increasing, the policy was to consolidate the rule.
> (3) Examples of conciliation — eight were listed.
> (4) Examples of oppression — seven were listed.[64]

Also, textbook content was consistent with the marking scheme:

> *The Manchus as a minor and backward race came to rule over the Han race* — a numerous race with a long-existing culture, [the reason] its reign could last for 260 years was not only due to its brave troops — the troops of the Eight Banners — but, more importantly, the Manchus were able to *assimilate Han culture*, and made use of policies of conciliation and oppression in their rule. (italics added)

In short, the examination questions, marking schemes and textbooks highlighted two characteristics of Qing rule: first, that the Hans were highly civilised, while the Manchus were aliens, backward and uncivilised; second, that the reason why the Manchus were able to rule for 260 years was because of their policies of conciliation and oppression in ruling the Han people. These Han-centred conclusions were in line with the curriculum, which made the same disparaging judgements on the Mongols and Manchus.

As in the first phase (1945–74), the implementation of the F1–5 curriculum was examination-oriented. Moreover, the style of assessment in the CEE remained basically unaltered — a test of students' factual recall in the form of essay and multiple-choice questions, and teaching was more or less confined to spoon-feeding students with a body of facts and established views. This, in fact, contradicted the curriculum aim 'to develop students' skills of analysis'. However, the factual nature of the implemented curriculum did match the other aims of the official curriculum, such as 'to understand the basic facts of the rise and fall of successive dynasties',[65] with dynastic history taken merely as the events and deeds of emperors and other key individuals who contributed to the prosperity and decline of the respective dynasties. The specified aim 'to know China's traditional culture',[66] was interpreted almost exclusively as meaning to know about the culture of the Han. Historical views were expressed as orthodoxy and were very often moralising, more so than in the first phase (1945–74), perhaps because the second phase was a period of transition to decolonisation and the colonial government wanted to give more emphasis to civic education (see Chapter 2 for a detailed analysis). Although in this phase the junior level and the senior level curriculum extended study to 1976, the avoidance of contemporary history by teachers and students alike led to an implemented curriculum which was decontextualised and depoliticised.

THE CURRICULUM FOR H-LEVEL AND A-LEVEL/AS-LEVEL

The Curriculum Development Process (H-Level and A-Level/AS-Level)

The HKEA was set up in 1978 as a quasi-autonomous government organisation, and since then has been responsible for the A-level and H-level examinations previously administered by HKU and CUHK respectively. In 1979, the A-level subject committee stated that 'The A-level/H-level examination syllabus should be drafted by the A-level/H-level subject committee with the help and guidance of the departments and units in the universities concerned'.[67] Consequently, as in the first phase, the A-level and H-level subject committee was dominated by university teachers, and there was little change in the sources of their membership. Throughout this second phase (1974–97), representatives from HKU headed the A-level subject committee, and in one way or another members of the committee were all associated with HKU's representatives. For example, committee members included ex-students of HKU: C. N. Leung (subject officer, HKEA), W. T. Ling (subject officer, ED), H. W. Poon (school representative),[68] F. Kan (HKU representative), and teachers from the Chinese department: W. Y. Tu, T. W. Lin, F. Jin and K. P. Ho. Moreover, there were many occasions on which meetings were held at the Chinese department of HKU[69] instead of at the HKEA. All this indicates that the A-level subject committee was the domain of HKU.

In these 23 years, the only changes made to the A-level Chinese History were: the introduction of AS-level to replace H-level; the requirement that students take two papers (each lasting for three hours) instead of three; the extension of the end-date from ~1600 BC to 1976; and the introduction of data-based questions. Yet even these changes were made only as a result of the broader curriculum reforms, with the subject committee itself making no attempt to initiate changes to the Chinese History curriculum. For instance, the introduction of the AS-level originated from the *Education Commission Report No. 2*, in which a recommendation was made to review sixth-form education. This led, in 1989, to the 'Sixth Form Education Working Group's proposal to standardise sixth-form education by replacing the H-level with the AS-level'.[70] The original H-level three-paper examination changed to a two-paper one for compatibility with other humanities subjects,[71] while the extension of the end-date from 1911 to 1976 was primarily aimed at matching the junior level and CEE curriculum, which had already done so.[72] D. C. Lam, the head of the ED's History section, recalled his telephone exchange with HKU's representative about bringing the A-level end-date into line with the AS-level: 'When I telephoned the HKU representative about extending the end-date to 1976 he was not at all eager to change. Yet it was not up to him to decide because the CEE had already extended its end-date'. Nor was the introduction of data-based questions an initiative of the subject committee. According to F. S. Tsang, the subject officer of HKEA, 'in reviewing the examination format, the HKEA proposed that A-level Chinese History should include either data-based questions or a project as a new form of assessment. In the subject committee meeting, members noted the introduction of data-based questions in the CEE and A-level/AS-level "History", and the committee decided to adopt data-based questions'. The static nature of A-level Chinese History was criticised by K. C. Au, a member of the A-level subject committee, as 'a 30-year no change conservative curriculum'.[73] In response to Au's criticism, HKU's representative made the following remark: 'The inclusion of new topics, for example, Ming and Qing, and further grouping of the syllabus (three papers changed to two) were already steps taken to update the syllabus. No further revisions were needed'.[74]

It should be noted that HKU representatives in the A-level subject committee were all specialists in ancient and medieval Chinese history, and the examination questions in the A-level matched HKU teachers' specialisations. The fact that the A-level curriculum was under the influence of HKU and the membership of the committee was stable help to explain the conservative approach to curriculum reform.

Just as HKU teachers determined the nature of the A-level syllabus, the H-level syllabus was drafted by CUHK academics and adopted without opposition by the members of the subject committee. C. C. Lo, H. B. So and K. T. Sun continued to be the major figures on the H-level subject committee (as they had been in the previous phase), with C. C. Lo as Chair of the committee from 1984 to 1992, when the H-level was abolished. In this second phase (1974–97), no major changes were made to the H-level syllabus, the only ones being the extension of the end-date from 1911 to 1949, and equal emphasis being given to dynastic history and theme-based cultural history (geography, institutions, intellectual thoughts, Chinese race and culture).

S. K. Tse, a teacher member at that time, made the following comments on who played dominant roles in the H-level subject committee:

> H-level had [a] close relationship with CU teachers' specialisms. They put great effort into keeping their areas of expertise in the H-level syllabus. That was why there were representatives of ancient and medieval history (e.g. C. C. Lo, H. B. So, K. T. Sun and T. S. Pong), but not any specialists in modern and contemporary history. As a teacher member, I once suggested changing the aims of the examination to 'testing students' ability of synthesis and analysis, and evaluating historical events and figures'. I also brought out the importance of including Hong Kong history in the syllabus. Yet these proposals were all rejected. They were very conservative and failed to respond to curriculum changes.

D. L. Luk interpreted H-level Chinese History's inertia as being due to the fact that:

> The H-level subject committee worked in harmony. Members respected K. T. Sun and C. C. Lo who were their former teachers ... They never insisted on changing anything which contradicted Sun's and Lo's views. The chairman was C. C. Lo who was an expert in Song history; hence every year at least one question on Song history was bound to appear in the examination. Yet I was sure no student would know how to answer it.

The H-level was CUHK's 'sovereign territory', and with Lo and Sun dominating the subject committee, the syllabus remained largely unchanged for more than 20 years. The A-level/AS-level and H-level were controlled in this way by HKU and CUHK respectively.

In view of this, the approach to curriculum planning for H-level, A-level/AS-level was highly centralised, but the decision-making, unlike the junior and upper secondary syllabuses, was in the hands of the respective university teachers rather than government officials. Table 4.3 (p. 104) helps to illustrate this.

The AS-level and A-level teaching syllabuses of 1991 and 1992 respectively were introduced as a result of the broader curriculum reforms which were taking place during this period. Letters were sent to schools asking for teachers' views on the revised curriculum, but this form of consultation was geared to promotion and implementation rather than a collection of views.[75] The Textbook Review Committee had no part to play in the A-level and H-level as there were no prescribed textbooks for the sixth-form level, and support given to teachers was confined to articles contributed by sixth-form teachers to the History newsletter.

Table 4.3 Approaches to curriculum development (H-level, AS-level and A-level) (1974–97)

Year	Level	Who initiated syllabus revision	Subject committee to produce a syllabus	Consultation with teachers	Government to approve textbook	Curriculum materials produced
1980	H-level	CUHK/HKEA	Yes	Yes	Reference books recommended	No
1986	H-level	CUHK/HKEA	Yes	Yes	Reference books recommended	No
1991	AS level	ED/HKEA/HKU	Yes	Yes	Reference books recommended	History newsletter
1992	A-level	ED/HKEA/HKU	Yes	Yes	Reference books recommended	History newsletter

The Curriculum (H-level and A-level/AS-level): Aims and Content

The *Education Commission Report No. 3* (1988) had recommended that the school system be changed to 6–5–2 (6-year primary, 5-year secondary and 2-year matriculation), and the 1-year H-level curriculum was thus abolished in 1993. The 2-year A-level curriculum was divided into A-level and AS-level (Advanced Supplementary Level) with the academic standard of the latter being lower than that of the former, two AS-level courses being equivalent to one A-level course. The teaching syllabuses for AS-level and A-level were first issued in 1991 and 1992 respectively. On the basis of data available, the analysis of the content of the H-level will focus on (1) the study of Chinese History as a continuous whole and (2) an orthodox historical perspective, while for A-level/AS-level, the focus will be on (1) the study of Chinese history as a continuous whole and (2) a Han-centred historical viewpoint. Table 4.4 (p. 105) illustrates the development of the H-level and A-level/AS-level Chinese History curriculum between 1974 and 1997.

H-Level

The study of Chinese History as a whole

The belief in the importance of studying Chinese History as a continuous whole continued to be a major priority of members of the subject committee. Hence, from 1974 to 1992, the curriculum was heavily burdened with content knowledge stretching from ~1122 BC to 1911, and extended to 1949 in 1980. The following minutes of meetings reveal the curriculum decision-makers' perceptions of Chinese History:

Committee members felt that in studying the subject, one should have a comprehensive knowledge of the essentials. If students were allowed to choose the topics, this meant students would concentrate on certain selected areas and they would have little knowledge of other aspects of history.[76]

Table 4.4 Development of the H-level and A-level/AS-level Chinese History curriculum (1974–97)

Level	H-level	A-level	
Year	1974–92 (H-level examination was abolished in 1993)	1976–90	1991–97 (AS-level examination was introduced in 1993)
Key curriculum documents	examination syllabus	examination syllabus	teaching syllabus and examination syllabus
Genesis	as entrance examination for CUHK	as entrance examination for HKU	A-S level and A-level teaching syllabuses issued in 1991 and 1992 respectively. A-S: paper 1 (Data-based questions were newly included as compulsory questions) A-level: papers 1 and 2
Aim	1974–82: no examination aims 1983–92: aims were to test students' ability in 1. understanding historical events 2. synthesis and analysis 3. evaluation	test students' general and advanced knowledge of historical themes	1. understand traditional Chinese culture 2. enhance skills of historical research 3. promote skills of evaluation 4. understand changes made in history 5. nurture good behaviour
Content arrangement	theme-based chronology – 1974–79: Zhou dynasty (~1122 BC) –1911 – 1980–92: Zhou dynasty (~1122 BC) –1949	theme-based chronology: Zhou dynasty (~1122 BC) to 1644	theme-based chronology: Shang (~1600 BC) to 1976
Curriculum emphasis	1974–85: geography, institutions, intellectual thoughts, Chinese race, culture 1986–92: economics as an additional theme	politics, foreign relations, Chinese race, institutions, scholarship and culture, historiography	'Chinese race' replaced by 'economic development'

S. K. Tse, a member of the H-level committee, confirmed the committee members' view of the nature of Chinese historical knowledge:

> The committee was chaired by a CUHK teacher, and members from the same institution were keen followers of Confucius. They stressed the importance of building a comprehensive historical knowledge on the part of students. Hence any proposal to reduce the content or compartmentalise Chinese History would meet strong opposition especially from these members.

Thus, as with F1–3 and F4–5, H-level students were required to study more than 3,000 years of history but, unlike these two levels, the H-level did not include contemporary history (post-1949) and just dealt with dynastic history and cultural history, where there were already established views.

An orthodox historical perspective

No teaching syllabus was ever issued for the H-level examination, and the examination syllabus was the only official document on its curriculum. The list of examination topics and statements reflected the state-centred, orthodox views originating in 'the 24 Dynastic Histories', and were similar to those listed in the F1–3 teaching syllabus: 'The five *barbarian tribes* invaded the Han territory', 'The *disorder* created by Empress Wu and Wei', 'The *prosperity* of Xuan Zong', 'The An Shi *uprising*', The *extension* of the Tang territory', 'The *extension* of the Han territory' (in contrast to 'the invasion of the Han territory by the barbarians), and 'The *disasters* caused by the barbarian troops'. Since students were only required to focus on these views in the examination, there was little room for them to express their personal views, nor were they expected to, and aims (1983–1992) such as 'to analyse or evaluate historical events or figures' became meaningless. The examination of such an extensive period of history, across the themes of politics, culture, intellectual thoughts, foreign relations, economic development and institutions, was aimed at selecting the best academic achievers to enter CUHK, while at the same time serving to indoctrinate students with the orthodox views of historical China.

A-level/AS-level

The study of Chinese History as a continuous whole

Before the H-level was abolished in 1993 and replaced by the AS-level, there was no A-level teaching syllabus, and the A-level examination syllabus was the only document defining the official curriculum. This syllabus prescribed the time-frame and provided a list of topics to be examined. The period of study in the first phase was reduced in the 1976 examination syllabus, with the end-date brought forward to 1644. However, with the introduction of the AS-level and A-level in 1991 and 1992 respectively, it was extended once again, this time to 1976. When asked about the changes made to A- level Chinese History, L. Y. Chiu, the chairman of the A-level subject committee, stated that:

> The A-level has made great changes over the last 20 years. The period of study has been extended from Qin [dynasty] Han [dynasty], to Sui [dynasty] Tang [dynasty], and later further extended to Ming [dynasty] and Qing [dynasty]. Since 1991 students have had to study up to 1976. Also included were topics such as economic development. In terms of academic requirements, the A-level is very demanding.

A Han-centred viewpoint

The Han-centred view expressed in the official syllabuses for F1–5 and the H-level was also included in the AS-level and A-level syllabuses, particularly regarding the distinctive characteristics of the Han culture. This can be seen in the first of the aims listed in the AS-level and A-level syllabuses: to help students 'understand traditional Chinese culture',[77] which was taken as the culture of the Han race. For example, the 'historical writings' which students were to study were mainly the work of Han writers.[78] Also, in the topic 'religion', it was stated that ' "Taoism" was the only religion that originated from ancient Chinese society and culture, hence it was necessary to study it in great detail'.[79] As for Buddhism, the syllabus emphasised that 'Buddhism was a foreign religion … it became most prosperous in the Sui and Tang dynasties because Buddhism was able to assimilate itself into the Han culture and in particular with Confucianism and Taoism'.[80] The religion of the Han race was hence differentiated distinctively from those of non-Han races.

The Curriculum (H-level and A-level/AS-level): Impact on Teaching, Learning and Examinations

The data on the actual implementation of the sixth form curriculum during this period have two limitation: first, there have been no earlier studies on the implemented curriculum; and second, there are no prescribed textbooks and marking schemes for the H-level and A-level/AS-level. However, enough information can be gleaned from examination reports, interviews, newspaper articles, minutes of meetings and examination questions to give a good idea of the effect of the curriculum on teaching and learning.

The study of Chinese History as a continuous whole

As there was so much to cover in the syllabus, and no prescribed textbooks, many teachers tended to focus on the examination, repeatedly getting students to do past examination papers, determining which topics usually appeared in them and cramming their students with 'model answers' for these topics. In the words of two experienced teachers:

> It was impossible to 'cover' the syllabus; therefore lessons were devoted to drilling students in examination skills. They were required to do the past examination questions, sometimes on an individual basis, sometimes as group work. Usually assignments were distributed before Christmas and students were to submit them after the holiday. After marking, students could exchange their assignments. These assignments could also be regarded as model answers. (S. C. Koo)

> I prepared a lot of 'notes' for F6–7 students. I referred to these 'notes' in my teaching. In fact all the essential 'points' in answering a particular question were included in the 'notes'. After I joined the HKEA in marking the A-level examination scripts, I was better informed of the requirements in the A-level. (F. S. Tsang)

It is not surprising that with the content of the curriculum spanning more than 3,000 years, and the emphasis of both syllabus and examination on the learning of traditional, officially prescribed views, teachers had little opportunity to promote critical thinking in their students.

Another consequence of the very extensive coverage was the avoidance of contemporary history, with teachers placing emphasis on the more familiar dynastic history. A feature article in a newspaper has the following comments:

> Although contemporary Chinese history is offered at the junior level, CEE and sixth-form, students know very little of this part of history. For the junior level, two lessons per cycle can hardly teach anything systematically to students. In the CEE class, both teachers and students try to avoid contemporary history. Instead, effort is put into certain dynasties about which questions are likely to appear in the examinations. The same things happen in the sixth-form. Hence it is not surprising to find a F7 student who knows nothing about contemporary Chinese history.[81]

An orthodox historical perspective

The following extract from the minutes of a meeting of the Chinese History H-level committee which discussed the level of difficulty of the examination questions illustrates the lack of confidence curriculum planners had in the ability of students to use originality and analysis in answering questions:

> As question 7 [There was a view that the Opium War was caused by the Qing government's restrictions laid on the foreign merchants. Do you agree? Criticise this view with supporting facts] required the candidates to comment on a statement made by a historian on the

> Anglo-Chinese war, this committee thought that this type of question was too difficult for Hong Kong H-level candidates. In fact, most of the candidates attempting the question could only make a general comment on the Anglo-Chinese war but could not comment with regard to the historian's statement.[82]

This shows that the decision-makers tended not to expect students to demonstrate a high level of ability in critical thinking, or to require students to question orthodox views.

Some teachers, however, did try to encourage their students to evaluate and analyse in spite of the limitations brought about by the nature of the syllabus and examinations, as shown in the following comment:

> Within the A-level parameters, I tried to encourage students to discuss issues that were related to the examination. It would be high-sounding if we simply ignored the examination. There was analysis but it was conducted within the parameters of the traditionally accepted views. (S. K. Shum)

However, normally teachers concentrated on priming their students for the public examination, by making them do past examination papers and cramming them with the established views of history that came up again and again:

> Being restricted by the examination, lessons are boring rather than stimulating. Teachers even give students past examination questions as revision guidelines. Views traditionally adopted were to be memorised rather than criticised.[83]

Since teaching and learning were confined to orthodox views, students were hardly likely to find the subject interesting and conducive to critical thinking.

The following examples show that orthodox views were embedded in the examination questions:[84]

> Explain the causes leading to 'the An Shi uprising'. (In the Tang dynasty the deeds of General An and Shih were considered as an uprising)[85]

> Give an account of the disasters brought by empress Wu and Wei and their impact. (There was an orthodox view on the control of power by women. Empress Wu and Wei were traditionally considered as creating disasters in the imperial court.)[86]

As a result of having to study 3,000 years of history and the need to reproduce traditional views on Chinese History, particularly those promoting a Han-centred viewpoint, there were repeated criticisms in the H-level and A-level examination reports that students tended to recite model answers, that their answers revealed unclear concepts and confused thinking, and that they were poor in organisation and analysis.[87]

A Han-centred viewpoint

In differentiating the Han race from the non-Han races, the following examination questions revealed a Han-centred viewpoint:

> Give an account of the policies of conciliation and suppression of the Manchus and their impact.[88]

> 'The Yuan dynasty and the Qing dynasty were set up by races residing near the frontier. Yet they adopted different policies in ruling the Han people'. Comment on their ruling policies.[89]

> 'The fall of the Yuan dynasty was a result of the adoption of the discrimination policy against the Han people'. Comment on the policy adopted by the Mongols.[90]

The above discussion shows that there was a gap between the aim and the assessment. While the aim specified 'through organising and synthesising related historical facts, to develop students' ability in critical thinking and evaluation', at the classroom level many students tended to memorise masses of factual accounts and orthodox views which were decontextualised and depoliticised.

CONCLUSION

During this phase (1974–97), the status of Chinese History as an independent subject was consolidated. Although the nature and role of the subject had already been defined when Chinese History finally became an independent subject in the school curriculum at all levels in 1967, in this phase they were further established. During this time, the curriculum development process was centralised and to a large extent determined by the bureaucratic establishment of the ED, and the F1–5 curriculum was controlled by the main decision-makers in the ED and HKEA (from 1978). The outcome was that individual officials and subject committee members became the dominant forces in curriculum development. The official curriculum, as defined by this dominant group in its meetings, emphasised both dynastic history and cultural history, which were chronologically arranged, and encompassed more than 3,000 years (~1600 BC to 1976). Orthodox views were presented that aimed at indoctrinating students into an uncritical acceptance of the curriculum's portrayal of the behaviour of certain historical figures. In addition, a Han-centred viewpoint was embedded in Chinese History's content. As for the H-level and A-level, the curriculum was predominantly controlled by CUHK and HKU respectively, as it was primarily designed to cater for university entrance. Apart from those changes which were introduced as a result of the broader curriculum reform, university members tended to look after the interests of their respective universities when considering curriculum change.

The biggest gap between the official curriculum and the implemented curriculum lay in the contrast between the intended aim of 'helping students to develop an objective attitude and skills of analysis' and the actual primary concern of both teachers and students which was how to 'swallow' the mass of facts and views for the examination. Another aspect of the curriculum was that traditional culture was equated with Han culture, and was given a high regard in both the intended and the implemented curriculum, although cultural history was given less attention in teaching and learning, and examinations.

Overall the following characteristics were more strongly embedded in the curriculum than in the first phase: viewing the study of Chinese History as sacred and indivisible; the predominance of a Han-centred orthodoxy; and a moralising function. These characteristics had their historical origins in 'the 24 Dynastic Histories', but once they were established in the curriculum, they became a 'tradition' of the subject which could hardly be removed. One of the results was that, during this phase, when the socio-economic-political changes in Hong Kong gave rise to a series of reforms in the curriculum, Chinese History remained largely unchanged.

5

A Period of Crisis and Opportunity for Chinese History as an Independent Subject (1997–2005)

During the second phase (1974–97), Chinese History was able to establish a strong subject culture and consolidate its independent status in the school curriculum. In this phase, the development of Chinese History after the handover of sovereignty to China is examined. This analysis can enhance our understanding of the politics of Chinese History, particularly the ways in which the subject community strived to protect the status and 'tradition' of Chinese History in the face of broader curriculum reform during this period.

THE CURRICULUM DEVELOPMENT PROCESS (F1–3)

When the CDI was established in 1993, Chinese History finally became an independent subject in the Humanities section, with a senior subject officer and an officer responsible for the subject's curriculum development (unlike before when Chinese History was subordinated to History within the Humanities section of the Advisory Inspectorate). Being a fully independent subject has been of considerable importance for Chinese History, especially when curriculum developers have wanted to initiate changes to the curriculum. This is because Chinese History officers can now submit a proposal directly to the CDC for curriculum revision without having to go through the head of the History section. In this way, the revision of the junior level syllabus was speeded up, and it took only half a year from the final draft to the introduction of the new syllabus in 1997 (it was originally scheduled to be implemented in September 2000). C. N. Leung, the first officer in charge of Chinese History in the CDI (1993–96), gave the rationale for the revisions to the syllabus:

> Following the handover, the aim to cultivate students' affection for the nation and its people was a must. ... The inclusion of moral/civic education was to remind teachers of the importance of incorporating this element into their teaching.

However, the speed with which the revised syllabus was introduced meant that resources such as textbooks were not available for teachers and students. Because of this lack of planning, queries were raised about the motives for the implementation of the new curriculum. An article in the *Apple Daily Newspaper* on 16 June 1998 reported teachers' discontent over the lack of relevant teaching resources for the revised junior form level Chinese History syllabuses to be implemented in September 1998; and the teachers queried whether the abrupt implementation was to please the SAR government.

At first, the proposed revision was criticised also by members of the CDC subject committee. F. S. Tsang, the HKEA officer, recollected: 'Members did not agree with the proposal put forward by C. N. Leung. We considered that, despite the so-called revision, the syllabus was still much the same as the one introduced in 1982. Hence it was "the same medicine differently prepared". When H. C. Wong took up the task, he specified the "linked dot and line approach" that highlighted each dynasty's characteristics. Added to this were the detailed illustrations of how to teach and the inclusion of moral and civic education in the topics. H. C. Wong considered that detailed prescription could help teachers. Wong's ideas were adopted in the syllabus.'

In spite of these objections, and because of the dominance of the CDI officials, the proposal was accepted by the committee and a draft syllabus was issued in 1996.

The development of the revised curriculum was a highly centralised process with the CDI initiating the revision and little attention being paid to the concerns of teachers. This can be seen when, in 1996, after the subject committee had finished reviewing the draft syllabus, a questionnaire was distributed in January 1997 to collect teachers' views. According to 'The report of the questionnaire survey' compiled by the CDI,[1] '53% of respondents agreed with the revision, while 44% of respondents agreed with the revision, but with reservations concerning some parts; for example, many of those with reservations felt that the overall content should be reduced and the difficult topics should be adjusted'. In spite of these reservations, however, the subject committee only made minor revisions to the syllabus: taking out the prehistoric period; changing the name of the topic 'the Confucian politics of the Eastern Han' to 'the unity and power of the Eastern Han'; and changing the name of the topic 'intellectual thought' to 'development of intellectual thought'. Otherwise, the report stated, 'for the sake of the completeness of the curriculum, and to take into account the consistency of the curriculum, the original version was to be kept'. The only teachers' views that were adopted by the subject committee concerned very minor issues; and in keeping with 'the consistency of the curriculum', students were again required to study the entire course of Chinese History, from the Xia (~2100 BC) to the contemporary period. Nonetheless, for the junior level, it was the first time that a questionnaire survey had been conducted to collect views.

As a result of the criticisms of the lack of teaching resources, the CDI produced three sets of teaching packages and videos for teachers and organised seminars to introduce the revised curriculum. Thus, in terms of teaching resources, the 1997 syllabus offered more curriculum materials to teachers than any of the previous syllabuses. However, the process by which the junior level Chinese History curriculum has developed from 1997 until the present time has been basically the same as in the first and second phases, i.e. mostly dominated by government officials and highly centralised.

The Curriculum (F1–3): Aims and Content

After 15 years of stability, the 1982 junior level syllabus was revised and introduced in 1997, when Hong Kong was returned to China. The revisions were aimed principally at meeting the political needs of the SAR government, in particular the building of a sense of national identification and the enforcement of the principle of 'one country, two systems'. In comparison with the first phase (1945–74) and second phase (1974–97), this syllabus included a number of novel ideas: first, the promotion of a sense of national identification as one of the stipulated aims; second, the inclusion of Hong Kong history; and third, reinforcement of the orthodox views of Chinese History and its moral function. At the same time, the newly revised curriculum retained the dominant features of the syllabuses in the previous phases, and thus the main features of the new curriculum were: (1) the study of Chinese History as a continuous whole; (2) a Han-centred cultural viewpoint; (3) an orthodox historical perspective and moral and civic education (but more explicit and with more emphasis than before); (4) a sense of national identification; and (5) Hong Kong history as peripheral to Chinese History. Table 5.1 illustrates the features of the 1997 F1–3 Chinese History curriculum.

Table 5.1 F1–3 Chinese History curriculum (1997)

Nature of curriculum document	Teaching syllabus
Genesis	Revised the aims and content of the 1982 syllabus to meet the SAR government's political needs after the handover.
Aims newly added	• develop the recognition of, and a sense of belonging to, the nation and its people so as to achieve the aim of national unification and nation-building • cultivate a sense of national identification through learning Chinese culture • cultivate students' good conduct and their sense of social responsibility
Content arrangement	Same as the earlier phases: Xia (~2100 BC) to the contemporary period.
Curriculum emphasis	Equal emphasis on dynastic history and cultural history. Hong Kong history was appended to the syllabus for teachers' reference.

The study of Chinese History as a continuous whole

As in the 1975 and 1982 syllabuses, the revised syllabus covered the period from the Xia (~2100 BC) to the contemporary period (end-date not specified), and stipulated the aim of studying Chinese History as:

> To know the basic facts of the rise and fall of all dynasties so that students can understand the background and changes of current events.
> (F1–3 Chinese History, CDC, 1997: 8)

Also, Chinese History continued to be based on dynastic-political history, with the following explanation given for such an arrangement:

> Dynastic-political history is used as the backbone, supplemented with cultural history. In studying this, students can gain a comprehensive knowledge of historical China. (ibid.: 2)

In other words, it was felt that in order to appreciate the essence of historical China, students needed to gain a comprehensive knowledge of the whole of Chinese history from the Xia (~2100 BC) to the contemporary period.

A Han-centred viewpoint

One of the long-standing aims of the syllabus was that:

> Through technological inventions, cultural exchange with foreign countries, and intellectual and religious thoughts, students come to understand that Chinese culture has the spirit of accommodating other cultures and making innovative creations. In the process of development, Chinese culture could assimilate other nations' cultures. (ibid.)

Once again, Chinese culture meant the culture of the Han, and despite the claim that 'Chinese culture has the spirit of accommodating other cultures ... [and can] assimilate other nations' cultures', the two non-Han administered dynasties, the Yuan dynasty (ruled by Mongols) and the Qing dynasty (ruled by Manchus), were seen as 'oppressors'. For instance, the stated aim of studying the Yuan dynasty was 'to understand the oppressive policy (against the Han people) of the Yuan administration', and the recommended teaching method was to foster situations where students 'in groups discuss the *improper* administrative policy of the Mongols' (italics added) (ibid.: 25); and similarly, in teaching the Qing dynasty, the theme was 'to inquire into the *oppressive* and *conciliatory* policies adopted by the Manchus towards the Han people' (italics added) (ibid.: 27). In order to reinforce the Han culture, 21 learning objectives with corresponding illustrations of events and people were listed in Section B (cultural history). One example of these objectives of studying ancient culture was 'to respect traditional culture' (implying Han culture), and the corresponding illustrations of events/people were to enable students 'to understand the deeds of Chinese ancestors, especially in creations and inventions' (ibid.: 37). Students were, therefore, expected to accept unquestioningly the greatness of traditional Chinese culture.

An orthodox historical perspective and moral and civic education

One novelty in the new syllabus was its emphasis on the role of Chinese History as a vehicle for moral and civic education. It was not just that the moral function of Chinese History was stated as one of the aims in this official syllabus, since the same moral function had also been included in the aims of the 1982 syllabus. For the first time, specific objectives of moral and civic education were set and illustrations were given of the good or bad behaviour of certain historical figures with the aim of transmitting the orthodox views on correct and incorrect values for students to emulate or condemn. In addition, certain topics were specified, together with advice on the teaching points and appropriate teaching-learning activities, and teachers were advised to refer to the prescribed manual even if they attempted to tailor the curriculum to suit the needs of the school. This contrasted with previous syllabuses, which had just given general suggestions on teaching methods.

One of the main decision-makers in drafting the 1997 syllabus, H. C. Wong, stated his belief that 'to cultivate students' values through Chinese History is a very normal thing'. He told the press that 'for the first time, the official Chinese History syllabus prescribed how to cultivate students' conduct through the subject'.[2] C. Chan, an inspector and member of the subject committee, also stressed the moral value of Chinese History:

> There are positive and negative personages in history. These historical figures can easily affect students' moral values. We should identify with the positive figures, but condemn the villains. There are lessons to learn from history. The guidance given in the new syllabus is to alert teachers to this important mission.

Table 5.2 (p. 118) illustrates examples of the values attributed to historical events/personages in the new syllabus.

In the new section devoted to specifying the teaching themes and the corresponding recommended teaching methods, established views were prescribed and students were expected to understand and reproduce rather than interpret them — for example, Xia Jie's *brutal* rule; Shang Zhou's *brutal* rule; Wang Mang *usurped* the Han throne; The *peaceful* reign of Zhen Guan and Kai Yuan; the North Song's long-existing *weaknesses*; and the Mongols' *oppressive* rule. This contradicted the aims stipulated in the syllabus, which emphasised the development of 'students' objectivity and skills of analysis'. Although the syllabus recommended that discussions be held with students, divergent thinking was restricted since students were expected to learn the established views which had already been prescribed by the curriculum developers. As a consequence of this, training was directed towards content-based technical skills, rather than the critical thinking skills which had been emphasised in the syllabus.

Table 5.2 The promotion of moral and civic education in the F1–3 Chinese History curriculum (CDC, 1997: 14–36)

Learning Objectives	Examples in Chinese History
To sharpen one's will, treasure life, understand that committing suicide is not a solution to problems	Xiang Yu failed and he committed suicide; this could not alter the situation.[3]
Respect freedom of speech	Qin Shihuang burnt books and buried scholars. People lost their confidence in the emperor and this led to the downfall of the Qin dynasty.
Learn to be patient and rid oneself of arrogance	Liu Bang was patient, and therefore he succeeded. Xiang Yu failed because he was arrogant.
Cultivate patriotic ideas. Do not harm the nation's interests for the sake of personal benefits.	Shi Jingtang ceded sixteen districts located in the northern sections of modern Hebei and Shanxi provinces.[4]

A sense of national identification

The most significant change made in the revised syllabus was a new aim: 'to cultivate in students a sense of national identification and a sense of belonging to China and its people'. Under colonial rule, this had been a sensitive issue which had been studiously avoided in the Chinese History curriculum, but now it was given great emphasis, and study of the culture and history of China was seen as a means of achieving this aim. As the syllabus stressed:

> One of the objectives of history teaching is, through understanding the nation's culture and history, to establish in students a sense of recognition and belonging to the nation. The ultimate aim is to unite the nation and build up the nation. (ibid.: 7)

Table 5.3(p. 119) adapted from the 1997 syllabus helps to illustrate the promotion of a sense of national identification and/or patriotism in the curriculum. It should be pointed out that, although the examples listed in the table were previously included in the 1975 and 1982 syllabuses, it was only in the 1997 syllabus that all these 'examples' were actually linked to the promotion of a sense of national identification and patriotism.

Table 5.3 The promotion of a sense of national identification/patriotism in the F1–3 Chinese History curriculum (CDC, 1997: 20–35)

Learning Objectives	Examples in Chinese History
Show concern for the nation's development.	The nation was partitioned into the South and North Dynasties. The Sui dynasty unified the nation and developed national power.
Wholeheartedly serve the nation.	Officials' deeds in defending the nation against the Jin and Mongols
Be selfless, and not gain personal benefits at the expense of the nation's interests.	Deeds of Gao Zong and Yue Fei
Wholeheartedly serve the nation and protect the nation's interest.	Deeds of Lin Zexu
Cultivate patriotic ideas.	Late Qing revolutionary movement
Cultivate patriotic ideas.	May Fourth Movement
Love peace. However, in the face of foreign invasion, one has to have a brave spirit, and be willing to sacrifice oneself for the nation.	War against the Japanese invasion
Strive for ethnic unity and national unification.	The establishment of the PRC

The examples of the concept of 'nation' given reflect that it comprised 'political', 'cultural', 'ethnic', 'geographical', and 'institutional' aspects. However, no reference was made to the current communist ideology. The revision was well received by the local press: 'The new syllabus has included the identification with China and the cultivation of a sense of belonging to the nation and these can help our next generation build up their attachment to our motherland'.[5] The *Sun Pao* editorial even recommended that 'the education of the idea of nationalism should be strengthened'.[6] It was apparent that the main curriculum developers intended to politicise and contextualise the Chinese History curriculum after the handover.

Hong Kong history

The third major curriculum innovation which distinguished this syllabus from all previous ones was the inclusion of Hong Kong history as part of the syllabus, albeit it only as an appendix. It was recommended that 'when teaching Chinese History the teacher can discuss the related [Hong Kong] topics with students so as to build up their local affection and ethnic identification'. However, the syllabus also stressed: 'Teachers should pay attention to the arrangement of time. It is not advisable that the teaching of Hong Kong history should affect the teaching of other topics in Chinese History'. The overall effect of this was to make it clear that Hong Kong history was to be regarded as a peripheral supplement to dynastic history. In a survey report conducted by the CDI, the subject committee stated: 'This subject should still use the history of one country as the framework. The primary aim was to study the history of the nation … Hong Kong history should be studied in relation to the relevant topics in Chinese History'.[7] The Chinese History Teaching Series produced by the CDI also emphasised that 'if for the sake of increasing the element of Hong Kong history, Chinese History has to be reduced drastically, this way of handling things is not desirable'.[8] Nevertheless, even with such a minor role in the Chinese History curriculum, it was thought that the inclusion of Hong Kong history could help students to understand the historical link between Hong Kong and China and the dependent nature of Hong Kong's relationship with the Mainland; and that Hong Kong was a part of China. Hence, the outcome of including Hong Kong history was that, while it saved Chinese History from the charge of being decontextualised, it did not affect the 'Chinese History system'. Chinese History was still regarded as sacred and indivisible, to be studied in its entirety.

The new junior level syllabus, therefore, had the following characteristics which distinguished it from previous syllabuses. First, moral and civic values were explicitly prescribed for individual topics and deeds of historical figures (in the 1975 and 1982 syllabuses no such links were made between moral and civic values and events/personages), and the recommended teaching methods were geared towards arriving at the prescribed orthodox judgements stipulated in the official syllabus. (This kind of detailed prescription was available only in this third phase [1997–2005]). Second, it promoted a stronger relationship between national identification and the teaching of individual topics. Third, Hong Kong history was included to supplement relevant episodes in Chinese History in order to bring out the so-called 'historical linkage between Hong Kong and China', and to enhance students' local feeling for Hong Kong and a sense of belonging to the nation. However, as a consequence, the curriculum was even more loaded with content than before, thus further reinforcing its highly academic orientation. This indicated that the curriculum developers had tightened their control of the curriculum, and teachers continued to be treated as functionaries whose job was to follow the guidelines laid down in the syllabus.

The Curriculum (F1–3): Impact on Teaching, Learning and Examinations

The study of Chinese History as a continuous whole

The period of study in the revised F1–3 syllabus stretches from the Xia (~2100 BC) to the contemporary period (end-date not specified) and consists of two parts — Part A is dynastic history and Part B is devoted to cultural history. It is recommended that 70% of the teaching time should be devoted to teaching Part A, and 30% to Part B. It is clear, however, that dynastic history is still the major focus in teaching, with teachers trying to cover as much as possible of the 4,000 years of history, and textbooks remain the major teaching resource, as the following comments of various teachers show:

> I follow the official syllabus and teach all the things contained in the *textbook*. I agree that students should have a good grounding in Chinese History in F1–3 and hence no part should be skipped in teaching. (italics added) (W. Y. Chung)

> I consider Part A as more important because it relates to the chronological development of historical China. Students' knowledge of dynastic history is more important because it provides the context within which an understanding of culture can develop. Therefore in my school we only select two topics to teach in Part B, and devote most of the time to teaching Part A. (S. W. Lau)

> All along, we do not refer to the syllabus when planning the scheme of work. We teach all the things contained in the *textbook*. It is inevitable that we have to 'gallop' from one dynasty to another in our teaching. Yet it is important for students to gain a comprehensive knowledge of Chinese History. (italics added) (K. W. Wong)

A Han-centred viewpoint

Just as in the first and second phases, textbook accounts of the two non-Han administered dynasties are based on orthodox Han-centred historical views of Chinese History, which portray the Mongols and the Manchus as inferior to the Han in terms of both administrative ability and culture, and as oppressive rulers of China. The following extracts from popular textbooks illustrate this:

> The Mongols were afraid of the Hans' superior culture and the people were not easy to administer. Hence they adopted oppressive policies … Yuan's downfall was due to its negligence of civil administration. They could only use force to suppress Han people … the Mongols' military strength shocked Europe and Asia, but they were poor in culture and administration.[9]

> It was not an easy task for the Manchus, as a minor race, to administer a highly civilised country … For the sake of enlisting the support of intellectuals and eliminating the opposing forces … a number of massacres were carried out … to prevent anti-Qing ideas spreading around.[10]

Similar Han-centred accounts of Mongol and Manchurian rule[11] can be found in other textbooks, such as those by Everyman's Book Company and Ling Kee

Publishing Company. Although this bias in discussing the non-Han dynasties contradicts the stipulated aim of 'achieving ... racial unity', teachers seem not to give much thought to why emphasis is placed on the ways the Han race was unfairly treated in the Yuan and Qing dynasties. In the words of one teacher:

> When I was a student my teacher taught me similar things about the rule of the Mongols and Manchus. Now I teach the same things to my students. I have no idea who stipulated such a view. We pay much attention to how the two minor races unfairly treated the Han people. I have never thought about whether this way of handling the topic is proper or not. (K. W. Wong)

The examination papers from a sample of 10 schools reveal that, whenever there were questions asked on the Yuan and Qing dynasties, they would in one way or another be related to the administrative policies adopted against the Han people. In one of these schools, there was an examination paper[12] that differentiated the Mongols from the Chinese — 'In the Yuan dynasty, *the Mongols adopted oppressive policies against the Chinese*. Give an account of the way in which the Han people and the Southerners (people living in the southern part of China) were treated differently in political affairs and legal matters'. (italics added)

An orthodox perspective and moral and civic education

As well as adopting a Han-centred approach to history, most textbooks follow the orthodox views, which have always been part of the Chinese History curriculum, as the following example illustrates:

> The brutal rule of Xia Jie — His rule was cruel. He abused the system of punishment and made his people suffer ... Later Shang Tang defeated Xia Jie.[13]

The above extract shows the prescribed critical judgement of Xia Jie without any evidence to support such a claim, and students are expected to remember such views rather than interpreting on the basis of evidence and argumentation. A similar approach is evident in the following extract:

> Wang Mang usurped the Han throne — Wang Mang used different methods to please the authorities. He aimed at seizing the imperial power ... At last he changed the official name of the nation to Xin.[14]

Wang Mang's deeds are viewed as *usurpation* because he was a relative of the empress (not the emperor), and hence his seizure of power is regarded as illegitimate. Two further examples illustrate the inheritance of traditional views, but this time expressing positive evaluations:

> The peaceful reign of Zhen Guan — when emperor Tai Zong was on the throne, he worked very hard to administer the country. He took care of people's livelihood and developed the economy. The Tang dynasty was able to prosper.[15]

> The peaceful reign of Kai Yuan — the emperor Xuan Zong made great efforts to build a strong nation. He was innovative and hence the power of the Tang dynasty reached a climax.[16]

The emperors Tai Zong and Xuan Zong are evaluated positively and, again, students are not expected to offer alternative interpretations of their administrations. Examples such as those cited above are commonly found in textbooks published by Ling Kee, Everyman's Books, Modern Education, and Hong Kong Educational Publishers, all of which have adopted the same orthodox views.[17]

Throughout the three phases, the incorporation of official views into the textbooks has been due to commercial considerations. According to one textbook editor, 'the company cannot afford to take the risk of being excluded from the recommended textbook list. Therefore we follow the official curriculum closely, and are very careful when putting forward historical views. It is not surprising to see the same line of argument adopted in all textbooks in Hong Kong'.[18] Ye Xiaobing, who came from Beijing, and was one of the authors of the most popular Chinese History textbook, made similar comments:

> I refer to the official syllabus when writing the textbook. In fact, the historical views incorporated in the textbook are not original. These are already well-established views. Many publishers would adopt similar views in their textbooks. That is why there are no major differences in views between textbooks.

When asked about the traditional views of historical events and people, several teachers declared that they followed the official line because of their own experiences as students and their reliance on the textbook:

> I follow the textbook's narration. Views such as *Wang Mang usurped the Han throne*, and *the peaceful reign of Zhen Guan* have been adopted for a long time. I have never thought about making alternative interpretations of these views. (W. Y. Chung)

> I take the orthodox views for granted. When I was a student my teacher never raised the issue of orthodox views. As a teacher, this has never occurred to me either. (W. H. Siu)

In one case, the teacher considered it was necessary to follow the traditional views for examination reasons:

> Since there are no public examinations at the junior level, we can ask students to challenge the orthodox views. Yet in the CEE students are expected to reproduce orthodox views. Therefore, to play safe, I would prefer not to make any new interpretations. (S. W. Lau)

This same unquestioning acceptance of traditional views of history is reflected in, and reinforced by, schools' internal examinations, as the following extracts from the examination papers of various schools show:

> Account for *Wang Mang's usurpation of the Han throne.*[19]

> What were the impacts of *the peaceful reign of Zhen Guan?*[20]

> Define '*the five barbarian tribes who invaded the Han territory*'.[21]

> Give an account of the *peaceful reign* of Kai Yuan.[22]

> Account for the *peaceful reign* of Wen Jing.[23]

> Account for the *peaceful reign* of Ming Zhang.[24]

With textbooks, teachers and school examinations all adopting an orthodox historical perspective, it is understandable that students had few chances to develop independent thinking.

As regards the integration of moral and civic education into the teaching of Chinese History, none of the teachers interviewed in this study referred to the illustrations given in the official syllabus, or to the charts of moral and civic values for certain topics in textbooks;[25] nor did any of them express a wish to make use of Chinese History teaching to inculcate moral or civic education any more than they had always done. According to them, 'there is not enough time to go through the topics, so there is no room to discuss with students the moral and civic values exemplified by events/personages'.[26]

Moreover, an analysis of the examination papers of nine schools revealed that not even one explicitly included moral and civic messages in the questions and expected answers. The main focus of the questions was factual recall, as shown in a few illustrations of so-called essay questions:

> Give an account of the policies devised by Ming Tai Zu that aimed at expanding his monarchical power.

> Give an account of the process of the downfall of the Ming dynasty and the entry of the Manchus across the border.

> What were the reasons leading to the Dong Lin party conflict?

> Why was Qin Shihuang able to unify China?

Why did Emperor Tai Zu carry out the centralisation policy?

What were Emperor Ming and Emperor Zhang's achievements?

It seems that the stipulated aim of moral and civic education in the official syllabus is less keenly pursued at the classroom level.

National identification

Many textbooks follow closely the views on 'national identification' in the 1997 official curriculum. In particular, since the handover, the Chinese Communist Party has been portrayed in a more favourable light. For example, the phrases 'allied with the Russians, *allied* with the Chinese Communist Party'[27] were used in editions after 1997, compared with the wording in the earlier editions 'allied with the Russians, *accommodated* the Chinese Communist Party'. The term 'allied' gives a higher status to the communists than 'accommodated'. On the post-1949 period, the current editions of textbooks have the wording, 'the *KMT retreated* to Taiwan',[28] whereas the earlier editions all used the phrasing 'the *National Government moved* to Taiwan'.

Also, the theme of 'national feeling' has been presented much more strongly in textbooks since 1997 than in the past. For instance, the topic 'May Fourth Movement' (1919) is described in the following ways:

> In the early republican period, in the face of internal and external pressure, people's *patriotic feelings* were agitated.[29]

> In the Paris Peace Settlement, China's demand could not be met. When the news was heard, the *whole nation was furious.*[30]

> The May Fourth Movement in 1919 was an anti-invasion *patriotic movement...* it enhanced the *nation's dignity ...*[31]

Another example is the description of the Opium War:[32]

> Opium was 'detrimental to China' was changed to 'detrimental to the *nation*'.

> The physical and spiritual health of the 'Chinese people' was changed to '*compatriots*'.

> The British ... ignored the virtue of *justice* by importing large amounts of high price opium to China.

> The *insulting* Treaty of Nanjing was signed.

> The treaty of Nanjing marked an era of *suffering* in the modern history of China.

In commenting on the Opium War, one popular textbook describes the Qing Commissioner Lin Zexu in the following terms: a *bright* official, the most *persistent* official, and *far-sighted*, and a picture of Lin Zexu destroying opium in Humen is also included. While the Commissioner is held up as a shining example, the textbook writer severely criticises Lin's adversary, Captain Elliot:

> He actively supported the export of opium to China for economic benefits, persuaded the British government to use force against China, and exhibited barbarous behaviour ...

While the promotion of 'national feeling' is evident in textbooks, politically sensitive issues, such as the 1989 June Fourth Incident, have been dealt with in a cautious manner by publishers in order not to provoke the PRC government. Among the four most popular Chinese History textbook publishers — Manhattan Press, Modern Education, Ling Kee and Hong Kong Educational — only the one from Manhattan Press mentions briefly 'in May 1989, young students and a large mass of people demonstrated at Tiananmen Square. In June, the government intervened and the incident was resolved'.[33] According to the textbook author, Ye Xiaobing, 'the best way to handle this topic was to put it as vaguely as possible'. Hence it seems that after the handover, publishers were more active in exercising self-censorship. Ye Xiaobing stated:

> I think as long as there is no value judgement on the June Fourth Incident, the ED will not interfere. I just give a simple account of the incident and that is why it is safe.

Despite its emphasis in the textbooks, it seems that teachers were less concerned with developing students' sense of national identification than with covering the syllabus:

> I do not specifically cultivate students' sense of national identification through teaching a particular topic, but I stress the importance of being an honest person, and to care about China's affairs. *Frankly, as before, most of the time I 'gallop' from one dynasty to another.* (italics added) (W. Y. Chung)

Another teacher expressed his unwillingness to relate the development of national identification with a communist state:

> Occasionally, I talk with students about national identification. I relate that with cultural aspects rather than political affiliation. I try to avoid the identification with the PRC because I myself find it difficult to identify with a communist state. (W. H. Siu)

One teacher did not even bother about national identification in his teaching:

> There is no difference between teaching political history and cultural history. I would not try to arouse students' emotions when I talk about Chinese culture nor would I intentionally bring about their sense of national identification when touching on the contemporary period. (K. W. Wong)

In the internal examination papers of these three teachers' schools, no questions were related to 'national identification', and an analysis of the examination papers of a further six schools[34] also revealed that 'national identification' is an aim of the intended curriculum that is largely ignored at the classroom level.

The above analysis shows that the emphasis on 'national identification' in the official curriculum has been implemented in textbooks, but is probably not being keenly pursued in class. Teachers seem to be following the well-established 'pattern' of teaching dynastic history rather than promoting a sense of national identification.

Hong Kong history

In response to the somewhat vague recommendations of the CDC on including Hong Kong history in the curriculum, Chinese History textbooks have played safe by integrating it into individual dynasties as very minor supplementary sections. In one textbook, for example, after the account of the Yuan dynasty, Hong Kong history is briefly appended as follows:

> At that time residents in the North took refuge to the South. The Man clan settled in Sun Tin and Tai Po, [and] the Liu, Hau and Pang also moved from different places to the New Territories in Hong Kong.[35]

Other textbook publishers such as Hong Kong Educational and Manhattan Press have adopted the same cautious approach, whereby Hong Kong history accounts for a very small proportion of the content of textbooks. Table 5.4 illustrates the weighting of Hong Kong history in three series of textbooks.

Table 5.4   Chinese History textbooks: Hong Kong history as peripheral to Chinese History

Publisher	Hong Kong Educational Publishing Co. (2000)	Manhattan Press (HK) Ltd. (2000)	Modern Education Publishing Co. (2000)
Form level	F2	F2	F2
Total no. of pages	177 pages	190 pages	165 pages
No. of pages devoted to Hong Kong history	7 pages	9 pages	6 pages

Chinese History clearly still dominates the curriculum, with the integration of Hong Kong history being peripheral and serving merely to interest students and provide them with a sense of familiarity. This curriculum arrangement conforms to the political agenda of the SAR government by emphasising that Hong Kong was historically part of China. Also, by including Hong Kong history in Chinese History, albeit a very brief coverage, the SAR government has avoided the criticism of maintaining a decontextualised and remote Chinese History curriculum after the handover.

One group of teachers[36] claimed that they did include Hong Kong history in their teaching, though only to a limited extent. Their ideas can be summarised as follows: (1) Chinese History is too remote and boring for students; (2) the inclusion of Hong Kong history enhances their interest in studying history; (3) Hong Kong history is peripheral, and the *main focus* should still be on Chinese History.

None of these schools, however, asked questions on Hong Kong history in internal examinations, while an analysis of the internal examinations of another six schools revealed that only one included a question on local history in its examination paper. This took the form of short questions and fill-in-the-blanks, and students were required to supply bits of information when answering questions such as, 'Why did the Pang clan emigrate to the South?' For the fill-in-the-blanks format, students simply needed to recall dates, and names of events and places. In these cases, the inclusion of Hong Kong history has in no way affected the predominant role of the study of Chinese History as a continuous whole in the implemented curriculum, especially in the examinations — and one wonders to what extent this situation is representative of teachers and schools generally.

To summarise, since the new junior level syllabus was introduced in 1997, the implementation of the curriculum has displayed the following features: first, the Han-centred orthodox historical view of Chinese History has continued to be the basis of the curriculum and is emphasised in textbooks, teaching and examinations; second, although Hong Kong history has been integrated into the curriculum, it is treated as peripheral to Chinese History, and merely serves to enhance students' interest and give them a sense of the relevance of Chinese History. Also, this study shows that teachers largely ignore moral and civic education in their teaching and assessment. Similarly, the newly included aim of promoting 'national identity' serves a largely 'decorative purpose' in teaching and assessment. Therefore, the new curriculum has not had a significant impact on the implemented curriculum. As with the curriculum in the previous two phases, the new F1–3 syllabus has an academic orientation.

INTRODUCTION OF THE REVISED FORMAT OF CEE QUESTIONS: 2001–05

Before the examination for the F4–5 (CEE) syllabus (introduced in 1990) in 1995, there were many complaints from teachers about the fact that there was little change in the question format and the marking scheme. For example, the minutes of subject committee meetings reveal that as early as 1994 members had discussed the revision of the question format, proposing that:

> Regarding the CEE questions and marking schemes, there could be sub-questions set to help candidates answer the questions from a low level to a higher level; and block marking rather than a point-reward-basis should be adopted. The CDC and CEE subject committees could form a joint working group called 'Question setting and marking' to follow up this issue.[37]

In an interview with the press, C. C. Choi, Secretary of the HKEA, made the following comments:

> CEE Chinese History has long been criticised for stressing memorisation. The subject committee, after discussion, has recommended that the objective of assessment should be on students' expression of views.[38]

According to F. S. Tsang, the HKEA Chinese History subject officer:

> The origin of the revision is from *schoolteachers*. In the seminars, they have made severe criticisms of the essay questions: no changes have been made to the format of questions, factual recall is stressed in the examination, the requirement of the examination has deadened students' interest in the subject, and there is no way to enhance their thinking skills. Teachers are very enthusiastic about changing the question format in the CEE. (italics added)

Dissatisfaction with the CEE questions continued to be expressed by members of subject committee at meetings in 1995 and 1997:

> Currently, many candidates tend to memorise the marking scheme rather than to understand history. To improve the situation, the first thing to do is to change the method of marking — 3 marks per point should not be continued. The marking scheme should not be in detail. A framework that lists the main points would suffice.[39]

The same criticism appeared in another subject committee meeting:

> In the examination paper — the pattern of questions and the way of marking remain unchanged. Candidates could easily predict the

questions and hence memorise the answers. ... It is recommended that the question formats should be varied.[40]

One should note that the revision of the CEE question format was initiated by schoolteachers, rather than by the bureaucracy — the ED or HKEA officers. The role played by the officials was one of coordination, including an exploratory study of the possible format of the questions, and promoting their implementation in the CEE. This situation was, therefore, quite different from the pattern that prevailed during the first and second phases.

Two working groups were set up to review the CEE Chinese History curriculum: one on 'setting and marking questions' and another on 'the review of the syllabus'. Both groups concluded that a new objective should be included in the examination syllabus: 'the student is to express personal views on historical knowledge'. In 1998, the Chinese History subject committee made the following recommendations:[41]

(1) Questions set should aim at reducing regurgitation, enhancing comprehension and stimulation of thinking skills.
(2) Types of questions should be varied.
(3) 'Expressing personal views' should be added and block marking be used in this part.
(4) Marking should be flexible, and not be confined to 3 marks for each point.

As a result of these recommendations, the CEE subject committee began to work on a new format for essay questions, and in April 1998 and November 1999, two sample question papers were sent to schools. The sample question papers required more specific answers and minute details of historical knowledge, e.g.

(1) Emperor Ming Tai Zu's abolition of the prime ministerial post led to the empowerment of the eunuchs. Explain the relationship between these two developments. (5 marks)
(2) From the perspective of appointing/dethroning the emperor, waging war, incriminating the loyal officials, levying heavy tax and corruption, and inducing the emperor to playful deeds, explain the damage caused by the eunuchs in the Ming dynasty. (15 marks)

These two questions in the new question format required more prescribed answers from students than before. For example, the question set in the 1983 examination for the same topic was actually less rigid:

Ming Tai Zu fiercely carried out autocratic rule. Give an account of his policy, (18 marks) and the impact on the Ming's political situation (9 marks).

There was also a newly added question which asked for students' personal views:

> Who do you think did the most severe damage: Wang Zhen, Liu Jin, or Wei Zhongxian? Compare their deeds. (8 marks)

The marking scheme specified that 'as long as the reasons stated were reasonable, marks can be given accordingly'. It can be seen that the new question format specified the intention of the question more precisely, and the questions were set in sequence, giving students directions for their answers. According to F. S. Tsang, the HKEA officer: 'the new format was to guide students to get hold of the core of the question'. To introduce the new CEE question format and the new teaching and learning strategies, a seminar was held by the ED on 3 July 1999, with more than 400 Chinese History teachers present. However, to the dismay of the officials, the seminar turned out to be a meeting of 'condemnation'. According to the subject officer of the CDI, H. C. Wong:

> Teachers are furious. They focus on the negative impact of the examination on students; that is, the questions are too difficult for students and such a change will depress the overall results of Chinese History. They blame the abrupt revision and claim that they themselves find it difficult to grasp the requirement of part 4 — expressing personal views.

F. S. Tsang, who was centrally involved in formulating the questions and was himself present at the seminar, complained that teachers were being self-contradictory in that:

> The new format was introduced as a result of teachers' requests. They (teachers) complain that the format of the CEE questions has not been altered for a couple of decades, and that these types of questions kill students' creative thinking. However, in reality, teachers only want good examination results for their students. In the seminar they said students could not cope with too many changes, and therefore it is better not to change anything at all.

After the seminar, the ED collated teachers' views and forwarded them to the secretary of the CEE subject committee.[42] The main criticisms were:

(1) The examination syllabus is content loaded. It is difficult to finish teaching the syllabus in a year and a half.

(2) The new question format (questions were structured from simple to complex, and included a part on students' personal views) requires students to have a clear understanding of historical events. This is beyond students' ability to handle.

(3) There are problems (lack of objective criteria in marking students' personal views) in the assessment criteria of the new question format.

(4) The reform was implemented hastily. Both teachers and students find it difficult to cope with the change. Support should be given to teachers.

The teachers' expression of their discontent in the seminar sent out a strong message to officials: the revised format needed to be clearly specified and teaching materials provided to help teachers prepare their students for the examination. As a result, a revised version of the sample questions and marking schemes was sent to schools. This new version included the following changes: unpopular questions were omitted — such as those on the culture of the Shang dynasty — and the part that required students to express personal views was reduced to a maximum of four marks out of a total of 25. Also, in 2000, the CDI issued a teaching package to help teachers familiarise themselves with the new question format, and set out the rationale for the revision:

> Since, in the old question format, only open-ended questions were asked, some minor, basic historical knowledge could hardly be touched upon. Asking questions on basic knowledge aims at widening students' learning perspective and enhancing their comprehensive knowledge of China's past.[43]

Officials used the following sample question to illustrate the requirements of the new question format:

(1) With which war do you associate the following 4 names? What was the other name of this war?
     Arrow ship incident (b) Ye Mingchen (c) Treaty of Tianjin (d) Treaty of Beijing
(2) From the perspectives of commercial interests and of the British and the Manchu officials' ways of handling things, explain the reasons leading to the war.
(3) From the perspectives of sovereignty, national defence, and economic conditions, analyse China's losses in its rights and interests.
(4) Based on this war, comment on the official Ye Mingchen. What are your views on him?

Since the four questions are related, if a wrong answer is given in (1), the subsequent answers in (2), (3) and (4) might be wrong. Therefore, without accurate historical knowledge, it was impossible to talk about analysis and comment.[44]

It was clear that the new question format demanded a more thorough knowledge of Chinese History and, with the requirement that students should express their personal views, interpretive ability was emphasised for the first time. Thus, in terms of intellectual requirements, the new CEE question format was more demanding than that of the 1975 and 1982 syllabuses.

The manner of introduction of the new question format shows that two different groups of teachers existed: the innovative and the conservative. For example, the innovative teachers assumed the role of initiators by expressing their discontent with the existing CEE question format in the media, seminars and subject committee meetings, as a result of which a decision was made by curriculum planners to change the question format to promote students' thinking. However, the more conservative teachers regarded this revision as harmful to their interests as it would mean a change in their long-established and internalised teaching patterns, which they feared might lead to a decline in their students' performance in examinations. Hence, once the new format had been formulated, these conservative teachers strongly condemned the proposed change. In this incident, the subject community, especially teachers, played a more active role in influencing the Chinese History curriculum than in the first and second phases. Paradoxically, it was schoolteachers who initiated the change to the CEE question format and it was also schoolteachers who were against the changes made. As noted in the revised sample questions, there was a compromise in which the part that required students to express personal views was reduced to four marks out of 25 (the original recommendation was flexible, ranging from four to 10).

The new essay question format introduced in the 2001 CEE has not led to a significant difference in student performance in the examination. As shown in the HKEA document 'Analysis of CEE results of all candidates by subject', students' performance in the 2001 Chinese History examination was slightly better than in previous years. For example, in 1999, 60.2% of candidates were awarded grade E or above; in 2000, it was 61.8%; and in 2001, the percentage went up to 63.4%. The fact that the change in the question format and the inclusion of the part that required students to express their views has not had an adverse effect on students' attainment may explain why teachers showed no great opposition to the questions set after the 2001 examination.

THE INTRODUCTION OF 'NEW HISTORY'

The broader curriculum reform undertaken by the SAR government in 2000 has had a significant impact on Chinese History (see Chapter 2). In April 2000, the CDI announced that there would be four options for schools to choose from concerning the place of Chinese History in the curriculum. One option was 'New History,' which brought together Chinese History and History as one subject. According to the two CDI senior officers, C. H. Lee (History) and H. C. Wong (Chinese History), 'soon after the Education Commission carried out a holistic review of education in 1998, the CDC began to review the curriculum. Since there were a lot of overlaps between Chinese History and History, the Chief Executive, K. K. Chan, asked the respective subject officers to review the two subjects and investigate a possible integration'. W. N. Bau, Chief Curriculum Development Officer in the CDI, stated that 'New History' was intended to link up the development of China with the rest of the world. Students could understand China from a new perspective. This could strengthen their sense of national identification and belonging to China.[45]

The pilot study and the drafting of 'New History' were controlled by the CDI officials and were not made known to the public. In 2002 the CDI completed New History's curriculum framework and appended it to the newly published PSHE curriculum guide. The outline of 'New History' (renamed 'History and Culture') shows that it takes a chronological approach, with five themes integrated across the history of China and the West, namely, political, economic, social, intellectual and ethnic. Chinese History's previous emphasis on the 'political' aspect of dynastic history no longer dominates the curriculum. With a drastic reduction in content, both concepts of history (for example, change and development, cause and effect relationships, and evidence) and concepts in history (for example, civilisation, culture, government, and revolution) have become the key concerns in the new curriculum. In terms of skills, 'New History' places more emphasis on historical methods and the comparative study of the culture of China and the West; and, in general, it aims to encourage students to view the history of China and the West from a global perspective.

In view of the political sensitivity of Chinese History and the possible resentment of the subject community (see Chapter 2), the government neither adopted a high profile in introducing this new curriculum nor published a 'History and Culture' curriculum guide for schools. According to the officer-in-charge, H. C. Wong, no further curriculum development of 'History and Culture' was carried out after 2003. It is up to individual schools to decide whether they would like to offer the subject, and the CDI will provide professional support for these schools on request. The CDI's passive role shows that it has been extremely cautious in handling the integration of Chinese History and History, fearing that the subject community might make use of this opportunity to start another furious attack on the government. Unlike the previous curriculum developments where teachers were involved in drafting the syllabus and revising the curriculum, the process for 'History and Culture' was a 'black box'. The ambiguous status of 'History and Culture' represents a 'victory' for the subject community in guarding the independent status of Chinese History after the handover.

THE INTRODUCTION OF 'KEY LEARNING AREAS' (KLAS): 'PERSONAL, SOCIAL AND HUMANITIES EDUCATION' (PSHE)

Another option for schools to choose regarding the place of Chinese History in the school curriculum was the KLA, whereby Chinese History would be included in 'Personal, Social and Humanities Education' (PSHE). The CDC's consultation document *Learning To Learn: The Way Forward in Curriculum Development* (November 2000) provided a detailed explanation of how the KLAs were arranged. There were six strands linking and integrating related knowledge content in PSHE, among which two were related to history: 'Time, Continuity and Change', and 'Culture and Heritage'. The learning objectives listed for the former were mainly directed towards the acquisition of skills. Content thus became a tool to train skills such as 'distinguishing between primary and secondary sources, fact and opinion, interpretation, and judgement'. For the other strand 'Culture and Heritage', the emphasis was on 'the uniqueness of Chinese culture', and the 'main virtues of Chinese culture' (Key Stage 3) and, through cultural interaction, the examination of one's own culture (Key Stage 4). This strand, therefore, aimed at fostering students' understanding of, and conformity with, Chinese culture. However, since 2002, the KLA PSHE has developed into a school-based curriculum which schools can refer to as a model when introducing their own curriculum development. In other words, the KLA PSHE can in no way threaten the independent status of Chinese History in the school curriculum.

THE NEW CEE (F4–5) CHINESE HISTORY CURRICULUM: 2004–08

In 2000, the subject community made a joint effort to politicise Chinese History in order to counteract the possible threat to its independent status. They argued that, with the return of Hong Kong to China after years of colonial rule, it was even more important for the subject to maintain its independence in order to play its important role in national education and as a symbol of national unity; integrating it with other subjects would take away this independence. The high profile adopted by the subject community in voicing opposition to the integration of Chinese History with History or as a strand in the KLA PSHE placed considerable pressure on the government (see Chapter 2). At the same time, the introduction of the revised format of the CEE questions was criticised as a piecemeal measure, which simply paid lip-service to improving the curriculum. Therefore, in 2000, a CDC-HKEAA Joint Working Group was set up to revise the F4–5 Chinese History syllabus. This revision indicated that the government supported the independent status of Chinese History, and hence it was another 'victory' for the subject community as the bastion of Chinese History's independence. Moreover, in order to reduce the possibility of disputes arising from the revision of the syllabus, the CDI even enlisted key members of the two Chinese History associations to join the Working Group. This new syllabus was introduced in 2004 and was first examined in the CEE in 2006, replacing the previous revised format of questions. However it will last only until 2008 because in 2009 a new senior secondary curriculum will be introduced, and the Chinese History curriculum will also have to be revised accordingly.

Both the new and old syllabuses require students to study the entirety of Chinese history, and both focus mainly on modern history and de-emphasise ancient and medieval history. For the new syllabus, however, there is a specific aim: 'to let students master the concept of time, continuity and change'.[46] Also, in order to allow enough teaching time, some topics, together with cultural history (included as part B in the old syllabus), have been discarded. These changes have not created discontent among the subject community, probably because representatives of the two teacher associations were members of the Working Group, and compromises were made regarding the revision of the syllabus.

The new syllabus is also less prescriptive than the old one. For instance, one of its stated objectives for students is: 'through knowing and *critically examining* the historical events and personages cultivate good conduct', which can be contrasted with the objective prescribed in the old syllabus: 'to cultivate good conduct through learning from the deeds of historical personages'. Also, less established views are presented regarding important historical figures; for example, in the old syllabus, Qin Shihuang and Han Wu Di were viewed as bad and good leaders respectively, while the new syllabus suggests examining historical figures from different perspectives. Nevertheless, in the interpretation of major historical developments, traditional, orthodox views still dominate, which limits alternative interpretations of Chinese history.

As in the old syllabus, the new one presents a Han-centred view of history, although the emphasis has been reduced, with statements such as 'the oppressive policy adopted by the Mongols' being deleted. Moreover, since the cultural domain has been discarded in the new syllabus, the superiority of the Han culture is not as prominent as in the old syllabus.

The new syllabus is more concerned with national identification than the previous one, and in this respect specifies its aims as: 'to foster a sense of responsibility to the society, nation and race'; and 'to enhance a sense of recognition and identification with the nation and the race'. However, it makes no reference to the Chinese Communist Party, nor does it use historical events and people to illustrate patriotic deeds.

Lastly, Hong Kong history is not included in either the old 1990 syllabus or the new one, which reflects the curriculum developers' perceptions of Hong Kong history and the cultivation of a Hong Kong identity as of little importance.

CONCLUSION

Shortly after the handover, the independent status of Chinese History faced a crisis, but the efforts made by the subject community turned the crisis into an opportunity. Chinese History has been able to maintain its separate status at both the junior and the senior level. For the junior level, it was intended that a sense of local and national identification be promoted, and so Hong Kong history was included as an appendix to the official syllabus. In addition, orthodox views, including the Han-centred interpretation of history and moral and civic education, were more precisely prescribed in the syllabus. However, while the inclusion of Hong Kong history has made students' learning more relevant, this study shows that, at the classroom level, teachers have not given much attention to national identification; and no questions on this aspect have been set in schools' internal examinations. Moreover, while teachers and textbooks continue to adhere closely to Han-centred interpretations of Chinese History, moral and civic education seem to be taken less seriously. Nevertheless, the new junior level syllabus has increased the amount of content to be covered.

The revised CEE question format was introduced with the intention of encouraging students to build up a comprehensive understanding of Chinese History. However, with the newly added section on 'expressing personal opinions', the demands on students are higher than before. In reaching this situation, teachers have played a dual role: on the one hand, they initiated the change and, on the other, they are implementing the curriculum in class. When teachers, especially the more conservative ones, realised that the change might harm their interests they expressed misgivings about the new format; and, as a result, only minor changes were introduced. This incident reflects the active role played by schoolteachers in the revision of the CEE question format, something which did not happen in the first and second phases.

The introduction of 'New History' and 'KLA–PSHE' have put the independence of Chinese History in crisis as an independent subject as in both curriculum initiatives the content of Chinese History will be reduced drastically. While 'New History' is based on a cultural framework, 'KLA–PSHE' stresses skills training, and in these two options the 'tradition' of studying Chinese History as a continuous whole no longer exists. However, the subject community played an active role in defending the status of Chinese History, arguing that after the handover the subject should become a core element of basic national education, and that an independent Chinese History reflects the state's sovereignty. The establishment of two teacher associations has meant that Chinese History teachers are better organised to oppose curriculum reforms which they think have an adverse effect on the autonomy of Chinese History. The introduction of the new CEE (F4–5) syllabus is an indication of the 'victory' of the subject community in protecting the interests of Chinese History in the face of curriculum reform in general and curriculum integration in particular.

6

Conclusion

CHINESE HISTORY FROM 1945 TO 2005: A SUMMARY

During the first phase (1945–74), after the establishment of the PRC, the colonial government was worried about the political struggle between the KMT and CCP extending to Hong Kong, and of particular concern was the possible influence of communism in Hong Kong in general, and in the field of education in particular. In order to counter this, the government exercised tight control of education, particularly in the 1950s and 1960s. However, its concerns regarding Chinese History were alleviated by the collaborative efforts of a group of conservative Chinese scholars who had taken refuge in Hong Kong after the communist takeover in 1949. These scholars followed an orthodox approach to Chinese History, which had its historical origins in 'the 24 Dynastic Histories', and took a traditional Han-centred historical view when interpreting Chinese History. They were not interested in modern Chinese history or politics, only in ancient cultural history. Once settled in Hong Kong, they committed themselves to transplanting their vision of Chinese culture in the British colony by writing textbooks and teaching Chinese History in primary and secondary schools and tertiary institutions, and were influential in keeping Chinese History depoliticised. In this way, the subject was allowed a good deal of autonomy by the government. In the 1950s, the Chinese History curriculum followed that of the Nationalist government, which was largely modelled on 'the 24 Dynastic Histories' of the imperial court. Pedagogy consisted of the transmission of orthodox views of individual events and personages with the aim of providing moral exemplars for students. With the emphasis on dynastic court politics, the period of study was confined to pre-1945 and excluded Hong Kong history, leaving the curriculum effectively depoliticised and decontextualised. Chinese History became an independent subject at A-level, H-level and CEE in 1967 in order to widen subject choice for students. The content of this new subject, and its depoliticised and decontextualised nature, supported the interests of the main parties concerned: the colonial government, the government of the PRC, and the local subject community. As a result, the subject was able to strengthen its position in the school curriculum.

The Chinese History curriculum remained unaltered throughout the second phase (1974–97) despite an attempt by the Education Department in 1975 to incorporate Chinese History into the proposed new Social Studies subject. When this recommendation was announced, the reaction of the Chinese History subject community was one of indignation, with some university teachers asserting in the press that it was a colonial plot to try to eradicate 'national education'. As a result of the dispute, the colonial government, conscious of its low level of legitimacy, adopted a more cautious approach to curriculum reform and a more accommodating attitude towards the Chinese History curriculum. As long as the subject did not create any political embarrassment to the government or affect its relationship with the government of the PRC, the subject was allowed to follow its own agenda. Remarkably, not only was Chinese History not integrated into Social Studies, but it became a common core subject at junior secondary level. Under the guardianship of the subject community, the curriculum throughout the second phase was virtually identical to that of the first phase, the only changes being the extension of the period of study and the inclusion of additional cultural themes. This lack of change was striking, particularly in view of the fact that many subjects in one way or another underwent major curriculum reform during the 1980s and 1990s. This was the case with History, for example, which, with the introduction of mass education in 1978, changed its emphasis from learning content to developing skills. Hong Kong history was also included in 'History' to make the subject more relevant to students' interests, and the subject was used to facilitate the implementation of project-based learning. The insulation of Chinese History from the broader pattern of curriculum change can be explained in terms of the harmonious match between the subject and the interests of the colonial government and the government of the PRC. After the Social Studies incident and throughout the second phase, Chinese History was left undisturbed by the reforming currents affecting other areas of the secondary school curriculum. Whether or not the subject should change, and if so how, were largely decisions which were made by the key members of the subject committees, and such decisions were taken (for example, the extension of the end-date to 1976) only after considering the possible impact on the colonial and PRC governments. This self-regulation on the part of the subject community was reflected in the depoliticised and decontextualised nature of the curriculum.

During the third phase (1997–2005), as a result of political imperatives arising from decolonisation, the Chinese History curriculum was revised to emphasise the aim of cultivating a sense of belonging to the nation and the people of China. At the same time, Hong Kong history was for the first time appended to the junior level curriculum. This promotion of national identity and ethnic solidarity are phenomena normally associated with decolonisation. Two years after the return of Hong Kong to Chinese sovereignty, however, the SAR government, seeing itself in a more legitimate position to review the education system, made tentative moves to reform the Chinese History curriculum. It proposed four options for the future development of the subject: leaving Chinese History as an independent subject; integrating it into PSHE; merging it with History to form a new subject called 'New History'; and making it a school-based curriculum. Three of these options threatened the status of Chinese History, and in the face of this crisis the subject community started a second 'protect our subject' campaign (25 years after the first one in 1975). This time a more active approach was adopted, with the two newly established teacher associations initiating media pressure on the government and seeking public support. With Beijing's official representative expressing her support for an independent Chinese History subject, the three interested parties were divided into two rival camps, with the Beijing official and the local subject community on one side, and the SAR government on the other side. There was considerable tension between the two camps and the Education Department defended itself by claiming that it had no intention of 'killing off' Chinese History and that it was up to the schools themselves to decide how they would prefer their students to study the history of China. Six months later, as can be seen in the proposed framework of 'New History' and 'PSHE', the Chinese History element was strengthened, with the curriculum reform consultation document's preamble stressing the importance of Chinese History education. Moreover, 'New History' was quietly shelved in 2003 after the completion of a pilot study. All this indicates that the SAR government was trying to seek a compromise with the subject community on the relative importance of Chinese History in the curriculum. The revision of the F4–5 Chinese History curriculum and its introduction to schools in 2004 further reconfirmed its independent status. These successful experiences are likely to prompt the subject community to continue to take an active role in protecting the autonomy of Chinese History.

THE ACADEMIC ORIENTATION OF CHINESE HISTORY

Chinese History has always focused on a body of facts, and, as was noted in Chapters 3, 4 and 5, over the last 60 years its time-frame and content knowledge have been continually expanding. This can be attributed to the chronological approach adopted by curriculum developers, who have insisted that Chinese History needs to be studied in its entirety before one can come to appreciate the essence of Chinese culture. One result of this is that the whole 3,000 years of history is repeated three times (F1–3, F4–5 and F6–7) in secondary schools in ever-increasing detail. Also, due to changes in the broader social and political contexts, the scope of study and the content became even more extensive in each successive phase. Another very important feature of Chinese History has been its focus on imperial court history, supplemented by cultural history. The rise and fall of dynasties are interpreted as being attributable mainly to the deeds of emperors and their court officials, while the social structure or relationships between the economic and political infrastructures at particular points in time are not referred to or used as analytical frameworks. As a result of the academic orientation of Chinese History, students are presented with a body of facts without any means of achieving genuine understanding and with little opportunity for critical analysis.

From the beginning, the content of Chinese History has been based on orthodoxy, moralising and a Han-centred interpretation of history. As noted in Chapter 1, Chinese History has its historical origins in 'the 24 Dynastic Histories'. As early as Confucius' *Spring and Autumn Annals*, historical narratives were full of conclusions regarding individual events, personal deeds and races. As Confucian historiography emphasised the exemplary function of history, the 'lessons' embodied in history were aimed at setting moral exemplars for emperors and officials. Another purpose of writing history, according to Confucius,[1] was to 'unite the Han people and differentiate them from the barbarians'. The moralising nature and Han-centred interpretation of history thus took shape as early as the Confucian period and were later incorporated into 'the 24 Dynastic Histories', which were then taken as the blueprint for the interpretation of the Chinese past. Since the purpose of 'the 24 Dynastic Histories' was to serve the interests of the state, individual events and the actions of important people in the imperial court were recorded in detail with a view to highlighting good or bad deeds and loyal or disloyal behaviour. In addition to traditional Chinese historiography, the traditionally conceived epistemology (see Chapter 1) tended to interpret the rise and fall of dynasties in terms of individual actions and events, while macro and structural perspectives, such as social, political and economic issues, were not used in historical analysis and explanation. Dynastic histories were thus filled with accounts of discrete events and personages through which orthodox views of the past and of 'correct behaviour' were established or reinforced.

These characteristics of dynastic histories were manifested in the Nationalist government's Chinese History syllabus[2] and textbook narratives, and were adopted in Hong Kong schools in the 1930s and 1940s, when Chinese studies was seen as a means of countering Chinese nationalism in order to avoid any threat to the stability of the colonial government. After 1949, Hong Kong, Mainland China and Taiwan used 'the 24 Dynastic Histories' as the major basis of their Chinese History curricula, each interpreting it according to its own political needs. In the case of Hong Kong, 'the 24 Dynastic Histories' became the traditional version of Chinese History, which specified 'the study of Chinese History as a continuous whole'. In this way, the orthodoxy, moralising function and Han-centred interpretation of history as exhibited in the Chinese History curriculum were a legacy of curriculum development in republican China. Hence, as shown in the official curriculum and its implementation, orthodox views of particular events and people, and racial and national identity were officially stipulated, and students had to learn these established views rather than interpret the past for themselves. Moreover, the moral instruction embedded in 'the 24 Dynastic Histories' was also incorporated into Hong Kong's Chinese History curriculum.

As a result, one of the principal functions of Chinese History has been as a moralising agent. Events and the actions of people offer a gallery of examples of moral and immoral behaviour for students to emulate or condemn. This was particularly evident in the second and third phases (1974–97, 1997–2005), when the official curricula stipulated which historical figures were 'good' or 'bad'. Also, the Han-centred interpretation of history throughout the three phases has devalued the rule of the Mongols and Manchurians while emphasising the superiority of 'Han culture', as can be seen in the official curriculum (e.g. the syllabuses and curriculum guidelines) and in teaching, learning and examination. In this way, the curriculum content of Chinese History throughout the period studied here has focused on a relatively static body of facts, and on orthodox views that aim at providing moral instruction to students and promoting a Han-centred view of history.

The academic nature of Chinese History is also reflected in the form of the curriculum. As shown in Chapters 3, 4 and 5, textbooks and CEE marking schemes have always been based on the reproduction of the traditional views, moral instruction and a Han-centred interpretation of history which have characterised the curriculum. Consequently, since teachers have generally depended to a large extent on textbooks and marking schemes, the influence of these features can be seen in the classroom. Teaching and learning have tended to emphasise memorisation and recitation, rather than interpretation. Also, individualised rather than collaborative learning has been the norm. Only recently, in the revised CEE (2001–05) and the 2006 CEE examination sample scripts has a small section been included (worth four marks out of 25 and six marks out of 20 respectively), that requires students to give their own views on historical events or personages. Although it is not specified that students are required to provide evidence to support their arguments, this is the first time in the last 60 years that students have been given a chance to 'interpret' Chinese History. In contrast, at the sixth-form level, data-based questions were introduced in the A-level in 1994, which meant that Chinese History at the most senior level followed its counterpart 'History' in using sources for both teaching and assessment. As noted in Chapter 4, this change can be attributed mainly to the ED's reform of sixth-form education in the early 1990s, which forced Chinese History's curriculum developers to revise the teaching of sixth-form Chinese History. Eventually, members of the sixth-form subject committee chose to introduce data-based questions in the A-level examination rather than adopt project-based assessment.

THE PATTERN OF CHANGE IN THE CONTENT OF CHINESE HISTORY

The present study has identified the special features of Chinese History's academic content as being: the study of Chinese History as a continuous whole; orthodox views aimed at providing moral exemplars for students; and a Han-centred interpretation of history. As for the form of the curriculum, Chinese History has always tended to emphasise individualised rote learning and examination-oriented study. It is argued that these features, which have formed an integral part of Hong Kong's Chinese History curriculum over the last 60 years, clearly illustrate the social characteristics of an academic curriculum as defined by Young (1971, 1998), which include literacy, individualism, abstractness and unrelatedness (see Chapter 1). This study has also shown that when Chinese History was first incorporated into the school curriculum, it was already academically oriented, and over the years the subject has become even more academic in both its content and form. This shows a different pattern from that posited by Goodson (1987b, 1988, 1994) and Ball (1985), who argue that as a result of the struggle for status, power and resources, and as examinations become directly linked to university departments, school subject groups move progressively away from utilitarian and pedagogic traditions towards embracing academic traditions. Also, the development of Chinese History in Hong Kong does not conform to Kliebard's (1991: 179) US pattern of the process of evolution of school subjects, in which 'traditional subjects like Mathematics, History and Classical languages are incorporated into the curriculum as academic disciplines, and in the process of development, move 'downward' so that they more closely approximate the interests of learners'. The pattern of development of Chinese History shown here also contrasts with two studies conducted in Hong Kong: Wong's (1992) study on the evolution of Social Studies, which agreed with the findings of Goodson, and Vickers' research (2000) into the history of the school subject 'History', which portrays a shift from a traditional academic emphasis towards the promotion of a more skills-based pedagogy. In contrast, the pattern of change in Chinese History since 1945 has been towards an ever-more entrenched academic orientation.

THE INFLUENCES THAT HAVE SHAPED CHINESE HISTORY'S PATTERN OF CURRICULUM DEVELOPMENT

In the 1960s, when Chinese History became an independent subject at F1–3, F4–5 and F6–7, its academic orientation was firmly established. It has subsequently remained largely unchanged despite the fact that in the last 30 years there have been significant socio-political-economic changes in Hong Kong — growth in population, economic transformation, the emergence of the middle class, and the introduction of mass education. The pattern of curriculum development of

Chinese History shows how, on the one hand, colonialism and decolonisation have provided a socio-political context within which the subject community has been able to define the nature and role of the subject and, on the other hand, how the nature and role of the subject so defined has had its historical origins in Chinese historiography. The ways in which curriculum decisions have been made have also played a dominant role in affecting the content of Chinese History.

Macro-level Influences (Colonialism and Decolonisation) and Meso-level Influences (Social, Political and Economic Factors)

The influence of colonialism and decolonisation on Chinese History from 1945 to the present has been evident in the aims and content knowledge set out in the curriculum. As far as the aims of Chinese History education in the colonial era were concerned, nationalism or national sentiment was taboo, and cultural identification rather than national identification was seen as a more viable reason for continuing Chinese History education in Hong Kong. It should be noted, however, that the representation of 'China' in Chinese History was ancient and abstract, detached from a real and tangible 'China' — although it could be said that this kind of abstractness was at least able to provide Hong Kong students with some sort of identity with China, albeit historical China.

However, since the handover, Chinese History has become a legitimating vehicle to promote national sentiment and, in contrast to the colonial period, 'national and ethnic identification with the state' has become a dominant aim of Chinese History education. As a result, a concrete 'here and now' 'China' has suddenly become identified in the official curriculum, even though the content knowledge has remained largely unchanged. In striving for an independent Chinese History subject, the subject community, specifically the teacher associations, even recommended at one point that 'Chinese History' be renamed 'National History' in order to signify the importance of the subject after China's resumption of sovereignty.

With regard to content, the Chinese History curriculum has been regulated to suit the government's socio-political needs at particular points in time. For example, in the 1950s, the curriculum followed that of the Nationalist government, at first focusing on the modern and contemporary period (1644–1945). The 1956 KMT/CCP riots, however, alerted the government to the need to depoliticise Hong Kong society, and it was thought that a principal means of achieving this was the depoliticisation of the school curriculum. As a result, the contemporary period was omitted from the curriculum for more than 30 years. Thereafter, Chinese History emphasised ancient rather than contemporary history. The scope of studies thus stretched from ~2100 BC (Xia) to 1911 in 1965 and later to 1945 in 1972 covering more than 3,000 years of history. Even when the end-dates of the CEE, AS-level and A-level syllabuses were extended to 1976 in the 1980s, after the PRC government had concluded its evaluation of the Cultural Revolution, students were only required to reproduce factual accounts of contemporary China, and were neither exposed to controversial issues nor asked to exercise independent thinking. This was most clearly reflected in the CEE questions that related to post-1949 history. After the handover, when the post-colonial administration felt the need to cultivate local and national sentiments, Hong Kong history was included in the junior level curriculum in order to establish the historical linkage between Hong Kong and China. Although the curriculum was for the first time contextualised, students were also potentially further burdened with the need to memorise factual knowledge of Hong Kong from prehistoric times to 1997.

Colonialism and decolonisation may have provided the context within which the Chinese History curriculum has evolved over the last 60 years, but the nature of its development challenges the most widely-held theories of colonial and postcolonial education. As noted in Chapter 1, proponents of the classic view of colonialism, or dependency theory, mainly focus on the negative socialisation of the colonised by the coloniser, achieved through alienation and/or devaluation of the indigenous culture, in particular its history. There is also said to be a 'positive socialisation of the coloniser on the colonised' (Memmi, 1965: 105), by which the colonial power emphasises its own history and customs in order to overwhelm the culture of the colonised and socialise them into its culture. However, far from being devalued in importance, the most telling feature of Chinese History in Hong Kong is the fact that it has been an independent subject in the school curriculum since 1967, and as such it has an even greater weighting than in Mainland China and Taiwan. The actual scope of study involved in Chinese History in Hong Kong has also been broader than in these two places. Moreover, in terms of the aims of Chinese History education, the first teaching syllabus introduced in 1975 and the subsequent syllabus revisions in 1982 (F1–3), 1990 (F4–5), 1991 (AS-level) and 1992 (A-level) all stipulated identification with Chinese culture and its value in Chinese History education. Hence, in terms of students' learning of 'national' history, Hong Kong students have not been disadvantaged when compared with other Chinese communities such as Mainland China and Taiwan. All these factors contradict the notion that colonial education in Hong Kong demoted the history of the native people, and show how history curriculum development in Hong Kong has not conformed to the Marxist view of colonial curriculum development.

Also, as regards Hong Kong, it cannot be argued that colonial education emphasised the 'positive socialisation of the coloniser on the colonised', at least with respect to British history. In contrast to Chinese history, British history, formerly included in the History syllabus, has never occupied a predominant position in either the CEE, H-level/AS-level or A-level. In fact, as early as the 1960s, British history was being reduced in the syllabus; and in 1984, British domestic history (except the Industrial Revolution, Liberalism, and Parliamentary reforms in Britain) was entirely excluded from the syllabus. This limited exposure to British culture could hardly have cultivated students' identification with the sovereign state.

It is also clear that the manner in which Chinese History developed as an independent subject does not support the revisionist interpretation of colonialism, which tends to view education as one of the 'benefits bestowed' on the colonised. This is seen in the ways in which the Chinese History curriculum was depoliticised and decontextualised — in other words, the 'benefits bestowed' were not unconditional. The colonial government had to ensure that the curriculum would neither threaten its administration nor upset Sino-British relationships. However, it is argued here that the continued existence of Chinese History as an independent subject was the result of collaboration between the colonial government and the subject community. Socio-political tensions existing after the establishment of the communist regime in China in 1949 prompted the colonial government to take steps to ensure that the Chinese History curriculum became depoliticised and decontextualised in order to prevent the promotion of subversive activities which might threaten its already weak legitimacy. With the collaboration of important members of the local subject community, the subject's role and nature were defined so as to meet the needs of both the colonial government and the subject community. In addition, the subject community continually regulated the Chinese History curriculum in order to adjust to shifts in the political context in Hong Kong and Mainland China, for example in extending the end-date of the syllabus to 1976 only when the PRC government had concluded its evaluation of the Cultural Revolution. This kind of collaboration and self-regulation on the part of the subject community, and the resulting Chinese History curriculum, can be interpreted as a form of collaborative colonialism. In the second phase, when political transition was underway, precautionary measures prevailed, with the main members of the subject community, as guardians of Chinese History, striving to maintain the status quo in the subject. As a result, during colonial rule, the curriculum helped to promote an identification with ancient cultural China, rather than with a modern political or ideological China. Once instituted, this educational aim became the 'tradition' of the Chinese History curriculum. The subject was thus characterised by an emphasis on ancient history and an absence of sensitive political issues. Students were to devote themselves to the chronologically arranged dynastic history and cultural history that were largely irrelevant to their experience and interests. It could be argued that colonialism did in this sense constrain the development of Chinese History to the extent that the quality of students' learning was somehow diminished. However, although the Chinese History curriculum had to be depoliticised and decontextualised to avoid involvement in modern Chinese politics and any threats to the colonial rule, the indigenous culture was by no means devalued.

While this study reveals a marked difference in the way colonialism was manifested in Hong Kong's Chinese History curriculum in comparison with school curricula in other colonial countries, the features of the curriculum do support some of the findings of local studies which have investigated the impact of colonialism on various subject curricula. For example, in reviewing cultural studies in Hong Kong in the pre-1960s, Luk describes the impact of Chinese History on students as a building up of 'a Chinese identity in the abstract, a patriotism of the émigré' (1991: 673). Sweeting and Morris (1993), in reviewing the nature of the curriculum in Hong Kong, argued that the school curriculum lacked clarity about national identity. Also Morris and Chan (1997) posited that education reform was geared to producing a depoliticised and decontextualised curriculum. This study also supports the findings of several local studies on curriculum development in the colonial period which view the phenomenon of collaborative colonialism as a major factor in the development of History and Chinese History in Hong Kong. For instance, Vickers (2000) used a collaborative model in his analysis of the local History curriculum, in which he found that a tacit collaborative contract existed between the government and those directly involved in curriculum development. Vickers, Kan and Morris (2003) also used the 'collaborative colonialism' model to explain Hong Kong's Chinese History curriculum development; and Kan and Vickers' (2002) study of the different historical visions of History and Chinese History found support for Robinson's 'collaboration theory' in which a colonialist elite helps to produce 'a collaborative contract' where 'the terms of such contracts are seldom dictated by the colonists, whose reliance on the collaborators often gives the latter considerable leverage and scope to pursue their own agendas' (1986: 30).

The present study, however, has expanded the 'collaborative colonialism' model referred to in the above three studies, and offers a fuller explanation of how and why the subject community collaborated with both the colonial government and the SAR government in the first two years after the return of sovereignty to China in the production of a decontextualised (during the colonial rule) and depoliticised Chinese History curriculum.

However, with regard to the collaborative role played by the subject community, it should be noted that Chinese History's 'collaborators' were not of the kind envisaged by Carnoy (1974) and Altbach and Kelly (1984) when they refer to colonial regimes using education to entrench a collaborationist native elite. Far from being elites under the British rule, these 'collaborators' were originally immigrants from Mainland China who took refuge in Hong Kong after the establishment of the communist regime in 1949. It was their aspiration to transplant Chinese studies, including Chinese History, from the Mainland to Hong Kong, and from about the 1960s Chinese History educators born and bred in Hong Kong were to varying degrees taught by these first-generation collaborators.

Consequently, when they themselves became important players, they inherited the 'tradition' of Chinese History and played a fuller collaborative role.

This study also shows that the situation in which Chinese History has found itself since the return of Hong Kong to China does not conform to the usual practices of decolonised education. Hong Kong differs from other decolonised states in that its people, for political and economic reasons, had preferred to be governed by the British administration than to be under the sovereignty of a communist regime[3] (see Chapter 2). Furthermore, since the handover, Hong Kong has become a Special Administrative Region (SAR) of China, and although, supposedly, 'Hong Kong people rule Hong Kong', it is still not an independent state. Decolonised education as manifested in Chinese History is characterised by compliance with the notion of 'one country, two systems'. For 'one country', the curricula for F1–3 and F4–5 were revised in such a way that only the PRC government is recognised as the legitimate state. However, it should be noted that the notions of 'one country', 'nation building', and 'national identity' as seen in the Chinese History curriculum are ethno-cultural, historical, and/or geographical, rather than political or ideological. Neither the official curriculum nor the implemented curriculum makes any reference to the PRC's communist ideology. In this sense, 'one country, two systems' is manifested in Chinese History, and this ambiguity in the definition of 'nation' in the curriculum offers an alternative interpretation of decolonised education. In the first two years after the handover, the revision of the Chinese History curriculum did support the notion of decolonisation being geared towards developing national identity and nation-building. However, the curriculum reform in 1998 and the introduction of four options for the subject's development have weakened, or at least threatened, the independent status of Chinese History, and with it 'the study of Chinese History as a continuous whole' is also under threat. In these circumstances, it is the subject community which has taken up the challenge and become a pressure group in an attempt to preserve the nature and role of Chinese History and its independent status in the school curriculum. In its struggle with the SAR government, the subject community has been able to make use of Chinese History's political significance to secure an ally in a senior Beijing official, and thus curriculum reform has become heavily politicised. The political pressure has forced the SAR government to make concessions regarding an integrated curriculum for Chinese History; and, as a result, the independent status of Chinese History has been reconfirmed through the introduction of the revised F4–5 curriculum in 2004 and a proposed new senior secondary Chinese History curriculum in 2009. The SAR government, under 'one country, two systems', has found itself in a difficult position with regard to Chinese History. There is no precedent in other former colonies for what has happened to the subject in Hong Kong, and in this respect it offers a new interpretation of decolonised education.

Micro-level Influences (Educational Interest Groups)

From 1952 onward, the ED's Syllabus and Textbook Committee (STC) was responsible for drawing up syllabuses and monitoring textbook publication, until 1972 when the Curriculum Development Council (CDC) was established to replace it in giving advice on matters relating to curriculum development. The subject committees in the CDC were administered by the ED's Advisory Inspectorate (AI), which meant that the bureaucratic establishment, especially the most significant people in the government bureaucracy, played the major role in the construction of the F1–5 curriculum.

In the ED bureaucracy before 1993, Chinese History was subordinated to History as a division in the Humanities section; in fact, it was not until the mid-1980s that a senior inspector post was established for Chinese History. In a restructuring of the AI in 1993, Chinese History became a subordinate part of Chinese Language, which meant that Chinese History was never given an independent identity in the Advisory Inspectorate. This lack of independent status impeded the subject's development, especially in the allocation of resources. However, with the establishment of the Curriculum Development Institute (CDI) in 1993, which took over curriculum development from the Advisory Inspectorate, Chinese History was made an independent division within the Humanities section. At the same time, the HKEA, as a quasi-autonomous government organisation, was responsible for the subject's public examination syllabuses, with HKEA subject officers exerting the most influence on the CEE subject committees. The fact that subject officers of both the Advisory Inspectorate and the HKEA were tenured staff reinforced the bureaucratic tendency to avoid change, and this type of conservative mentality is directly linked to the fact that there have been so few changes to the Chinese History curriculum since 1945.

The H-level (later replaced by the AS-level) and the A-level were spheres of influence for academics from the History Department of CUHK and the Chinese Department of HKU respectively. For example, for more than 30 years, representatives from HKU exerted the main influence on the A-level Chinese History curriculum, while representatives from CUHK were in charge of the H-level subject committee for more than 20 years. The content of H-level and A-level syllabuses was thus directly linked with the areas of expertise of the staff of the two universities. With the abolition of the H-level in 1993, the sixth-form subject committee came under the controlling influence of HKU's representatives, whose interpretation of the nature and role of Chinese History has consequently directly affected the development of the subject at sixth-form level.

There have been different degrees of centralisation in the approach to curriculum development over the last 60 years. During the first phase (1945–74), there was complete centralisation, with the power of decision-making in syllabus revision resting with the subject committee, which was largely dominated by key players in the ED. In the process, teachers were neither consulted nor provided with curriculum materials to assist them in their teaching. During the second phase (1974–97) there were nominal consultations in the form of questionnaires and the production of teaching materials, but the rationale for the final draft of syllabuses was not revealed to the public. No explanation was given by the subject committee for its choice of a particular approach in preference to the approaches that had been proposed by teachers in various questionnaire surveys. The decision-making process for the junior level curriculum revision and the new CEE question format in the third phase (1997–2005) was similar to that of the first two phases, except that far more curriculum materials were produced. In the course of curriculum development for the proposed 'New History' and 'PSHE', a working group was established, which acted as an intermediate agency between the superordinate agency (decision-makers) and the subordinate agency (implementers), and functioned as a buffer zone in the face of disputes over the new initiatives.

Throughout the three phases of the development of Chinese History, the local subject community has been most anxious to preserve both the independent status of the subject and the traditional methods of teaching Chinese History (this is especially evident in the third phase). It has also tried to ensure that the examinations would not be too difficult for students since this would reduce the popularity of the subject. The result of this has been that questions requiring memorisation of facts have appeared repeatedly in the public examinations. Members of the subject community have been able to exercise control over the curriculum for the last 60 years as insiders as well as outsiders. As insiders, they have participated in various subject committees and influenced the making of the curriculum, while as outsiders they have exerted pressure on the government through the media and striven to gain public support to protect the independent status of the subject.

The centralised top-down decision-making process in the development of the Chinese History curriculum has facilitated the control of the curriculum by key members of the subject community, and this study supports Marsh's (1997) identification of the features of centralisation of curriculum decision-making in general, and Morris' (1995b) and McClelland's (1991) argument on curriculum development in Hong Kong in particular. The role played by the main decision-makers in the development of Chinese History is depicted by Young (1971: 52) as follows: 'those in position of power will attempt to define what is to be taken as knowledge, how accessible to different groups any knowledge is, and what are the accepted relationships between different knowledge areas, and between those who have access to them and make them available'. For Chinese History, it has always been government subject officers or academics who have been the key members in the subject community, and who have defined the aims and content of the subject. Once the subject secured its position in the school curriculum, their determination to ensure 'the study of Chinese History as a continuous whole' became a 'tradition' of the subject. Not only is it fully implemented in the curriculum, but it is repeated at each stage of education from junior secondary level to sixth-form. According to the main curriculum developers, only through following a chronological approach can students come to appreciate the greatness of China and its civilisation. The emergence of this 'tradition' of Chinese History's content knowledge corresponds to the findings of a study undertaken by Kliebard (1986). In his work on the US curriculum from 1893 to 1958, Kliebard discerned a number of dominant traditions within the school curriculum, and came to the conclusion that 'by the end of the period covered the traditional school subject remained an impregnable fortress'. In the case of Chinese History in Hong Kong, this 'impregnable fortress' is not only evident in its resistance to encroachment from other subjects, but in the fact that its curriculum has also remained largely unchanged over the period covered in this study.

It was only in the course of serious disputes about the subject's status with the (SAR) government that two Chinese History teacher associations were established by the subject community, and this kind of 'safeguard the subject' establishment is unique in the history of school subjects in Hong Kong. This differs from the role of teacher associations portrayed by Goodson (1988): 'Teacher associations have long been highly active in the process of the subject's development'. Prior to that, except for the Social Studies incident in 1975, joint efforts within the subject community were rare. This study therefore supports the interpretation by Bucher and Strauss (1976), who argue that school subject associations often develop at a particular time when there is an intensification of conflict over school curriculum and resources, and over recruitment and training — except that in this case the teacher associations are mainly concerned with the subject's independent status. It also expands on local studies on the influence of teacher associations on curriculum development. For example, in their earlier work, Wong (1992) and Morris (1995b) argue that the absence of influential intermediate groups, such as teacher associations, affected curriculum development in Hong Kong. The extent to which the new Chinese History teacher associations have exerted their influence on education policy has been remarkable.

The history of Chinese History revealed in this study is different from the way in which Goodson interprets the history of school subjects in England. He argues that, fundamental to an understanding of the history of school subjects, is the struggle between various stakeholders — including politicians, teachers, academics and inspectors — for status, power and resources. However, Goodson overlooks or downplays the importance of conviction or belief in influencing the various people involved. In the case of Chinese History, the main members of the subject community do believe in the importance of Chinese History (however deluded they may be), and hence strive to fight for its independent status. Moreover, the minor changes made in the Chinese History curriculum over the last 60 years fail to support the argument that it can simply be attributed to those involved struggling for power.

To conclude, studying the last 60 years of the development of Chinese History helps to illuminate the origins of the present curriculum. As has been argued in Chapter 2, Chinese History is a socially constructed subject in the sense that during the colonial period it was academically oriented, decontextualised and depoliticised. Since the return of the sovereignty to the PRC, as a result of socio-political factors which have an impact on the curriculum, it has become even more academic and shifted towards contextualisation, but remained depoliticised. In the initial period of its development, key members of the subject community — university academics, schoolteachers and officials — in collaboration with the colonial government, helped to shape the notion that Chinese History should be studied as a continuous whole. Thereafter, this curriculum approach and emphasis has been firmly adhered to by the subject community; and the government bureaucracy and the centralised top-down decision-making process have both facilitated and reinforced this 'tradition'. Since the handover, the subject community has formed two teacher associations to counteract the SAR government's attempts to weaken or threaten the status and/or the sacred and indivisible 'tradition' of the subject. Whether or not Chinese History's 'tradition' can be maintained does not simply involve a struggle between the subject community and the SAR government as the stance of the PRC government will also have a decisive influence. In this respect, the Chinese History issue has become a test of the validity of 'one country, two systems'.

Notes

INTRODUCTION

1. The *Spring and Autumn Annals* covered the history of the period from 722–481 BC. There have been disputes among historians as to whether the author was Confucius.
2. Culture can be divided into spiritual culture and material culture. The former refers to the political and moral disciplines of the nation (or race), where loyalty and filial piety were the essence of the ideology. Material culture refers to, for example, four inventions in particular (the compass, gunpowder, paper-making, and movable-type printing), as well as art, science, technology and literature. Historically, culture in China has been taken as identified with the culture of the Han race.
3. At different times, Tu Weiming makes use of different ideas to reinterpret Confucian thoughts. According to him, 'moralism' and 'rationalism' are among the many ideas he has used to interpret Confucian thinking. See Tu, 1999: 19–38.
4. He Bingdi suggests the use of 'humanism' to interpret Chinese culture (see He et al., 1998: 73–102).
5. Tu Weiming specifies the relationship between political legitimacy and Confucian studies through an illustration of the interpretation of Confucian thoughts by political leaders such as Lee Kuan Yew, Jiang Zhongzheng and Jiang Zemin.
6. Orthodoxy refers to the views prescribed in 'the 24 Dynastic Histories'.
7. 'The 24 Dynastic Histories' were histories of the imperial dynasties, or more precisely histories of the imperial families. Altogether there were 3249-*juan* (thread-bound volumes, usually containing a much shorter text than a volume in modern book publishing).
8. The Six Classics are: the *Book of History*, the *Book of Odes*, the *Book of Changes*, the *Book of Rites*, the *Book of Music* and the *Spring and Autumn Annals*. These six books are Confucian classics which followers of Confucianism must read and abide by.
9. In 1935, the *Education Journal* in China (vol. 25, no. 5) published an issue on 'Experts nation-wide express views on classical studies'. Various views were given, but the majority were in favour of including classical studies in primary and secondary schools since they represented the essence of Chinese studies and could serve as the medium to promote moral education.

10. In the *Education Journal* (1941, vol. 31, no. 11), renowned historians expressed their views on the aims of history education in the face of the Japanese invasion. Qian Mu, Chen Lifu, Li Dongfang, Miao Fenglin and others stated that history education should aim at promoting patriotism and nationalism.

11. The book was compiled from Qian Mu's lecture notes when he was teaching in Peking University. He placed great emphasis on the role played by intellectuals during adverse periods in history.

12. According to 'The History of the History Department, New Asia College' (K. T. Sun, 1983), New Asia College was established 'to enhance the study of Chinese culture'.

13. For example, in the history syllabus issued in Beijing in 2001, the aims of history teaching do not include the law of 'class analysis'.

14. The Chinese Studies Committee was appointed by the government in 1952 to make recommendations on Chinese Studies in Hong Kong. It is discussed in detail in Chapter 2.

15. Confucian classics were all written in classical style Chinese, which had a highly condensed vocabulary and refined literary style.

16. Qian Mu used the chronological approach when writing *The General History of China*. His main reference was taken from 'the 24 Dynastic Histories'. See *The General History of China*, 1947: 1.

17. Hong Kong, Mainland China and Taiwan all have distinct transliteration systems, and therefore names that appear in the study are translated according to the relevant system. For Cantonese names, initials are used for the first names (e.g. K. C. Au).

CHAPTER 2

1. The main riot which took place in Kowloon on 10 October 1956 was a conflict between the KMT and CCP. On 13 October, the Chinese Premier Zhou Enlai expressed to the British ambassador in Beijing his dissatisfaction with the Hong Kong government's treatment of the KMT members in the riot. Some KMT rioters had been arrested. See *Hong Kong Pictorial History*, Hong Kong: Tai Dao Publishing Limited, 144.

2. *Hong Kong Hansard*, 1950: 41, cited in Lau, 1982: 36.

3. In April 1966, a protest against a rise in Star Ferry fares led to riots which included looting and arson. Also, in 1967, when the Cultural Revolution reached its height in China, communist unions in Hong Kong took the lead in labour disputes and later broadened the disputes into an anti-colonial administration movement. Order was restored at the end of 1967.

4. For Anglo-Chinese Schools, Chinese History became an independent subject in 1956 (F6–7), 1960 (F1–3) and 1965 (F4–5). For Chinese middle schools, it was in 1962 (F1–3), 1965 (F5) and 1967 (F4–5).

5. Reported in *Sing Tao Evening Post*, 30 September 1973.

6. Reported in *Workers' Weekly*, 17 September 1973. 'Peiping' is a term referred to by the national government and/or KMT. 'Beijing' is used after the establishment of the PRC in 1949.

7. Front page, *Oriental Daily*, 7 March 1975.

8. Louise Mok, Principal Inspector, Social Studies and P. S. Chan, Senior Inspector, History.

9. Reported in *Oriental Daily*, 8 March 1975.

10. The views were expressed by Dr Y. S. Yu and Dr C. I. Tang, both professors at New Asia College of the Chinese University of Hong Kong which was founded by Qian Mu, a rightist.

11. In 1982, 1984, 1985 and 1986, when there were disputes between China and Japan, there were newspaper articles discussing the lack of instruction on contemporary Chinese history in local schools.

12. Feature article, *Wen Wei Bao*, 22 June 1975.

13. Junior secondary Chinese History syllabus, CDC, 1982: 22.

14. Minutes of the CEE Chinese History subject committee, 28 May 1984 and 28 January 1986.

15. Minutes of the CEE Chinese History subject committee, 25 February 1987 and 29 April 1987.

16. This document was found in the press cuttings file, Advisory Inspectorate, dated 15 October 1990.

17. There were editorials and joint declarations from university teachers attacking Wong's recommendation.

18. Reported in *Ming Pao*, 8 July 1994.

19. Reported in *Wen Wei Bao*, 26 September 1996.

20. F1–3 Chinese History syllabus, CDC, 1997: 8.

21. Ibid.

22. *Hong Kong Economic Journal*, 8 January 2000. The author was K. H. Yip, a Chinese History professor in the Hong Kong Baptist University.

23. For example in the 'Rationale for Development' it states 'Hong Kong, as a SAR of China and an international financial centre, is in need of a new generation of residents who possess an enhanced sense of national identity and cultural understanding as well as a global perspective. Elements of learning in the contexts of Chinese history and culture need to be strengthened in the curriculum as early as possible in all types of schools' (*Learning to Learn*, Consultation Document, CDC, November 2000: 4). Also, in the 'Summary', it states: '… included Chinese History elements as essential contents for learning , ibid.: 18).

24. The aim is stated in the Association's homepage http://www.hktache.org, translated from Chinese.

25. Members of the Society's preparatory committee included 10 Chinese History panel chairs, three vice-principals, three teachers and nine lecturers from the tertiary institutions.

26. The results of the survey undertaken by the Association revealed that more than 90% of teachers thought that a comprehensive national history education could enhance students' national identity and that Chinese History should become a core course for junior secondary students.

27. *Learning To Learn*, Consultation Document, CDC, November 2000: 42.

28. Y. F. Sum, *Ming Pao*, 20 April 2000.

29. Hong Kong Teachers' Association of Chinese History Education, reported in *Da Gong Bao*, 28 November 2000.

CHAPTER **3**

1. Since the minutes of meetings before 1969 are not available, the percentage is based on the attendance at meetings held in 1969–71.
2. Minutes of meeting, Chinese History subject committee (CEE), 18 March 1969.
3. Letter sent to the Chairman of the CEE Chinese History subject committee, 19 May 1969.
4. I cannot identify any curriculum guideline for F1–5 when Chinese History became an independent subject in 1960. From the textbook written by K. L. Wong in 1963, the syllabus ran from the pre-historic period (~2100 BC) to 1945.
5. *Recommended History Guidelines for 5-year Chinese Middle Schools*, ED, 1962: 2–3.
6. In the 1958 CEE examination syllabus (English), it specified that the syllabus was to match the A-level requirement. In 1965, the Chinese middle schools set up a five-year curriculum. In 1967, when Chinese History emerged as an independent subject in the CEE (Chinese), the examination handbook set out that it matched CUHK's entrance requirements.
7. It should be noted that D. C. Lam headed the History section in which Chinese History was subordinated to History. He had not studied Chinese History at university.
8. Anglo-Chinese schools examination syllabus, 1965: 13.
9. Ibid.
10. CEE (English) examination syllabus, 1966: 12.
11. Here the 'Yuan Empire' was a derogatory term that indicated the invasions by Mongols. For those dynasties administered by the Han race, the word 'empire' was seldom used.
12. Annual Reports (1968–74), Examination Section, ED.
13. Ibid.
14. Ibid.
15. The examples included have been referred to in the official curriculum.
16. Marking scheme, CEE (English), ED, 1971.
17. Ibid., 1973.
18. CEE (English) question, 1970.
19. This topic was listed in, for example, K. L. Wong's textbook, Book 5: 13.
20. K. L. Wong (1963) *Chinese History*, Book 5, Hong Kong: Wang Fung Books, 15; and Sun K. T. (1965) *Chinese History*, Book 3, Hong Kong: Everyman's Bookstore, 45.
21. Ibid.: 35 and 47.
22. K. T. Sun (1960) *Chinese History*, year 2, Hong Kong: Everyman's Book Company, 8–14.
23. Y. C. Chan (1972) *Chinese History*, part 2, Hong Kong: Ling Kee Publishing Company, 171–72.
24. CEE (English) question, 1972.
25. Marking scheme, ED, 1972.
26. K. T. Sun (1960) *Chinese History*, year 4, first term, Hong Kong: Everyman's Book Company, 11–12.
27. Interview with L. Y. Chiu.
28. The A-level focused on remote periods of history (~1122 BC to 1911), which matched the expertise of staff, not a single one of whom specialised in modern Chinese history. Information about the course can be found in the University's calendars 1956–74.
29. *Chinese History for Anglo-Chinese Schools*, First Form, First Semester, Everyman's Publishing Company, 1960.
30. H-level syllabus, 1967–74.
31. Interview with L. Y. Chiu.

32. The analysis starts from 1956 because in that year the A-level Chinese History emerged as an independent subject.
33. A-level examination syllabuses, 1956–74, and H-level examination syllabuses, 1965–74.
34. In view of the absence of data on the A-level during this period (the syllabus only specified the time-frame and aspects of content to be examined, without referring to any events or people), only the H-level syllabus is referred to as a source of data.
35. H-level examination syllabus, 1965.
36. The subjects listed for students' rating were Chinese Language, Mathematics, Chinese History, World History and English.

CHAPTER 4

1. An introduction to Chinese History teaching, internal document, Advisory Inspectorate, ED, undated.
2. Chinese History syllabus (F1–3), CDC, 1975: 3.
3. *History Bulletin*, No. 5, ED, 1979: 68.
4. Chinese History syllabus (F1–3), CDC, 1975: 3 and 1982: 6.
5. Ibid. (1982: 6).
6. Ibid.: 19.
7. Ibid.: 16.
8. Ibid., 1975: 32.
9. Curriculum circular, No. 21, Chinese History, CDI, ED, 1993: 12.
10. Ibid.: 15.
11. Syllabus for Chinese History, F1–3, CDC, 1975: 3.
12. Syllabus for Chinese History, F1–3, CDC, 1982: 6.
13. Ibid.: 13.
14. Ibid.: 18.
15. Ibid.: 26.
16. Ibid.: 30.
17. Ibid.: 31.
18. In the Yuan dynasty, there was prejudice against the Han race in appointing officials.
19. Chinese History syllabus (F1–3), CDC, 1975: 32.
20. Ibid.: 31.
21. Chinese History syllabus (F1–3), CDC, 1975: 38.
22. Ibid.: 35.
23. Four questions would be set from the Shang dynasty to the Ming dynasty (~1600 BC– 1643). Another four questions would be set from the Qing dynasty (1644) to 1976.
24. Minutes of meeting, Chinese History subject committee, 23 May 1983.
25. Chinese History syllabus (F4–5), CDC, 1990: 7.
26. Reported in *South China Morning Post*, 6 June 1989.
27. Minutes of meeting, Chinese History subject committee (CEE), 11 October 1996.
28. Minutes of meeting, Chinese History subject committee (CEE), 7 December 1996.
29. Chinese History syllabus (F4–5), CDC, 1990: 11.
30. Ibid.
31. Chinese History syllabus (F4–5), CDC, 1990: 6.
32. Ibid.: 11.
33. Ibid.: 15.

34. Ibid.: 12.
35. Ibid.
36. Chinese History syllabus (F4–5), CDC, 1990: 6.
37. All Chinese History textbooks contained similar narratives, e.g. *Chinese History* (1993), Book 4, Everyman's Book Company, 124 and 126; *Chinese History* (2000), Book 2, Hong Kong Educational Publishing Company, 32 and 72; and *Chinese History* (2000), Book 2, Modern Education Company, 28 and 78.
38. Report of the Chinese History seminar (F4–5), ED, 1998: 9.
39. Mong (pseudonym), *Wen Wei Bao*, 22 July 1980.
40. Ibid., 17 March 1981.
41. W. C. Liu, *Ming Pao*, 2 April 1986.
42. Reported in *Ming Pao*, 5 November 1994.
43. S. S. Yung (a Chinese History teacher), *Economic Journal Newspaper*, 21 August 1984.
44. Report of a survey in *Oriental Daily*, 19 November 1982.
45. Cho Fung (pseudonym), *Economic Journal Newspaper*, 1 March 1985.
46. Reported in *South China Morning Post*, 10 June 1990.
47. CE reports, 1980–97.
48. Ibid.
49. Y. H. Cheng, *Economic Journal Newspaper*, 31 July 1982.
50. *Young Post*, 13 May 1986.
51. Flora Kan (Lecturer, HKU), *Hong Kong Standard*, 30 May 1990.
52. Marking scheme, Chinese History (CEE), 1981.
53. Ibid., 1991.
54. Jennifer (pseudonym), *Sing Tao Yat Po*, 13 August 1989. This article was kept in an ED file and marked 'Distribution AD (CIS)' which reflected that officials did pay attention to the views expressed in the article.
55. Chinese History syllabus (F1–3), CDC, 1982: 6.
56. Chinese History syllabus (F4–5), CDC, 1990: 6.
57. Permitted teacher (pseudonym), *Ming Pao*, 27 July 1988.
58. Minutes of meeting, Chinese History subject committee (CEE), 11 October 1996.
59. The question was set in 1970, 1973, 1975, 1983, 1985, 1987, 1991, 1994, 1996, 1998 and 1999.
60. This was the 1983 CEE marking scheme. There was no major difference between this one and those that appeared in different years.
61. *Chinese History*, Book 3, Ling Kee Publishing Company Limited, 1983: 171–73.
62. *Chinese History*, Book 3, Everyman's Book Company, 1980: 174.
63. The question was set in 1972, 1976, 1979, 1981, 1982, 1983, 1987, 1990, 1992, 1993, 1997 and 2000.
64. Marking scheme, CEE, 1987.
65. Chinese History syllabus (F4–5), CDC, 1990: 6.
66. Ibid.
67. A-level subject committee minutes, 30 October 1979.
68. Members from schools, if they had graduated from HKU, were mostly Chiu's ex-students.
69. For example, the meetings held on 23 September 1982, 24 September 1985, 30 September 1986 and 10 October 1987 were at HKU's Chinese Department.
70. All students were to follow a two-year sixth form programme. CUHK could no longer offer a four-year degree course.

71. Minutes of meeting, A-L subject committee, 30 September 1986.
72. Examination regulation and syllabus, A-L., 1994: 152.
73. 'History education', in Wong H. W. (1993) *Secondary School Curriculum Development*, Hong Kong, Commercial Press, 153.
74. Interview with L. Y. Chiu.
75. The HKEA officer (1979–93) C. N. Leung told me that letters sent to schools aimed at notifying them of the proposed changes to the existing curriculum. As expected, very few schools responded to the letter.
76. Minutes of meeting, Chinese History subject committee (H-level), 7 November 1980.
77. Chinese History syllabus (A-level), CDC, 1992: 6.
78. Ibid.: 14–15.
79. Ibid.: 16.
80. Ibid.: 15–16
81. K. Y. Law, *Wen Wei Bao*, 8 July 1996.
82. Minutes of meeting, Chinese History subject committee (H-level), 6 October 1987.
83. K. Hung, *Ming Pao*, 14 March 1986.
84. It should be noted that the question format of the A-level was different from the CEE. In particular, A-level tended to ask more 'evaluation' questions, and hence illustrative examples were far fewer than in the CEE.
85. Examination question, A-level, 1986 and 1987.
86. Ibid., 1986 and 1992.
87. H-level and A-level examination reports, 1980–89.
88. Examination question, H-level and A-level, 1989.
89. Examination question, A-level, 1988.
90. Ibid., 1997.

CHAPTER 5

1. The report of the questionnaire survey on the revised syllabus of the F1–3 Chinese History, CDC, 1997.
2. Reported in *Wen Wei Boa*, 17 January 1997.
3. Chinese History syllabus (F1–3), CDC, 1997: 16. The Chu state and the Han state were at war. Chu's Xiang Yu was defeated by Han's Liu Bang. Xiang committed suicide in the Wu river.
4. Chinese History syllabus, F1–3, CDC, 1997: 22. Shi Jingtang was a non-Han. At that time there were territorial conflicts between the Han and the non-Han people. The objective might imply that the 'nation' was taken as the Han's nation and hence even the non-Han people should put the interests of the Han as their top priority.
5. C. W. Chan, *Wen Wei Bao*, 1 February 1997.
6. Editorial, *Sun Pao*, 24 February 1997.
7. Survey report on the revised Chinese History syllabus (1997), CDC, paragraph 3.2.2.
8. Chinese History Teaching Series, Humanities Section, CDI, ED, vol. 5: 3.
9. *Chinese History*, Book 2, Modern Education Publishing Company, 2000: 83–88.
10. Ibid.: 12.
11. *Chinese History*, Book 4, Everyman's Book Company Limited, 1997: 179, 211. *Chinese History*, Book 4, Ling Kee Publishing Company Limited, 1998: 165, 196–98.

12. Terminal examination paper, F2, 1999, Confucius Hall Middle School.
13. *Chinese History*, Book 1, Manhattan Press (HK) Limited, 1999: 44.
14. Ibid.: 106.
15. Ibid., Book 2, 16.
16. Ibid.: 21.
17. *Chinese History*, Book 2, Hong Kong Educational Publishing Company, 2000: 20, 25; *Chinese History*, Book 2, Modern Education Publishing Company, 2000: 18, 20; *Chinese History*, Book 4, Everyman's Book Company, 2000: 13, 17; *Chinese History*, Book 4, Ling Kee Publishing Company, 1998: 50, 108 and 111.
18. C. F. Kwan, previously editor of Chinese History textbook, Modern Educational Publishing.
19. School A, F1 final examination, 2000.
20. School B, F2 mid-term examination, 1999.
21. School A, F1 mid-term examination, 2000.
22. School C, F2 mid-term examination, 1998.
23. School D, F1 final examination, 2000.
24. School E, F1 final examination, 1999.
25. Textbooks incorporating the official charts of moral and civic values include, for example, Hong Kong Educational Publishing Company, 2000, Modern Education Publishing Company and Manhattan Press HK Limited, 1999.
26. S. W. Lau, K. W. Wong, W. H. Siu and W. Y. Chung.
27. For example, *Chinese History*, F4, Manhattan Press (HK) Limited 1997: 146; *Chinese History*, F4, Everyman's Book Company Limited 2000: 122; *Chinese History*, F3, Hong Kong Educational Publishing Company, 2000: 108.
28. *Chinese History*, F4, Manhattan Press (HK) Limited 1997: 192; *Chinese History*, F4, Everyman's Book Company Limited 2000: 152; *Chinese History*, F3, Hong Kong Educational Publishing Company, 2000: 144.
29. *Chinese History*, F 3, Manhattan Press (HK) Limited, 1997.
30. *Chinese History*, F3, Everyman's Book Company Limited, 1997.
31. *Chinese History*, F5, Ling Kee Publishing Company Limited, 1999.
32. This part is taken from Kan and Vickers, 2002: 80–81.
33. *Chinese History*, F. 3, Manhattan Press (HK) Limited, 2000: 163.
34. These six schools were: Schools A, C, E, F, G and H.
35. *Chinese History*, Book 2, Modern Education Publishing Company, 2000: 85.
36. S. W. Lau, K. W. Wong, W. H. Siu and W. Y. Chung.
37. Minutes of meeting, Chinese History subject committee (CEE), 12 October 1994.
38. Reported in *Wen Wei Bao*, 3 April 1998.
39. Minutes of meeting, Chinese History subject committee (CEE), 11 February 1995.
40. Minutes of meeting, Chinese History subject committee (CEE), 20 September 1997.
41. Recommendation of the 2001 CEE Chinese History examination syllabus, minutes of meeting, Chinese History subject committee (CEE), 13 January 1998.
42. Minutes of meeting, Chinese History subject committee (CEE), 15 September 1999.
43. Senior form Chinese History Teaching Series, CDI, 2000: 6.
44. Ibid.
45. Reported in *Apple Daily*, 7 April 2000.
46. *Chinese History Curriculum and Assessment Guide (F4–5)*, CDC-HKEAA Joint Working Group, 9.

CHAPTER **6**

1. This was recorded in *The Spring and Autumn Annals* (see Chapter 1).
2. See Appendix III, IV and V, Report of the Chinese Studies Committee, ED, 1953: 54–55.
3. This was the case especially after the June Fourth Incident in 1989. In the early 1990s there was a massive increase in emigrants seeking overseas passports.

Bibliography

The official documents (include syllabuses, marking schemes, reports, policy papers, meeting minutes, and circulars/newsletters to schools) that are referred to in the course of this study include:

OFFICIAL DOCUMENTS

Minutes of meetings

- Chinese History subject committee (CEE, 1969–2005)
- Chinese History subject committee (H-level, 1967–1992)
- Chinese History subject committee (A-level, renamed Sixth Form in 1993, 1970–2005)

Policy papers

- White Paper on Secondary Education in Hong Kong Over the Next Decade (ED, 1974)
- Overall Review of the Hong Kong Education System (ED, 1981)
- A Perspective on Education in Hong Kong: Report by a Visiting Panel (Llewellyn Report, 1982)
- Education Commission Reports No. 1–7
- *Learning to Learn* (CDC, 2000 and 2001)
- Chief Executive's Policy Addresses, HK Government (1997–2005)

Reports

- Education Department (1953). The Report of the Chinese Studies Committee. Hong Kong: Education Department.
- Education Department Annual Reports (ED, 1938–2005)
- Examination Reports (ED, 1968–78)
- Examination Reports (HKEA, 1979–2005)
- Report of the Chinese Studies Committee (ED, 1953)
- Survey Report of the Revised Chinese History Syllabus (ED, 1997)
- Report of the Chinese History Seminar (ED, 1998)
- Report of the Questionnaire Survey on the Revised Syllabus of F1–3 Chinese History (ED, 1997)

Teaching syllabuses

- Recommended History Syllabus for 5-year Chinese Middle Schools (ED, 1962)
- Recommended History Syllabus for Chinese Middle Schools and Anglo-Chinese Schools (ED, 1970)
- Chinese History Syllabus, F1–3 (1975, 1982, 1997)
- Chinese History Syllabus, F4–5 (1990, 1997)
- Chinese History Syllabus, AS-level (1991)
- Chinese History Syllabus, A-level (1992)
- Chinese History Curriculum and Assessment Guide (S4–5) (2003)

Examination syllabuses

- Chinese History Examination Syllabus (CEE, English and Chinese) (1945–2005)
- Chinese History Examination Syllabus (H-level) (1967–1992)
- Chinese History Examination Syllabus (AS-level) (1993–2005)
- Chinese History Examination Syllabus (A-level) (1956–2005)

Marking schemes

- Chinese History Marking Schemes (CEE, 1970–2005)
- Chinese History Marking Schemes (H-level, 1967–1992)
- Chinese History Marking Schemes (AS-level, 1993–2005)
- Chinese History Marking Schemes (A-level, 1960–2005)

Circulars/Newsletters to schools, ED

- Recommendations on Chinese History Teaching (ED, 1995)
- Chinese History Teaching Series (ED, vol. 1–5)
- History Newsletter (ED, no. 1–4)

NEWSPAPER ARTICLES

Sing Tao Yat Pao, Wah Kiu Yat Pao, Ming Pao, Wen Wei Bao, Da Gong Bao, Oriental Daily, Popular Daily, Economic Journal, South China Morning Post, A Daily, Apple Daily and *Sun Pao* (tracking from 1965 [when Chinese History became an independent subject in CEE (English)] up until the present)

OTHER SOURCES

- Textbooks (Manhattan Press, Everyman's Book Company, Hong Kong Educational Publishing Company, Ling Kee Publishing Company and Modern Education Publishing Company)
- MEd theses
- 'A Research Project on History in Hong Kong Middle and Secondary Schools' (Noah, E. F., 1966)
- New Asia Colleges Twentieth Anniversary, the Chinese University of Hong Kong (1969)
- Articles and commentaries on Chinese History

PUBLICATIONS

References to articles and reports in local newspapers are given in the notes section and are not listed again here.

Published sources marked with * are written in Chinese and quotations from these sources are translated from Chinese.

Altbach, P. G. (1992). *Publishing and Development in the Third World*. Oxford: Hans Zell.

Altbach, P. G. and Kelly, G. P. (eds.) (1978). *Education and Colonialism*. New York: Longman.

Altbach, P. G. and Kelly, G. P. (eds.) (1984). *Education and the Colonial Experience*. New Brunswick: Transaction Books.

Apple, M. W. (1993). *Official Knowledge: Democratic Education in a Conservative Age*. New York: Routledge.

Apple, M. W. and Beyer, L. E. (eds.) (1988). *The Curriculum: Problems, Politics, and Possibilities.* Albany: State University of New York Press.

Archer, M. (1981). Educational politics: A model for their analysis. In Broadfoot, P., Brock, C. and Tulasiewicz, W. (eds.) *Politics and Educational Change: An International Survey.* London: Croom Helm.

Au, K. C. (1993). History education. In Wong, H. W. (ed.) *Secondary School Curriculum Development.* Hong Kong: Commercial Press, 139–60.

Au-yeung, N. C. (1987). *Recent Developments of the Official Curriculum for History in Hong Kong Anglo-Chinese Secondary Schools.* Unpublished MEd dissertation, the University of Hong Kong.

Ball, S. (1984). Imperialism, social control and the colonial curriculum in Africa. In Goodson, I. and Ball, S. (eds.) *Defining the Curriculum: Histories and Ethnographies.* London: Falmer Press.

Ball, S. (1985). Relations, structures and conditions in curriculum change: A political history of English teaching 1970–85. In Goodson, I. (ed.) *International Perspectives in Curriculum History.* London: Routledge.

Becher, T. and Maclure, S. (1978). *The Politics of Curriculum Change.* London: Hutchinson.

Bernstein, B. (1975). On the classification and framing of educational knowledge. In Young, M. (ed.) *Knowledge and Control: New Directions for the Sociology of Education.* London: Collier-Macmillan.

Betts, R. (2001). *Decolonization.* London: Routledge.

Bray, M. (1994). Decolonization and education: New paradigms for the remnants of empire. *Compare,* 24(1): 37–51.

Bray, M. (1997a). *Education and Colonial Transition: The Hong Kong Experience in Comparative Perspective.* Paper presented at the IXth World Congress of Comparative Education, The University of Sydney, Australia, 1–6 July 1996.

Bray, M. (1997b). Education and decolonization: Comparative perspectives on change and continuity. In Cummings, W. K. and McGinn, N. F. (eds.) *International Handbook of Education and Decolonization: Preparing Schools, Students and Nations for the Twenty-First Century.* Oxford: Pergamon Press.

Bucher, R. and Strauss, A. (1976). Profession and process. In Hammersley, M. and Woods, P. (eds.) *The Process of Schooling.* London: Routledge and Kegan Paul.

Carnoy, M. (1974). *Education as Cultural Imperialism.* New York: McKay.

Carr, E. H. (1961). *What is History?* London: Penguin.

Carroll, J. (1999). Chinese collaboration in the making of British Hong Kong. In Ngo, T. W. (ed.) *Hong Kong's History.* London: Routledge.

*Chan, M. K. (1989). The restoration of British education: Commission Report No. 3 and the issue of transitional connection. *The British Sunset in Hong Kong.* Hong Kong: Hong Kong Economic Journal.

Chan, M. K. (1992). Foreword. In Postiglione, G. (ed.) *Education and Society in Hong Kong: Toward One Country and Two Systems.* Hong Kong: Hong Kong University Press.

Cheng, K. M. (1996). Educational policymaking in Hong Kong: The changing legitimacy. In Postiglione, G. (ed.) *Education and Society in Hong Kong: Toward One Country and Two Systems*. Hong Kong: Hong Kong University Press.

Cheng, K. M. (1997). The policymaking process. In Postiglione, G. and Lee, W. O. (eds.) *Schooling in Hong Kong: Organization, Teaching and Social Context*. Hong Kong: Hong Kong University Press.

*Cheng, S. C. (1982). The education policy and its future orientation. In The Federation of Higher Education Students and The Hong Kong Chinese University Student Union (eds.) *The Perspective of Hong Kong Education*. Hong Kong: Wide Angle.

*Cheung, H. K. (1987). *The Development of World History in Hong Kong*. Unpublished MA dissertation, the Chinese University of Hong Kong.

Chiang Monlin (1924). *A Study of Chinese Principles of Education*. Shanghai: Commercial Press.

*Choi, P. K. (1987). *Sociology in Education*. Hong Kong: Wide Angle.

*Chou Liangkai (1993). *The Thinking of Historiography*. Taiwan: Zheng Zhong.

Clark J. (1990). National identity, state formation and patriotism: The role of history in the public mind. *History Workshop Journal*, 29 (Spring): 95–102.

Clignet, R. (1984). Damned if you do, damned if you don't: The dilemmas of colonizer-colonized relations. In Altbach, P. and Kelly, G. (eds.) *Education and the Colonial Experience*. New Brunswick: Transaction Books.

Coatsworth, J. (1982). The limits of colonial absolutism: The state in eighteenth century 'Mexico'. In Spalding, K. (ed.) *Essays in the Political, Economic and Social History of Colonial Latin America*. Newark, DE: Latin American Studies Programme, University of Delaware.

Cohen, L. and Manion, L. (1994). *Research Methods in Education* (fourth edition). London: Routledge.

Collingwood, R. G. (1946). *The Idea of History*. Oxford: Oxford University Press.

*Dai Baocun (1985). A review of the nation's historical research. *Secondary School History Education*, 15(2): 1–5.

Dirks, N. (1992). Introduction: Colonialism and custom. In Dirks, N. (ed.) *Colonialism and Culture*. Ann Arbor, MI: University of Michigan Press.

Eckert, C. (1991). *Offspring of Empire*. Seattle, WA: University of Washington Press.

Eggleston, S. J. (1977). *The Sociology of the School Curriculum*. London: Routledge and Kegan Paul.

Eisner, E. W. (1994). *The Educational Imagination*. New York: Macmillan College Publishing Company.

Eisner, E. W. and Vallance, E. (eds.) (1974). *Conflicting Conceptions of Curriculum*. California: McCutchan Publishing Corporation.

Elmore, R. and Sykes, G. (1992). Curriculum policy. In Jackson, P. W. (ed.) *Handbook of Research on Curriculum*. New York: Macmillan.

Esland, G. (1971). Teaching and learning as the organization of knowledge. In Young, M. (ed.) *Knowledge and Control: New Directions for the Sociology of Education*. London: Macmillan.

Esland, G. and Dale, R. (1973). *School and Society*, Course E282, Unit 2, Milton Keynes: Open University Press.

Evan, R. (1994). Educational ideologies and the teaching of history. In Leinhardt, G. Beck, I. and Stainton, C. (eds.) *Teaching and Learning in History*. New Jersey: Lawrence Erlbaum Associates.

Fagerlind, I. and Saha, L. (1989). *Education and National Development* (second edition). Oxford: Pergamon Press.

*Fan, K. (1995). The impact of Hong Kong's educational policies on secondary school Chinese Language teaching materials: An examination of the 1950s to 70s. In Siu, P. K. and Tam, T. K. (eds.) *Education Quality: A Collection of Essays*. Hong Kong: Hong Kong Education Research Association.

Fanon, F. (1969). *The Wretched of the Earth*. Harmondsworth: Penguin.

Fehl, N.E. (1966). *History in Hong Kong Middle and Secondary Schools: A Research Project of the Chinese University of Hong Kong*. Hong Kong: The Chinese University of Hong Kong.

Fehl, N.E. (1971). *Some Problems in the Relation of Chinese History and World History*. Paper presented in International Conference in the Chinese University of Hong Kong.

*Feng Tianyu and Chou Jiming (1996). *The Secrets of Chinese Culture*. Hong Kong: South China Press.

Fieldhouse, D. K. (1983). *Colonialism 1870–1945: An Introduction*. London: Macmillan.

Freire, P. (1972). *Pedagogy of the Oppressed*. London: Penguin.

Fullan, M. (1991). *The New Meaning of Educational Change*. London: Cassell.

Furnivall, J. S. (1956). *Colonial Policy and Practice*. New York: New York University Press.

Ginsburg, M, Cooper, S., Raghy, R. and Zegarra, H. (1990). National and world-system: Explanations of educational reforms. *Comparative Education Review*, 34(4): 474–99.

Giroux, H. A. (1981). *Ideology, Culture and the Process of Schooling*. London: Falmer Press.

Goodson, I. (1983). *School Subjects and Curriculum Change*. London: Croom Helm.

Goodson, I. (ed.) (1985). *Social Histories of the Secondary Curriculum: Subjects for Study*. Philadelphia: Falmer Press.

Goodson, I. (1987a). On Curriculum Form. Mimeograph: University of Western Ontario.

Goodson, I. (1987b). *School Subjects and Curriculum Change*. London: Falmer Press.

Goodson, I. (1988). *The Making of Curriculum*. London: Falmer Press.

Goodson, I. (1991). Social history of curriculum subjects. In Lewy, A. (ed.) *International Encyclopedia of Education*. Oxford: Pergamon Press, 58–63.

Goodson, I. (1994). *Studying Curriculum*. Buckingham: Open University Press.

Goodson, I. and Marsh, C. (1996). *Studying School Subjects*. London: Falmer Press.

Gordon, P. and Lawton, D. (1978). *Curriculum Change in the Nineteenth and Twentieth Centuries*. London: Hodder and Stoughton.

Green, A. (1997). Education and state formation in Europe and Asia. In Kennedy, K. (ed.) *Citizenship Education and the Modern State*. London: Falmer Press.

Guba, E. G. and Lincoln, Y. (1994). Competing paradigms in qualitative research. In Denzin, N. K. and Lincoln, Y. S. (eds.) *Handbook of Qualitative Research*. London: Sage.

*Han Fuzhi (1993). A critique of Chinese History education. *Jing E Quarterly*, 5(1): 4–10.

Hargreaves, J. D. (1988). *Decolonisation in Africa*. London: Longman.

*He Bingdi, Gao Kun, Chen Yuan, and Qiu Chengtong (1998). *China and the World in the 21st Century*. Hong Kong: Commercial Press.

Hogwood, B. and Gunn, L. (1984). *Policy Analysis for the Real World*. London: Oxford University Press.

* Hu Chongzhi (1988). *Historical Knowledge and Social Changes*. Taiwan: Lian Jing.

*Hu Shih (1935). The theoretical construction of new literature. In Tsai, Yuanpei (ed.) *The Introduction of New Literature in China*. Shanghai: Oriental Studies, 15–52.

*Huang, Ray (1988). *China: A Macro History*. Taipei: Yun Chen Cultural Enterprise.

Hung, Y. C. (1982). *A Study of the Implementation, in a Sample of Hong Kong Secondary Schools, of the History Curriculum Recommended by the Curriculum Development Committee for Forms I to III*. Unpublished MEd dissertation, the University of Hong Kong.

Hurst, P. (1983). Implementing educational change: A critical review of the literature. EDC Occasional Paper, 5. London: Department of Education in Developing Countries, Institute of Education, University of London.

Husbands, C. and Pendry, A. (1992). *Whose History? School History and the National Curriculum*. Norwich: University of East Anglia.

Jenkins, K. (1991). *Re-thinking History*. London: Routledge.

Jennings, R. E. (1977). *Education and Politics: Policy-making in Social Education Authorities*. London: B. T. Batsford.

Kah, G. H. (1991). *En Route to Global Occupation: A High Ranking Government Liaison Exposes the Secret Agenda for World Unification*. Lafayette, LA: Hunting House Publishers.

Kan, F. L. F. (2002) *Chinese History in Hong Kong: The Secondary School Curriculum, 1946–2001*. Unpublished PhD thesis, the University of Hong Kong.

Kan, F. L. F. and Vickers, E. (2002). One Hong Kong, two histories: 'History' and 'Chinese History' in the Hong Kong school curriculum. *Comparative Education*, 38(1): 73–89.

Kelly, G. P. and Altbach, P. (1984). *Education and the Colonial Experience*. New Jersey: Transaction.

Kerr, J. F. (ed.) (1968). *Changing the Curriculum*. London: University of London Press.

King, A. (1973). *The Administrative Absorption of Politics in Hong Kong: With Special Emphasis on the City District Officer Scheme*. Hong Kong: Centre of Asian Studies, the University of Hong Kong.

King, A. (1981). *Social Life and Development in Hong Kong.* Hong Kong: The Chinese University Press.

*King, A. (1992). *Chinese Society and Culture.* Hong Kong: Oxford University Press.

Kliebard, H. (1986). *The Struggle for the American Curriculum 1893–1958.* Boston: Routledge.

Kliebard, H. (1991). Constructing a history of the American curriculum. In Jackson, P. W. (ed.) *Handbook of Research on Curriculum.* New York: Macmillan.

Kliebard, H. and Franklin, B. (1983). The course of the course of study: History of curriculum. In Best, J. H. (ed.) *Historical Inquiry in Education: A Research Agenda.* Washington, DC: American Educational Research Association.

Kopf, D. (1984). Orientalism and the Indian educated elite. In Altbach, P. G. and Kelly, G. P. (eds.) *Education and the Colonial Experience.* New Brunswick: Transaction.

*Kwan, W. K. (1982). Our perspectives on contemporary education problems. In The Federation of Higher Education Students and The Hong Kong Chinese University Student Union (eds.) *The Perspective of Hong Kong Education.* Hong Kong: Wide Angle.

*Lam, N. (ed.) (1980). *Liang Qichao's Three Historical Works.* Hong Kong: Joint Publishing.

Lau, S. K. (1982). *Society and Politics in Hong Kong.* Hong Kong: The Chinese University Press.

*Law, H. L. (1955). *The History of Chinese Nation.* Taipei: Chinese Culture Press.

Law, W. W. (1997). The accommodation and resistance to the decolonization, neocolonization and recolonization of higher education in Hong Kong. In Bray, M. and Lee, W. O. (eds.) *Education and Political Transition: Implications of Hong Kong's Change of Sovereignty.* Hong Kong: Comparative Education Research Centre, the University of Hong Kong.

Lawton, D. (1980). *The Politics of the School Curriculum.* London: Hodder and Stoughton.

Lee, P. (1994). History, autonomy and education. *Teaching History.* London: The Historical Association.

Lee, P. (1995). History and the national curriculum in England. In Dickinson, A. and Gordon, P. (eds.) *International Yearbook of History Education.* London: The Woburn Press, 73–123.

Lee, W. O. (ed.) (1997). *Education and Political Transition.* Hong Kong: Comparative Education Research Centre, the University of Hong Kong.

Leung, Y. M. (1992). Education in Hong Kong and China: Toward convergence? In Postiglione, G. (ed.) *Education and Society in Hong Kong: Toward One Country and Two Systems.* Hong Kong: Hong Kong University Press.

*Li Guoqi (1970). The aim and mission of history education. *Contemporary China,* 3: 42–44.

*Li Longgeng (1987). The teaching of modern Chinese history and patriotic education in secondary schools. In Cang Rong and Zhou Fazeng (eds.) *A*

New Exploration of Research on History Teaching. Second series. Beijing: People's Education Press, 183–90.

*Liang Souming (1999). *The Essence of Chinese Culture* (seventh edition). Hong Kong: Joint Publishing.

*Liao Longsheng (1995). Research on senior secondary history education in Mainland China. *Research on the Education Policy and Content of Senior Secondary Education.* Teacher Research Centre, National Taiwan University, 3(6): 35–54.

*Liu Zhiqin and Wu Tingjia (1992). *A General Review of Chinese Cultural History.* Taipei: Wen Jin.

Lovat, T. and Smith, D. L. (1990). *Curriculum: Action on Reflection.* Wentworth Falls, NSW, Australia: Social Science Press.

*Luk, H. K. (1982). A few issues on Hong Kong education in the eighties. In The Federation of Higher Education Students and The Hong Kong Chinese University Student Union (eds.) *The Perspective of Hong Kong Education.* Hong Kong: Wide Angle.

Luk, H. K. (1987). *Schooling and Modernisation in Hong Kong: The Chinese Studies Curriculum and Cultural Heritage.* Discussion Draft. Hong Kong: School of Education, the Chinese University of Hong Kong.

Luk, H. K. (1991). Chinese culture in the Hong Kong curriculum: Heritage and colonialism. *Comparative Education Review,* 35(4): 650–68.

*Luk, H. K. (1995). Hong Kong history and Hong Kong culture. In Sinn, E. (ed.) *Culture and Society in Hong Kong.* Hong Kong: Hong Kong University Press.

*Luk, H. K. (1996). 'Colonial education and the so-called political apathy'. *Ming Pao Daily News,* 9 August 1996.

MacKenzie, J. (1984). *Propaganda and Empire.* Manchester: Manchester University Press.

Mangan, J. A. (1988). *Benefits Bestowed? Education and British Imperialism.* Manchester: Manchester University Press.

*Mao Weiran (1987). Using 'Three Faces' as guidelines to reform history teaching. In Cang Rong and Zhou Fazeng (eds.) *A New Exploration of Research on History Teaching.* Second series. Beijing: People's Education Press, 13–21.

Marsh, C. and Huberman, M. (1984). Disseminating curricula: A look from the top down. *Journal of Curriculum Studies,* 16(1): 53–56.

Marsh, C. (1997). *Perspectives: Key Concepts for Understanding Curriculum 1.* London: The Falmer Press.

Marsh, C. (1997). *Planning, Management and Ideology: Key Concepts for Understanding Curriculum 2.* London: The Falmer Press.

Maw, J. (1994). Understanding ethnocentrism: History teachers talking. *Teaching History.* London: The Historical Association.

McClelland, J. A. G. (1991). Curriculum development in Hong Kong. In Marsh, C. and Morris, P. (eds.) *Curriculum Development in East Asia.* London: The Falmer Press.

McCulloch, G. and Richard, W. (2000). *Historical Research in Educational Settings.* Buckingham: Open University Press.

Memmi, A. (1965). *The Coloniser and the Colonised.* Boston: Beacon Press.

Meyer, J. W., Kamens, D. H. and Benavot, A. (eds.) (1992). *School Knowledge for the Mass.* London: Falmer Press.

Morris, P. (1992). Preparing pupils as citizens of the Special Administrative Region of Hong Kong: An analysis of curriculum change and control during the transition period. In Postiglione, G. (ed.) *Education and Society in Hong Kong.* Hong Kong: Hong Kong University Press.

Morris, P. (1995a). *The Hong Kong School Curriculum: Development, Issues and Policies.* Hong Kong: Hong Kong University Press.

Morris, P. (1995b). Curriculum development in Hong Kong. *Education Paper 7,* Faculty of Education, the University of Hong Kong (second edition). Hong Kong: The University of Hong Kong.

Morris, P. (1997). School knowledge, the state and the market: An analysis of the Hong Kong secondary school curriculum. *Curriculum Studies,* 29(3): 329–49.

Morris, P. and Chan, K. K. (1997). The Hong Kong school curriculum and the political transition: Politicisation, contextualisation and symbolic action. In Bray, M. and Lee, W. O. (eds.) *Education and Political Transition: Implications of Hong Kong's Change of Sovereignty.* Hong Kong: Comparative Education Research Centre, the University of Hong Kong.

Morris, P. and Sweeting, A. E. (1995). Education and politics: The case of Hong Kong from an historical perspective. *Curriculum Development in Hong Kong* (second edition). Hong Kong: Faculty of Education, the University of Hong Kong, 142–67.

Morris, P., Kan, F. L. F. and Morris, E. (2000). Education, civic participation and identity: Continuity and change in Hong Kong. *Cambridge Journal of Education,* 30(2): 243–62.

Morris, P., McClelland, G. and Wong, P. M. (1998). Explaining curriculum change: Social studies in Hong Kong. In Stimpson, P. and Morris, P. (eds.) *Curriculum and Assessment for Hong Kong.* Hong Kong: Open University of Hong Kong Press.

Morrissey, M. (1990). *Curriculum Reform in the Third World: The Case of School Geography.* Mona, Jamaica: Institute of Social and Economic Research.

Musgrove, F. (1955). History teaching within a conflict of cultures, *History,* 15 (140): 300.

Nadel, G. and Curtio, P. (1966). *Imperialism and Colonialism.* London: Macmillan.

*Ng Lun, N.H. (1997). Education in retrospect. In Huang, G. W. (ed.) *Hong Kong History: New Perspectives.* Hong Kong: Joint Publishing.

Ngo, T. W. (1999). *Hong Kong's History.* London: Routledge.

Noah, E. F. (1966). *History in Hong Kong Middle and Secondary Schools: A Research Project of the Chinese University of Hong Kong.* Hong Kong: The Chinese University of Hong Kong.

Olson, A. G. (1992). *Making the Empire Work: London and HM Interest Groups, 1690–1790.* Cambridge, MA: Harvard University Press.

Pellen, K. (1991). History: Educational programs. In Lewy, A. (ed.) *International Encyclopedia of Education.* Oxford: Pergamon Press, 743–45.

Pennycook, A. (1998). *English and the Discourse of Colonialism.* London: Routledge.

Phillips, R. (1998). *History Teaching, Nationhood and the State.* London: Cassell.

Pierson, H. (1992). Cantonese, English, or Putonghua: Unresolved communicative issue in Hong Kong's future. In Postiglione, G. (ed.) *Education and Society in Hong Kong: Toward One Country and Two Systems.* Hong Kong: Hong Kong University Press.

Plumb, J. H. (1969). *The Death of the Past.* London: Macmillan.

Pong, H. W. (1988). *A Study of Values Teaching in Junior Secondary History Curriculum in an Aided Secondary School in Hong Kong.* Unpublished MEd dissertation, the University of Hong Kong.

*Pong, L. W. (1987). *The Development of Chinese History Curriculum in Hong Kong.* Unpublished MA dissertation, the Chinese University of Hong Kong.

Postiglione, G. (ed.) (1992). *Education and Society in Hong Kong: Toward One Country and Two Systems.* Hong Kong: Hong Kong University Press.

*Qian Mu (1947). *The General History of China* (third edition). Shanghai: Commercial Press.

*Qian Mu (1979). *Chinese Nation and Culture as Revealed in Chinese History.* Hong Kong: The Chinese University Press.

*Qin Xiaoyi (1985). *History Education and Nation Building.* Proceedings of International Conference on History Education, Taiwan.

*Qiu Tiansheng (1978). How to enhance national spirit through history teaching. *Secondary Education,* 29(3): 26–31.

Robinson, R. (1986). The excentric theory of imperialism: with or without empire. In Mommsen, W. and Ostrhammel, J. (eds.) *Imperialism and After.* UK: Vintage.

Said, E. (1994). *Culture and Imperialism.* UK: Vintage.

Schlesinger, A. (1992). *The Disuniting of America.* Norton: New York.

Silver, H. (1983). *Education as History.* London: Methuen.

*Siu, P. K., Wong, H. C., Chow, Y. F. and Ling, W. T. (1975). Chinese History essay questions in the last five years. *Xueji,* 5: 117–39. Hong Kong: Chinese University of Hong Kong.

Skilbeck, M. (1992). Economic, social and cultural factors. In Lewy, A. (ed.) *The International Encyclopaedia of Curriculum.* Oxford: Pergamon Press, 122–25.

Slater, J. (1988). *The Politics of History Teaching.* London: Institute of Education.

Slater, J. (1989). *The Politics of History Teaching: A Humanity Dehumanized?* Special Professorial Lecture, London: Institute of Education.

Sun, K. T. (1983). *The History of the History Department.* Hong Kong: New Asia College.

Sweeting, A. E. (1990). *Education in Hong Kong, Pre-1841 to 1941: Fact and Opinion.* Hong Kong: Hong Kong University Press.

Sweeting, A. E. (1991). Politics and the art of teaching history in Hong Kong. *Teaching History*, 64: 30–37.

Sweeting, A. E. (1993). *A Phoenix Transformed: The Reconstruction of Education in Post-war Hong Kong*. Hong Kong: Oxford University Press.

Sweeting, A. E. (1994). Hong Kong education within historical process. In Postiglione, G. and Leung, Y. M. (eds.) *Education and Society in Hong Kong: Toward One Country and Two Systems*. Hong Kong: Hong Kong University Press.

Sweeting, A. E. (1995). Hong Kong. In Morris, P. and Sweeting, A. E. (eds.) *Education and Development in East Asia*. New York: Garland.

Sweeting, A. E. (1998). Education and development in Hong Kong. In Stimpson, P. and Morris, P. (eds.) *Curriculum and Assessment for Hong Kong*. Hong Kong: Open University Press.

Sweeting, A. E. (2004). *Education in Hong Kong, 1941 to 2001: Visions and Revisions*. Hong Kong: Hong Kong University Press.

Sweeting, A. E. and Morris, P. (1993). Educational reform in post-war Hong Kong: Planning and crisis intervention. *International Journal of Educational Development*, 13(3): 201–16.

Taba, H. (1962). *Curriculum Development: Theory and Practice*. New York: Harcourt Brace.

Tan, J. (1993). *History of the History Curriculum under Colonialism and Decolonisation: A Comparison of Hong Kong and Macau*. Unpublished MEd dissertation, the University of Hong Kong.

Tan, J. (1995). *The History Curriculum in Hong Kong and Macau under Decolonisation*. Paper presented at the International Symposium on Education and Socio-Political Transitions in Asia, Comparative Education Research Centre, the University of Hong Kong.

Tanner, L. N. (1982). Curriculum history as usable knowledge. *Curriculum Inquiry*, 12: 405–11.

Thomas, R. M. (1983). The symbiotic linking of politics and education. In Thomas, R. M. (ed.) *Politics and Education: Cases from Eleven Nations*. Oxford: Pergamon.

Thomas, R. M. and Postlethwaite, T. N. (1983). Describing change and estimating its causes. In Thomas, R. M. and Postlethwaite, T. N. (eds.) *Schooling in East Asia: Forces of Change*. Oxford: Pergamon Press.

Thompson, J. T. (1976). *Policy-making in American Public Education: A Framework for Analysis*. New York: Prentice Hall.

Tsang, S. (1988). *Democracy Shelves: Great Britain, China, and Attempts at Constitutional Reforms in Hong Kong*. Hong Kong: Oxford University Press.

Tse, K. C. (1999). Civic and political education. In Bray, M. and Koo, R. (eds.) *Education and Society in Hong Kong and Macau: Comparative Perspectives on Continuity and Change*. Hong Kong: Comparative Education Research Centre, the University of Hong Kong.

*Tse, K. K. (1984). Analysing Hong Kong's education policy. In Lam, C. W., Fong, K. Y. and Cheung, K. W. (eds.) *Perspectives of Hong Kong Education*. Hong Kong: Wide Angle.

*Tsin Sin (1924). A study of Chinese principles of education. In Chiang Monlin (ed.) *The Works of Mencius, Book VII*. China: Commercial Press.

*Tsun, K. Y. (1973). Chinese History teaching and multiple choice questions. *History Bulletin*, 4:31. Hong Kong: Education Department.

*Tu Weiming (1989). *The Prospect of the Third Stage Development of Confucian Studies*. Taipei: Lian Jing.

*Tu Weiming (1999). *Ten Years' Opportunity for Confucian Studies: A Re-evaluation of East Asian Values*. Hong Kong: Oxford University Press.

*Tu Weiyun (1981). *A Discussion with Western Historians on Chinese Historical Studies*. Taipei: Dong Da Book Store.

*Tu Weiyun (1995). *The Two Circumstances of History*. Taipei: Dong Da.

*Tu Weiyun (1998). *A History of Chinese Historical Study* (second edition). Taipei: San Min Book Store.

Vickers, E. (2000). *History as a School Subject in Hong Kong: 1960s–2000*. Unpublished PhD thesis, the University of Hong Kong.

Vickers, E. and Kan, F. L. F. (2003). The re-education of Hong Kong: Identity, politics and education in postcolonial Hong Kong. *American Asian Review*, 21(4), 179–228.

Vickers, E., Kan, F. L. F. and Morris, P. (2003) Colonialism and the politics of 'Chinese History' in Hong Kong's schools, *Oxford Review of Education*, 29: 95–111.

*Wang Gangwu (1998). The political change of Hong Kong. In Liu, Q. F. and Kwan, S. C. (eds.) *Hong Kong in Transition: The Continued Search for Identity and Order*. Hong Kong: The Chinese University Press.

*Wang Zhongfu (ed.) (1997). *Understanding Taiwan's Textbooks*. Taiwan: Taiwanese History Society.

Watson, K. (1982). Colonialism and educational development. In Watson, K. (ed.) *Education in the Third World*. London: Croom Helm.

Watson, K. (1993). Rulers and ruled: Racial perceptions, curriculum and schooling in colonial Malaya and Singapore. In Mangan, J. A. (ed.) *The Imperial Curriculum: Racial Images and Education in the British Colonial Experience*. London: Routledge.

White, C. (1994). The aims of school history. *Teaching History*. London: The Historical Association.

Whitehead, C. (1988). British colonial educational policy: A synonym for cultural imperialism? In Mangan, J. A. (ed.) *Benefits Bestowed? Education and British Imperialism*. Manchester: Manchester University Press.

Wirt, F. and Harman, G. (eds.) (1986). *Education, Recession, and the World Village: A Comparative Political Economy of Education*. Philadelphia: Falmer Press.

*Wong, C. L. (1996). *The History of Chinese Education in Hong Kong.* 2nd edition. Hong Kong: Joint Publishing.

*Wong, F. L. (1957). *The Mission of Chinese History and Culture.* Hong Kong: China Book Store.

Wong, P. M. (1992). The Evolution of a Secondary School Subject in Hong Kong: The Case of Social Studies. Unpublished PhD thesis, the University of Hong Kong.

*Wu Jingxian. (1987). The aim of history education: Experiences and ideological inculcation. In Cang, Rong and Zhau, Fazeng (eds.) *A New Exploration of Research on History Teaching.* Second series. Beijing: People's Education Press, 22–31.

*Wu, Y. F. (1973). Problems of Chinese history teaching and learning. *Stadium*, 4: 172.

Young, M. (1971). *Knowledge and Control.* London: Collier-Macmillan.

Young, M. (1975). An approach to the study of curricula as socially organized knowledge. In Young, M. (ed.) *Knowledge and Control: New Directions for the Sociology of Education.* London: Collier-Macmillan.

Young, M. (1977). Curriculum and change: Limits and possibilities. In Young, M. and Whitty, G. (eds.) *Society, State and Schooling.* PA: Falmer Press.

Young, M. (1998). *The Curriculum for the Future.* London: Falmer Press.

*Yu Yingshi (1987). *Modern Interpretation of Traditional Chinese Thoughts.* Taipei: Lain Jing Publishing.

*Zhang Huabao (1993). *The Sociology of History.* Taipei: San Min.

*Zhang Xiaoqian (1978). National spirit and Chinese history education. *The Revival of Chinese Culture Monthly*, 11(7): 7–9.

*Zhang Yuan (1996). History teaching needs reforming. *Tsing Hua Journal for History Education*, 5.

Index